CIVIL RELIGION TODAY

Civil Religion Today

Religion and the American Nation in the Twenty-First Century

Edited by
Rhys H. Williams,
Raymond Haberski Jr., *and*
Philip Goff

NEW YORK UNIVERSITY PRESS
New York

NEW YORK UNIVERSITY PRESS
New York
www.nyupress.org

© 2021 by New York University
All rights reserved

References to Internet websites (URLs) were accurate at the time of writing. Neither the author nor New York University Press is responsible for URLs that may have expired or changed since the manuscript was prepared.

Library of Congress Cataloging-in-Publication Data
Names: Williams, Rhys H., editor. | Haberski, Raymond J., 1968– editor. | Goff, Philip, 1964– editor.
Title: Civil religion today : religion and the American nation in the twenty-first century / Rhys H. Williams, Raymond Haberski Jr., Philip Goff, [editors].
Description: New York : New York University, [2021] | Includes bibliographical references and index.
Identifiers: LCCN 2021016772 | ISBN 9781479809844 (hardback) | ISBN 9781479809851 (paperback) | ISBN 9781479809882 (ebook) | ISBN 9781479809868 (ebook other)
Subjects: LCSH: Civil religion—United States—History—21st century.
Classification: LCC BL2525 .C584 2021 | DDC 201/.720973—dc23
LC record available at https://lccn.loc.gov/2021016772

New York University Press books are printed on acid-free paper, and their binding materials are chosen for strength and durability. We strive to use environmentally responsible suppliers and materials to the greatest extent possible in publishing our books.

Manufactured in the United States of America

10 9 8 7 6 5 4 3 2 1

Also available as an ebook

CONTENTS

Introduction: Beyond Bellah   1
Raymond Haberski Jr., Rhys H. Williams, and Philip Goff

1. The Past and Future of the American Civil Religion   19
Philip Gorski

2. The Utilitarian Context of American Civil Religion   35
Mark Silk

3. Sacrifice, Service, and Civil Religion Now   50
Rosemary R. Corbett

4. Regions and Civil Religion(s) in America   76
Arthur Remillard

5. Seeing Bellah's Civil Religion through a Black Feminist Lens   95
Korie Little Edwards

6. Civil Religion and the Problem of Origins   118
Wendy L. Wall

7. Uncle Sam, the Statue of Liberty, and Images of National Identity   137
Rhys H. Williams

8. George Washington, Miguel Hidalgo, and Transnational Civil Religion at the U.S.-Mexico Border   163
Elaine A. Peña

9. Civil Religion in Indianapolis   180
Arthur E. Farnsley II

Acknowledgments   213

About the Contributors   215

Index   217

Introduction: Beyond Bellah

RAYMOND HABERSKI JR., RHYS H. WILLIAMS, AND PHILIP GOFF

Many scholars who have written about civil religion in America have had their own Robert Bellah moment. Typically, scholars asked Bellah to read their work and reflect on their interpretation of a term that Bellah almost single-handedly made famous in academic circles. However, those who had contact with Bellah also heard him say that he was quite ready for the academy to move beyond him and his connection to civil religion. Indeed, he would have been happy if many of us had moved "beyond Bellah" by the mid-1970s, or less than a decade after he had become the center of debates and discussions in the United States about American civil religion. Alas, that was not to be. In this volume, we are collectively asserting that there is still useful analytic life in the concept more than a half century later. Some scholars here argue that the need for "civil religion" is particularly acute at the end of the first quarter of the twenty-first century.

The Winter 1967 issue of *Daedalus*, the journal of the American Academy of Arts and Sciences, published Bellah's essay "Civil Religion in America," in which he argued that "American civil religion is not the worship of the American nation but an understanding of the American experience in the light of ultimate and universal reality."[1] For reasons still debated, Bellah's language captured better and more evocatively what other scholars had been trying to say for many years: that Americans believed their nation was more than the sum of its political actions and social ills. He pointed to many ways in which religious symbolism and ideas permeated Americans' thinking about their nation, their history, and their government. Further, Bellah seemed to ask if civil religion provided a way for generations of Americans to imagine they were involved in, if not united through, a common moral experience and whether that might offer hope for the fractious time in which he was writing.

For most scholars, the significance of civil religion is tied to that essay. According to Google's Ngram, civil religion and Bellah have a determinative relationship. From the mid-1960s through the early 1980s, Bellah's original essay on civil religion launched an academic industry that debated, expanded, contested, and revised the idea of American civil religion. More importantly, prior to Bellah's essay, very few scholars much less the general public used the term, even though it had originated with one of greatest modern philosophers, Jean-Jacques Rousseau (more on this below).

The timing of Bellah's essay was significant. He seized upon a term that seemed especially well suited to describe the middle years of the American Cold War combined with social and political convulsions around the Vietnam War and the civil rights movement. It was also a period in which religious belief and practice in the United States shifted for a variety of reasons: Americans had turned to religious leaders and institutions to make sense of the catastrophic destruction of the Second World War and the existential conflict with the Soviet Union; mainline Protestantism dominance had diminished, leaving a vacuum to be filled by other sources of transcendent thought; and the federal government inserted Godspeak into national symbols, such as currency and the Pledge of Allegiance. Those who commented on and studied such religiosity often did so by either looking at the practices, symbols, and liturgies that suggested a religious dimension to the nation or critiquing such expressions for degrading what they considered "real" religion. Bellah expanded this conversation in a novel way.

Sociologist Matteo Bortolini has ruminated on the popularity and dominance of Bellah's discussion of civil religion. Bortolini observes that "the appeal of Bellah's thesis probably partly depended on his use of the expression 'civil religion' itself and on his ability in reframing and naming the object as a discussion that had been going on in the 1950s and 1960s."[2] Bellah's essay also seemed uniquely interesting to scholars across disciplinary boundaries. While the essay is often characterized as an example of midcentury American studies, it drew attention almost immediately from historians of the United States and philosophers, theologians, as well as Bellah's colleagues in sociology. The first and still immensely useful example of this broad interest was a collection of essays published in 1974 and edited by Russell Richey and Donald Jones that, Bortolini contends, "validated" Bellah's civil religion, thus making it a target for all future work on civil religion. Bortolini explains, "The conceptual fitness of BCR [Bellah's civil religion] as a tool for understanding America's history and present condition was one of the main focuses of the ACR [American civil religion] debate. The condensed version of the original civil religion thesis was the target of recurring criticism: Bellah was attacked for his functionalist approach, fuzziness of concepts, lack of empirical research, scanty attention devoted to the evangelical tradition, and value-laden analyses."[3] And yet nothing has really replaced Bellah's civil religion as an analytic, prescriptive, and popular concept. Why?

Civil religion is a strange beast; it can often appear to mean almost anything to anyone at any time. The term can be helpful to political theorists for what it suggests about normative beliefs in or ideas about a nation. Sociologists find it useful because it provides a way to describe a sense of belonging and, at the same time, a rationale to see how groups can suffer alienation from an often overbearing majority. Theologians appreciate the way civil religion plays with the human need for transcendence and the search for divinity within a world dominated by political expediency. And historians find the term evocative for the way it reduces complex events to a usable past. Clearly, civil religion is, itself, a complicated term, but one that can cover up as much as it reveals about the nature of American life and history. Not surprisingly, Bellah's initial use of the term was born from conflict.

Bellah's essay sprang, he said, from "concern with the American Vietnam War," but he admitted that at the time he wasn't "fully aware of the new religious phenomenon" that he had observed. "It was a sense of moral crisis in the United States being engaged in a war that had such negative qualities to it that made me [ask], was there anything in our past that would help us avoid this catastrophe we were in."[4] Indeed, the Vietnam War made Bellah realize that the United States was in the midst of a period of profound doubt about the faith Americans had in the nation itself. Vietnam tested the fundamental existence and operation of an American creed. Bellah declared the crisis the "third time of trial." The first time of trial was "the question of independence," the second was the "issue of slavery"; each experience brought forth figures and symbols that contributed to a collective understanding of American morality and pointed a way forward as a more just nation. Importantly, such experiences provided landmark statements on both the shortcomings and the promise of the United States. Figures such as Washington, Jefferson, and, most profoundly, Lincoln reflected on struggles and sacrifices made by Americans who would not reap the benefits of their efforts. Following World War II, "every president since Roosevelt," Bellah observed, "has been groping toward a new pattern of action in the world, one that would be consonant with our power and our responsibilities."[5] Bellah's idea of civil religion, then, looked both backward at seminal American experiences as well as forward to ways Americans might evaluate contemporary crises and wars. Ironically, Bellah never intended for his essay to stand as the American version of Rousseau's work, but "Civil Religion in America" became a text far more influential than Rousseau in the American context.

That influence, though, was a burden. Almost from the moment his essay appeared Bellah sought to distance himself from what became the popular implications of the term—that America had a collection of ideals that generations of its people could appeal to as a kind of normative faith. Obviously, Bellah had good reason to disavow such a notion. If Americans were to believe in an elusive, illusionary, singular American civil religion, the nation would avoid facing tough problems and contending with difficult solutions. It would unreflectively justify, not thoughtfully critique, the nation's actions.

Bellah's loathing of Richard Nixon's administration and the escalation of the war in Southeast Asia led him to become the first person to try to find an American civil religion "beyond Bellah." The work that set this new course was his 1975 collection of essays, *The Broken Covenant*. He attempted to reorient how civil religion operated, shifting the emphasis from an optimistic understanding of foundational moments and documents to a more skeptical reading of the space between national ideas and actions. As he wrote in an email to Haberski, Bellah thought "no reader of *The Broken Covenant* has to my knowledge given it the common misinterpretation that 'Civil Religion in America' has received. [*The Broken Covenant*] begins by saying that the civil religion is 'an empty and broken shell,' so can't be simply a celebration of [the nation]." Taken together, then, Bellah's two major statements on American civil religion provided plenty of fodder for the debate over the term and Bellah's role in that debate.

The title of Bellah's 1975 book suggests an anachronism at the heart of the civil religion debate. In arguing that Americans understood their history through a covenant, Bellah at least assumed two mutual reinforcing ideas: that Americans had conscientiously fused faith and reason into a moral superstructure and that this structure helped conjure into existence a cultural entity understood as America. Bellah used this intellectual construction to understand how times of moral crisis pushed Americans to evaluate their commitment to each other. In one sense, Bellah could sound naïve about the consensus he assumed existed in the American past, but he also stated plainly an observation that in the mid-1970s at least was worth hearing: "The meaning of the American experience will remain forever opaque to those who, once they see through the most simple-minded version of American idealism, can find only violence and self-interest in its stead."[6] In the midst of war and social unrest, Bellah pressed Americans to imagine or find the moral imagination necessary to see something beyond themselves and their turbulent times. In one of the few reviews to acknowledge the development of Bellah's thinking about civil religion, sociologist Pierre Hegy concluded that "the reintegration of faith, myth, and symbols among the 'data' of social life and sociological research will give visions to the blind and hope to the desperate; it will allow the sociologist to be again a prophetic voice in his society. All these new perspectives are made possible by the not-yet totally 'broken' Covenant outlined by Bellah."[7] But Bellah was mostly frustrated by his role in the civil religion debate.

Bortolini argues that *Broken Covenant* failed to shift the conversation over civil religion in a direction that Bellah found constructive or that gave him a less prominent role as a progenitor of the civil religion that so many scholars found fruitful to critique. When Bellah's various attempts to move beyond the 1967 essay on civil religion gained him little attention, "he decided to abandon the discussion," Bortolini explains. "As Bellah's ideas on the ACR [American civil religion] started to change, a gap opened between the flesh-and-blood Robert Bellah and his much more influential avatar. While it assured the real Bellah of a continuous flow of material and symbolic capital, the existence of 'BCR's Bellah' did not help him in disseminating his new, modified ideas on ACR. When the chasm between the two became psychologically unbearable, the real Bellah abandoned the fictional one and left the debate."[8] Bellah's physical departure from the stage, however, had little effect on the vigorous debate over civil religion.

For nearly twenty years, from 1968 through the late 1980s, scholars introduced new ways to describe the phenomenon that Bellah had made so compelling. Robert Handy noted that by the late 1970s a "five-fold, somewhat overlapping typology of civil religion" emerged: civil religion as folk religion, as the transcendental universal religion of the nation, as religious nationalism, as democratic faith, and as Protestant civic piety.[9] And James Mathisen offered a periodization of the civil religion debate in honor of the twentieth anniversary of Bellah's essay. He suggested that there were four periods that characterized interest and contestation of the term: the period from 1963 to 1967, in which the "ground rules" of the debate were set; from 1974 to 1977, when civil religion enjoyed its "golden age" as a discourse; from 1978 to 1982, as American civil religion plateaued and began to be integrated into other debates about public religion and civic faith; and finally from 1983 through 1988, when the discussion or perhaps interest in civil religion began to wane. Mathisen's timeline made sense given his point of view from the late 1980s, but since that time applying and testing civil religion comparatively and theoretically as well as historicizing Bellah's original use of the term have attracted a good deal of attention.

From the 1990s to the present, civil religion has appeared in American religious history as well as histories of almost every major period, from Puritans to Reagan; in regional histories and the history of sport; in studies on war, U.S. foreign policy, and various national settings; and through the ideas of nationalism, patriotism, fascism, and communism. In other words, the discussion instigated by Robert Bellah shows no signs of retirement, though Bellah was surely happy to no longer be at the center of the debate over civil religion in the United States or anywhere else.[10]

As we have noted, Bellah's original formulation of American civil religion inspired both an empirical and a conceptual literature. Survey researchers, particularly in the 1970s, searched for evidence of ACR in the opinions of ordinary Americans, and more recently other researchers have done likewise for a variety of other nations. In both cases, the search centered on how publics considered the sacred dimensions of their nations and how that was different from institutionalized, confessional faiths. Other scholars did content analysis, for example, on the inaugural addresses of U.S. presidents, charting patterns in the ways presidents bring up references to the divine in that most ritualized of U.S. national ceremonies. Still other studies have examined architecture, public ceremonies, or monuments and statues in order to find examples of civil religious understanding of the American past and present.[11] At the conceptual level, scholars have wrestled with cognates of "civil religion," such as "American exceptionalism," "religious nationalism," and "legitimating myths" and the relations among them, all trying to find adequate formulations for expressing the general but varied ways in which religion relates to politics and national identity. Furthermore, scholars such as Stanley Hauerwas, David Sehat, and Dylan Weller have pointedly critiqued the conflation of the national and the divine, the political and the religious, the pluralistic and the deistic to the detriment of both religious and nonreligious Americans. Weller points out, "We cannot have it both ways. . . . Regardless of the position one adopts, in an age of steadily decreasing theistic belief, the future of American civil religion is uncertain."[12]

This volume continues that trend by going "beyond Bellah" conceptually and empirically, using an interdisciplinary cast of scholars, employing varying sets of methods and data, and moving across both regions and historical periods. Chapters explore the ideological roots of civil religion and more recent elaborations of the concept that further define and specify dimensions of the notion. Other chapters think about civil religion in a United States that is now a half century beyond the time Bellah wrote. Vietnam is long-ago history, even as the cultural battles about it still powerfully inform American politics. Political assassinations, which seemed almost unimaginable to many Americans when John F. Kennedy was killed in 1963, became distressingly commonplace. Racial tensions and issues connected to inequality have continued to bedevil the body politic, resulting in both an African American president and a furious backlash against the promotion of racial equality.

The major changes to American religious, political, and cultural life since Bellah's 1967 essay help form much of the context, and often the inspiration, for much of the scholarly work that follows in this volume. In many ways, religion and politics (broadly construed) have become ever more tightly interwoven, partisan, and explicit in the past few decades than they were during the Cold War, making the idea of civil religion all the more salient, even as it may be even more contested. Three major trends in American religion since the late 1960s when Bellah wrote seem particularly pertinent to us. First has been the fading of the Protestant "mainline" and its supplanting by Protestant evangelicalism as the culturally dominant religious expression. Second is the significant expansion of non-Christian religious options, much of which has been driven by new sources of immigration. Third has been the rise of religious "nones" and various forms of nonreligion. Each of these has been closely connected to political changes.

The first change we note is that the constellation of mainline Protestant denominations that dominated social and religious life in the postwar era—Episcopalians, Presbyterians, United Methodists, ELCA Lutherans—began to shrink as a percentage of the population and in terms of public influence. The reasons for this varied. Some denominations became embroiled in controversies over the Vietnam War and other social issues in ways that cost them members. Some scholars and church people claim that members left as the mainline denominations began offering a too-watered-down, culturally comfortable version of the faith. And it is empirically the case that declining birth rates and low rates of retention of young people led to aging—and shrinking—mainline churches. At the same time, evangelical Protestant denominations, such as the Southern Baptist Convention and the Assemblies of God, abetted by the rise of nondenominational megachurches, were growing rapidly. Again, there were several reasons for this, from theology to fecundity, but the demographic facts have been clear. The end result has been that white Protestant America has assumed a more conservative face, theologically, socially, and politically. The type of organized Protestant influence that helped pass the 1964 Civil Rights Act, for example, shifted to pressure to restrict abortion, keep same-sex marriage illegal, and have prayer in public schools.

As these shifts were emerging within American Protestantism, the composition of American immigration was changing significantly. Starting with the 1965 Hart-Celler Act that reformed the national quota system for immigration (a system that had kept legal immigration rates low since the early 1920s), the social and religious composition of newcomers to the United States changed. Immigrants from Europe became secondary to those from Asia, the Middle East, and Latin America. While the significant numbers of new Americans from Latin America meant that the majority of immigrants remained Christian, the United States began to receive large numbers of Muslims, Hindus, and Buddhists. Given both their different religious practices and their ethnoracial visibility, the number of non-Christian immigrants now in the United States is often overestimated; Muslims, Jews, Buddhists, and Hindus together remain under 10 percent of the U.S. population. But their public and social presence and significance have never been more prominent.

Finally, the past two decades in particular have witnessed a dramatic rise in the number of Americans who claim no religious identity at all. Social scientists call them "nones" in a type of shorthand, arising from a common question on social surveys that asks people for their religious identity and provides an option labeled "none." The percentage of nones has risen from the single digits in the 1970s to around 25 percent today, a dramatic upward slope. Overwhelmingly, those considering themselves "nones" have some type of religious belief or spiritual life—only about 5 percent of Americans call themselves atheist, and only 3 to 4 percent agnostic. Nonetheless, a quarter of American people do not identify with a religious tradition and are unconnected to a religious institution. Taken together, these three changes mean that the religious institutions that dominated American life when Bellah wrote no longer do so.

Each of these changes in religion is connected to changing aspects of American politics. High rates of immigration and immigration characterized by more non-Christians and non-Europeans have been the basis for immigration-related political contention in the first two decades of the twenty-first century that was unseen since the early twentieth century. Whether the United States is or should be a "Christian nation" is again a hot-button electoral issue. And as American religion, particularly American Protestantism, bifurcated more clearly into liberal and conservative wings, political differences followed suit. In a major political realignment since the late 1960s, the American South switched from the Democratic Party to the Republican in response to desegregation, voting rights, and gender politics, becoming the "deepest red" of the red state / blue state shorthand. White evangelical Protestants, once the base of support for Democrats and populists such as William Jennings Bryan, enthusiastically backed President Donald Trump. A clear divide has emerged between coastal, urban, and formally educated voters on one hand, and "heartland," small-town / rural, and less educated voters on the other. That these differences began to be reflected in religious affiliational differences as well as religious belief and attendance patterns further focused the tensions. Indeed, the polarization of religion and its increasing alignment with politics is regularly credited as some of the impetus for more Americans to call themselves "nones." This has been particularly true among young and liberal Americans, who are also more likely to be more educated. A result of all this is that by the second decade of the twenty-first century, the institutional center of American politics was largely missing electorally.

However, along with these changes in the religious and political contexts between 1967 and 2020, there remain some recurring theoretical and analytic issues that still resonate in the idea of civil religion, resonate in these chapters, and resonate in scholarly literatures more generally. A key debate, often implicit but nonetheless important, is the extent to which civil religion, in whatever form, is an ideology that is used self-consciously in pursuit of certain political ends, or whether civil religion is more like a culture, a widespread and generally accepted system of norms, values, and understandings that is often effective precisely because it is assumed rather than articulated, the accepted background rather than the foregrounded "figure."

The French philosopher Jean-Jacques Rousseau is credited with the phrase "civil religion" in his work *The Social Contract*. As noted by a number of scholars, Rousseau initially conceptualized civil religion as the articulation and propagation of some sacred principles that would bind the affections of the masses to the state, particularly in conditions where confessional religion was unable to do so or to serve as a basis for cultural unity.[13] In that sense, Rousseau's civil religion could be considered "ideology"—a belief system designed to support a regime and promoted by the regime itself. It has been called "political religion" by some scholars.[14]

On the other hand, Bellah's own approach had much more in common with Émile Durkheim's sociology, in which religion was a product of a "collective conscious" that was an expression of the collectivity. While it could certainly reinforce the moral appropriateness of the existing regime, its efficacy comes from its sources in the collective itself.

In that regard, civil religion was for Bellah much more like "culture"—a normative system widely dispersed throughout a people, providing a unifying identity and commitment to the collective.[15] Bellah's primary data for his initial article were speeches by American presidents, thus implying that civil religion is indeed a set of beliefs and practices sponsored by political elites for the benefit of the state and the national status quo. And yet much of the rest of Bellah's conceptualization neither was self-congratulatory nor emphasized political power and its distribution within the American nation or state. It portrayed the American presidents as reflecting a religious impulse deep within the national body politic, not creating it. And it portrayed the civil religion they articulated as being a politico-moral critique as well as a cultural system that bound citizens to the status quo.

The literature on civil religion has often followed one of these two paths, although not necessarily self-consciously. Most prominent have been debates on whether civil religion was primarily a "prophetic" or a "priestly" religion, to use sociologist Max Weber's distinction.[16] That is, does the religious message anoint the nation with special favor and reward it for its "chosenness," or does it use a transcendent standard of justice to criticize contemporary failings, calling the nation to be better than it is? Bellah did not view priestly versions to be true to the spirit of civil religion, and Philip Gorski largely agrees—a thoroughly priestly religion without any prophetic component is not a true civil religion.[17] But given that the main thrust of the civil religion literature has been focused on finding sources of American unity,[18] whether its priestly or prophetic usages, its effects in advancing group agendas through the fissures in American political power are less examined.

Some of the contributors to this volume reflect aspects of this analytic difference between civil religion as ideological theme and civil religion as cultural impulse. For example, Wendy Wall examines the clear attempts by midcentury elites to build a "politics of consensus" that functioned as an ideology. But it would misrepresent our contributors to assign them to a simple ideology or culture approach as if it were an either/or choice. For example, Mark Silk's chapter shows how both utilitarian concerns and confessional commitments were woven throughout the Founders' considerations of religion in the political life of the new nation. Art Farnsley demonstrates that a type of civic religion permeated

Indianapolis, serving local elites' interests in branding the city even as it reflected popular understandings among many. Korie Little Edwards examines how Bellah's civil religion can serve to support a white hegemonic understanding of American identity, even as that is neither the intention nor often recognized by those articulating civil religion as an idea. Indeed, this is one of the ways in which this volume brings conceptual development and analytic complexity to our understandings of "civil religion at fifty."

The Current Volume

The conference to discuss "Bellah at fifty," which first brought together the scholars who contribute to this volume, was in November 2016, just before the presidential election. Not surprisingly, there was much talk both about the election and about various civil religious themes that had emerged in the discourses of various campaigns. Unlike both Obama campaigns in 2008 and 2012, there were few "Bellah-esque" civil religious themes running through the Hillary Clinton–Donald Trump matchup. Clinton presented herself as competent and able to wear the mantle of being the first woman U.S. president but did not articulate a vision of the nation that had many transcendent overtones. Trump's message was about "making America great again," but with remarkably few homages to the Founders or those who had sacrificed for the nation, or even much religion talk at all. He promised to make America a "winner" again, but the emotions involved were insecurity, fear, belligerence, and sometimes vengeance, not hope, pride, or even a celebratory triumphalism.

The situation changed somewhat after Trump took office. While the president himself continued to struggle to articulate any vision of the nation that wasn't a seeming extension of his own personal fortunes, including petty grievances and graceless victories, many of his allies filled some of that void. Trump's support among white evangelical Protestants was remarkably strong during the election and held surprisingly steady afterward, and many visible clergy supporters, such as Robert Jeffress of Dallas, Mark Burns of South Carolina, and Paula White of Florida, infused his administration and even President Trump personally with religious significance. Notably, however, that significance was a decidedly Christian one and regularly ignored or denied the religious pluralism that Bellah believed civil religion required. It was an exclusionary "Christian nationalism," rather than a transcendent "religion of the nation," and was almost thoroughly devoid of self-critique. These developments reopened scholarly interest in understanding civil religion and scholarly debates about how best to conceive of it.

Thus, the authors engaging the concept of civil religion in this volume do so in an America that has significant differences in its connections between religion and politics than did the one Bellah was considering. Certainly there was conflict when Bellah was writing, and engaging the conflict of his moment was part of his entire purpose. But the landscape of that conflict has shifted in many ways, and even our authors who are doing more historical work are doing so from the framework of this new setting. The extent to which these social changes have implications for how we think about and research civil religion is one of the central questions of this volume.

Conceptual Heritage and Development

Thinking about civil religion both conceptually and as empirical practices, we see the book as being made up of three sections. The first section is on the conceptual heritage of the notion of civil religion and how others working from Bellah's framework have developed his view. Focusing on the historical development of different ways in which religion can support national identity, Philip Gorski revisits his important work in *American Covenant* to make critical distinctions among civil religion and its rival meaning systems—religious nationalism and liberal secularism.[19] Gorski argues that neither of the latter two systems has the right balance of inclusion and solidarity. Religious nationalism offers a rich culture of solidarity and national identity, but by practicing a religious and political exclusion that closes the nation. Liberal secularism, on the other hand, has the virtue of offering a potentially inclusive nation to many diverse groups of people and individuals, but struggles to provide significant meaning in terms of what it means to belong to the national community. Civil religion has historically, and can again, strike a balance between those poles. Mark Silk examines the ways in which a utilitarian understanding of religion informed many of the American Founders when they thought about the role of religion in the new republic. For Silk, the Founders' view of civil religion was useful more than true, at least to those trying to craft the institutional infrastructure of a new nation-state. Finally, Rosemary Corbett offers a bit of history about Bellah as he first considered and then developed his concept of civil religion. She provides the context in which he first worked, some insights into what motivated him, and how he sought to respond to critiques during his career. In addition, Corbett teases out some key theoretical themes in Bellah's civil religion work and how those themes both enabled and also limited the concept.

Critical Challenges

The second section offers "critical challenges" to Bellah's basic conceptualization of American civil religion. Chapters here view Bellah's formulation, while provocative, as overly inclusive—geographically, socially, and historically. Arthur Remillard disputes the notion of a single "American" civil religion, covering the nation, and instead sees multiple religious constructions of political community, largely varying by region and historical experience. For Remillard, presuming there is only one civil religion covers too much ground, too loosely. Geographic location and history matter, and it posits too much to try to cover it all. Korie Little Edwards, on the other hand, calls attention to what Bellah's formulation did not include directly, the experiences of African Americans, and the perspective on the nation that emerged from those experiences. Whereas Bellah was trying to produce a vision that could see the nation as whole, Edwards notes that the nation itself historically did not want Black perspectives or Black voices represented. The social location from which Bellah wrote went underexamined in the analysis of the civil religion concept and left it only partial. Finally, Wendy Wall, writing as a historian, notes that civil religion has been partly hemmed in by its disciplinary origins in Durkheimian sociology, with its attention to unifying cultural traits and solidarity in collectivities. Also, Wall notes, Bellah's American civil religion is unselfconsciously historical. He was writing at the end of a lengthy period in which U.S. institutional elites were deliberately constructing a "politics of consensus" that posits the origin of ACR in the nation's founding. If ACR is to be a sociocultural reality for the United States now, it will need to update itself for our times.

Civil Religion in Practice

The third section turns from direct conceptual considerations to studies of civil religion "on the ground," as it were. The chapters examine civil religion as it can be seen in the lived practices of communities and other groups of political actors. Rhys Williams studies two icons often thought to embody the nation—Uncle Sam and the Statue of Liberty. While each, as a singular figure, presents the nation as a unity, in practice the uses of the different symbols have been tied in different ways to explicit political messages and implicit images of national character and purpose. Both offer "legitimating myths" of the nation, but very different ones. Williams shows their usage in political debates about immigration and its impact on the United States. Intriguingly, Elaine Peña then shows another way to think about the use of embodied symbols to represent a nation. By examining both the past and present of an annual ceremony on the International Bridge in Laredo, Texas, Peña provides an example of civil religious expression that is transnationally produced and binationally managed. Far from the exclusionist message that often encompasses the idea of "American exceptionalism," the chapter describes an event and a relationship that manages to celebrate two histories and civil religious understandings simultaneously. Finally, Arthur Farnsley examines the history and development of downtown Indianapolis and the ways in which memorials and monuments were planned, executed, and moved over time. Rooting civil religious messages in architecture and material culture, Farnsley reveals an interesting confluence of strategic planning and cultural assumption that helped to align that most "heartland" of cities with a vision of a moral, worthy, and unified nation.

We are under no illusion that this volume will end debates about civil religion—we neither expect nor hope to be the last word. Rather, we believe there is still life in the concept of civil religion, and when considered carefully it can continue to offer understandings of the American nation and its history, identity, and public life.

NOTES
1 Robert N. Bellah, "Civil Religion in America," *Daedalus* 96 (Winter 1967): 1–21.
2 Matteo Bortolini, "The Trap of Intellectual Success: Robert N. Bellah, the American Civil Religion Debate, and the Sociology of Knowledge," *Theoretical Sociology* 41 (2012): 192n7.

3 Bortolini, "Trap of Intellectual Success," 193.
4 Robert N. Bellah, "In God We Trust: Civil and Uncivil Religion in America" (interview), *Encounter* (Radio National Australia, 2000).
5 Bellah, "Civil Religion in America," 16.
6 Robert N. Bellah, *The Broken Covenant: American Civil Religion in Time of Trial* (New York: Seabury Press, 1975), 49.
7 Pierre Hegy, review of *The Broken Covenant: American Civil Religion in Time of Trial* by Robert N. Bellah, *Review of Religious Research* 19, no. 2 (Winter 1978): 218.
8 Bortolini, "Trap of Intellectual Success," 202.
9 Robert T. Handy, "Theological Table-Talk: A Decisive Turn in the Civil Religion Debate," *Theology Today*, October 1, 343–44. This typology also appears in Russell E. Richey and Donald G. Jones, eds., *American Civil Religion* (New York: Harper & Row, 1974), 4–18.
10 For reviews and critiques of both the idea of and the scholarly literature about civil religion during different periods, see—just as a sample—Phillip E. Hammond, "The Sociology of American Civil Religion: A Bibliographic Essay," *Sociological Analysis* 37 (Summer 1976); Gail Gehrig, *American Civil Religion: An Assessment* (Storrs, CT: Society for the Scientific Study of Religion, 1979); N. J. Demerath III and Rhys H. Williams, "Civil Religion in an Uncivil Society," *Annals of the American Academy of Political and Social Sciences* 480 (July 1985): 155–66; James A. Mathisen, "Twenty Years after Bellah: Whatever Happened to American Civil Religion?," *Sociological Analysis* 50 (Summer 1989): 129–46; Robert Wuthnow, *The Restructuring of American Religion* (Princeton, NJ: Princeton University Press, 1988); Carolyn Marvin and David W. Ingle, "Blood Sacrifice and the Nation: Revisiting Civil Religion," *Journal of the American Academy of Religion* 64 (1996): 767–80; Marcela Cristi, *From Civil to Political Religion: The Intersection of Culture, Religion, and Politics* (Waterloo, ON, Canada: Wilfrid Laurier University Press, 2001); Peter Luchau, "Towards a Contextualized Concept of Civil Religion," *Social Compass* 56 (2009): 371–86; Raymond J. Haberski, *God and War: American Civil Religion since 1945* (New Brunswick, NJ: Rutgers University Press, 2012); Rhys H. Williams, "Civil Religion and the Cultural Politics of National Identity in Obama's America." *Journal for the Scientific Study of Religion* 52 (June 2013): 239–57.
11 For just a few examples of these types of empirical research, see Ronald C. Wimberley, D. A. Clelland, T. C. Hood, and C. M. Lipsey, "The Civil Religious Dimension: Is It There?," *Social Forces* 54, no. 4 (1976): 890–900; Cynthia A. Toolin, "American Civil Religion from 1789–1981: A Content Analysis of Presidential Inaugural Addresses," *Review of Religious Research* 25, no. 1 (1983): 39–48; Wade Clark Roof, "American Presidential Rhetoric from Ronald Reagan to George W. Bush: Another Look at Civil Religion," *Social Compass* 56, no. 2 (2009): 286–301; Peter Gardella, *American Civil Religion: What Americans Hold Sacred* (New York: Oxford University Press, 2014).

12 Dylan Weller, "Godless Patriots: Toward a New American Civil Religion," *Polity* 45, no. 3 (July 2013): 376. See also David Sehat, *The Myth of American Religious Freedom*, updated ed. (New York: Oxford University Press, 2016), 283–85, and Stanley M. Hauerwas, "Freedom of Religion: A Subtle Temptation," *Soundings: An Interdisciplinary Journal* 72, nos. 2–3 (Summer/Fall 1989): 330–34.
13 See Demerath and Williams, "Civil Religion in an Uncivil Society"; Cristi, *From Civil to Political Religion*; Ronald Beiner, *Civil Religion: A Dialogue in the History of Political Philosophy* (New York: Cambridge University Press, 2011); Anthony Squiers, *The Politics of the Sacred in America: The Role of Civil Religion in Political Practice* (Cham, Switzerland: Springer, 2018).
14 Cristi, *From Civil to Political Religion*.
15 Rhys H. Williams, "Religion as Political Resource: Ideology or Culture?," *Journal for the Scientific Study of Religion* 35, no. 4 (1996): 368–78.
16 See, for example, Martin E. Marty, "Two Kinds of Two Kinds of Civil Religion," in Richey and Jones, *American Civil Religion*; Martin E. Marty, *Religion and Republic: The American Circumstance* (Boston: Beacon, 1989); Wuthnow, *Restructuring of American Religion*.
17 Bellah, *Broken Covenant*; Philip Gorski, *American Covenant: A History of Civil Religion from the Puritans to the Present* (Princeton, NJ: Princeton University Press, 2017); see also chapter 1, by Gorski, in this volume.
18 Williams, "Civil Religion and the Cultural Politics of National Identity"; Rhys H. Williams and Todd Nicholas Fuist, "Civil Religion and National Politics in a Neoliberal Era," *Sociology Compass* 8, no. 7 (2014): 929–38.
19 Gorski, *American Covenant*.

1

The Past and Future of the American Civil Religion

PHILIP GORSKI

The United States has not been this deeply divided since the late 1960s. Indeed, by some measures, it is more polarized today than at any time since the Civil War—so polarized that American democracy itself now seems at risk.[1] The "culture wars" of the past may have generated political gridlock. But the culture warriors never cast doubt on the democratic process itself.[2] Trump did so. And there are probably more Trumps in our future.

This is why America's civil religious tradition has never been more needed than now—nor more threatened. It is needed because it constitutes the vital center of our public life, a shared language for articulating our common dreams. It is threatened because the core values of that tradition have been steadily hollowed out: a mature liberalism has too often regressed to a juvenile libertarianism, a reasoned patriotism into a loud-mouthed jingoism, a balanced secularity into a truculent secularism. Our civic virtues seem to be devolving into political vices.

There is plenty of blame to go around. But the nation's economic, cultural, and political elites are especially culpable. They have consistently confused their class interests with the common good. It must be added that the political right is more at fault than the political left.[3] The leaders of the Republican establishment and the religious right abandoned the vital center long ago in a ruthless quest for cultural and electoral hegemony, passing on the bill to their followers in the process. Trump returned it to them, marked "unpaid."

Americans like to "move on" and "turn the page" and "put it in the past." But that will not do, not this time. Too often past generations have bequeathed their moral debts to future generations. Debts accrued by Puritan holy warriors, southern slave owners, northern robber barons, and many, many others. The interest on these debts has grown truly staggering: residential segregation and mass incarceration, growing inequality and global warming, failed wars and frayed alliances.

This is not the only truth about America though. There are, too, the "self-evident truths" of the Founders: the Puritan truths of mercy, humility, and charity, and the Revolutionaries' truths of equality, justice, and liberty. Most have honored these values mainly in the breach. But a few have lived up to them. And it is to their credit that these ideals are still alive, and why some of us must try once more to live up to them.

What Is American Civil Religion?

The French philosopher Jean-Jacques Rousseau first set forth the "civil religion" idea over two centuries ago. But as we have seen, it was the late sociologist Robert Bellah who originally injected it into our national conversation just fifty years ago.[4] For him, as for me, civil religion is best understood as an agnostic form of political theology, an attempt to situate national purposes within a transcendent frame of reference.

In the case of the American civil religion (ACR), this frame may be understood in religious and/or secular terms because the ACR has religious as well as secular sources. The religious source is the prophetic religion of the Hebrew Scriptures. Prophetic religion in this sense should not be confused with "prophecy belief" of a contemporary sort. The former draws primarily on "latter prophets" such as Amos, Isaiah, and Jeremiah, who excoriated the Israelites for their sins and called them back to the covenant. "Let justice roll down like waters, and righteousness like a mighty stream" (Amos 5:24). The latter pulls mainly on apocalyptic texts such as Daniel and Revelation, which speak of a cataclysmic struggle between good and evil. Justice shall be done and the righteous lifted up.

The secular source of the ACR is civic republicanism.[5] It must be clearly distinguished from classical liberalism. For classical liberals, the main purpose of a political order is to ensure individual rights and promote private happiness. The only thing that citizens owe one another is to leave each other alone to the enjoyment of their just desserts. The best life is a life of private pleasures. For civic republicans, by contrast, the main purpose of a political order is the exercise of self-governance. Citizens are morally accountable to one another, and the best life is one dedicated to the common good. When the Founders spoke of the "pursuit of happiness," it was *public* rather than private happiness they had in mind.

Prophetic religion and civic republicanism have been entwined in each of the nation's two foundings: one Puritan, the other Revolutionary. The Puritans envisioned their New England as a "New Israel." It would be founded on a sacred covenant with God—or, rather, a series of covenants. The most famous of these was outlined by John Winthrop, the future governor of the Bay Colony, onboard the *Arbella*, before it set sail for the New World: "To follow the counsel of Micah, to do justly, to love mercy, to walk humbly with our God. For this end, we must be knit together, in this work, as one man. We must entertain each other in brotherly affection. We must be willing to abridge ourselves of our superfluities, for the supply of others' necessities. We must uphold a familiar commerce together in all meekness, gentleness, patience and liberality."[6] Should they adhere to the terms of their covenants, the Puritans believed, God would protect them and make them a "light unto the nations." Should they break it, however, God would punish them and make of them an example for all the world to see. The Puritans were also proto-republicans. Shortly after arriving in Massachusetts, Winthrop instituted a more inclusive system of communal governance. It was imperfectly inclusive—only male property holders could be full citizens. But it was also far more inclusive than in "old" England. Republican institutions soon became an integral part of the "New England way."

The American Revolution did not loosen the Puritan synthesis of prophetic religion and civic republicanism. On the contrary, it tightened the knot still further, transforming the inchoate "godly republicanism" of the New England way into a full-blown "Hebraic republicanism." The Puritan fathers actually had little knowledge of the theory or history of republican governance, in either its ancient or early modern forms. The intellectual leaders of the American Revolution were deeply conversant with both. They could quote Cicero and Polybius but also Machiavelli and Harrington (see chapter 2 by Silk in this volume). They understood that republics are sustained by virtue and endangered by corruption. They knew that the longevity of a republic depended not only on constitutional design but also on civic piety.

This has been well known since the rediscovery of the republican origins of the American Revolution a half century ago.[7] Less well known is the fact that the Revolutionary generation had a deeper knowledge of prophetic religion as well. During the seventeenth century, Christian scholars in the West learned Hebrew and Christian theologians began studying the Talmud. The Revolutionary generation was particularly influenced by a heterodox school of rabbinical commentary, which argued that the republic was the form of government that God had chosen for his people. The key text was 1 Samuel 8. There, the prophet Samuel warned the Israelites that a king would send their sons to war, put their daughters to work, seize their land, and, finally, make them into slaves again. "And in that day you will cry out because of your king, whom you have chosen for yourselves, but the Lord will not answer you in that day" (1 Samuel 8:18). Building on this interpretation, some Revolutionary-era thinkers argued that the "Hebrew republic" was the first and best republic, older and more perfect than its Greek and Roman successors.[8] It was more perfect because it rejected monarchy as idolatry and because it was based on divine rather than human law. They believed that the American Republic would recover the Hebraic ideal. In contrast to Continental republicans, such as Machiavelli and Rousseau, who claimed that Christianity and republicanism were antithetical, then, many of the American Revolutionaries saw them as complementary.

Civil Religion qua Dynamic Tradition

In *The Broken Covenant*, Bellah defined the ACR as America's "founding myth." In *American Covenant*, I redefine it as a dynamic tradition.[9] I do so because the myth concept suggests that the ACR was static. It was not. It has been repeatedly recuperated and rearticulated during periods of crisis and change. During the Civil War, for example, Frederick Douglass argued that the nation's founding documents were in fact antislavery documents. This was explicit in the Declaration's plain assertion that "all men are created equal." And it was implicit in the Constitution's omission of the world "slavery."

Following Douglass's lead, Abraham Lincoln would later argue that the Constitution had to be read through the lens of the Declaration and that the spirit of their preambles governed the interpretation of their articles. From this scriptural hermeneutic, Lincoln derived not only an argument against slavery but also a defense of the Union. Did the Constitution not speak of "We, the People, of the United States" rather than of "the peoples of these United States," he pressed?

Of course, the promise of racial equality contained in the Emancipation Proclamation and the Thirteenth and Fourteenth Amendments would be retracted almost as soon as it was issued. It would be almost a full century before there was a nationwide, and basically successful, effort to honor that commitment. But when Martin Luther King Jr. and other leaders of the civil rights movement made the case for racial equality, they often invoked secular and religious scripture to argue their cause. "I have a dream," King famously declared, "that one day this nation will rise up and live out the true meaning of its creed: 'We hold these truths to be self-evident: that all men are created equal.'" Later in that same speech, he insisted that "we will not be satisfied until 'justice rolls down like waters, and righteousness like a mighty stream.'" Elsewhere, he would emphasize the need for Protestants, Catholics, and Jews to join together in the quest for racial reconciliation.[10] In this way, King rearticulated the founding traditions in a more universalistic fashion that emphasized not just racial equality but also social justice and spiritual ecumenicism.

In *The Broken Covenant*, Bellah had concluded that the ACR had become an "empty and broken shell." But it returned, phoenix-like, in March 2008. Enveloped in a political crisis sparked by the incendiary words of his then pastor, Jeremiah Wright, a young presidential hopeful named Barack Hussein Obama would renew this peculiarly American blend of sacred and secular scripture. Obama spoke of the "original sin of slavery" and of the need to build a "more perfect union." He spoke of "marching" and "wandering" on the way to a better America. And he spoke as well of the need for reconciliation between all of America's races and creeds, not just Black and white, but people of all hues, not just Christians and Jews, but non-Christians and nonbelievers too. In this way, Obama rearticulated the founding traditions in a still more universalistic fashion that acknowledged America's increasing racial and cultural diversity.[11]

A Theory of Tradition

I refer to the ACR as a dynamic tradition rather than a founding myth. To some self-described "traditionalists," this may seem like a contradiction in terms. For them, a tradition is a tradition precisely insofar as it is unchanging. Some "progressives" may find this conceptual coupling equally perplexing. For them, progress is inherently opposed to tradition. The idea of a dynamic tradition attempts to capture the truths of traditionalism and progressivism without succumbing to their conceits.

For traditionalists, a tradition is like a spring. The water is purest at the source. The further one moves from the source, the muddier the water becomes. So it's best to hunker down near the spring or, having lost one's way, to retrace one's steps. For progressives, a tradition is more like a swamp. Over time, the once pure spring becomes a stagnant pool, as the detritus of the past accumulates and rots. There is no point searching for the original spring, says the progressive. It's better to move on in search of new lands.

In my view, a healthy tradition is more like a great river. It begins at a source or, more often, at multiple sources. But it gains in depth, breadth, and strength over time. It grows broader as it cuts through new landscapes. It grows stronger as new streams join it. And it grows deeper as the river bottom erodes to bedrock.

Sometimes we must go back to the sources. About that the traditionalists are right. But not because the truth is to be found there. About that the traditionalists are wrong. The truth is not in the purity of the source; it is in the flow of the river. The point of retracing our steps is not to get to the source so much as to follow the flow.

Consider an example: human equality. This ideal is enunciated in the source documents of American political tradition. Is the meaning of this ideal really exhausted by the "original intent" of the nation's Founders? After all, their stated intention was to limit human equality to white men and deny it to white women and Black slaves. It took a fratricidal Civil War and numerous civic struggles to conclusively demonstrate the contrary. Even today, some remain unconvinced.

Sometimes traditions become stagnant. About that the progressives are correct. But "moving on" is not the only possible response. About that they are mistaken. One can also return to the source and attempt to free it again. This can be done in two ways: by clearing away the debris or by drilling down more deeply.

Consider an example: the Progressive Movement itself! From the Puritans to the abolitionists, American Protestantism had been the wellspring of reformist movements through much of the nation's history.

With the collapse of Reconstruction and the onset of Jim Crow, however, this wellspring had become completely choked with racial detritus. Some Progressives decided to "move on." But others chose to drill deeper. That is what W. E. B. Du Bois did for much of his life. He often used Christian sources to criticize racist Christians. What would racist whites do if they encountered a colored Christ in their midst? This was the premise of a series of short stories he published over the years.[12]

For traditionalists, history moves in circles. We drift away from the source and then circle back to where we started. All history consists of movement and return. For progressives, history moves in straight lines. When tradition holds us back, we slough it off. All history is composed of resistance and emancipation. In the philosophy propounded here, history moves in spirals. Paradoxically, moving backward is often the only way to move forward. Reenvisioning the future often requires confronting memories of the past—like statues of the Confederacy.

The Civil Religious Tradition and Its Rivals

In *The Broken Covenant*, Bellah spoke of America's "founding myth" in the singular. I have already noted one reason for preferring the plural: America was founded at least twice, first by the Puritans and then by the Revolutionaries. There is also a second reason: America actually has three traditions of political theology. The ACR is one. The other two are religious nationalism and radical secularism.[13] Modern-day religious nationalists understand the United States as a "Christian nation" founded on "Judeo-Christian principles" that are now threatened by "irreligion" and "immorality." Radical secularists counter that the United States is a "secular democracy" founded on "Enlightenment principles" that are now threatened by "theocracy" and "superstition." The historical roots of both traditions go deep.

Religious nationalism is rooted in the Bible and doubly so. The first root has already been noted: a heterodox reading of the apocalyptic texts popularly known as "prophecy belief." On the orthodox reading of these texts originally set out by Saint Augustine and other church fathers, the apocalyptic texts are to be read figuratively and allegorically. The violent struggles between the forces of good and evil described in the texts are actually recurring struggles that take place in the human heart. On the heterodox reading that has become dominant among American evangelicals, these struggles will take place on an earthly stage and the forces of good and evil will assume physical form, probably at some date in the not too distant future. Prophecy believers interpret the apocalyptic texts literally and predictively rather than allegorically and figuratively.

The second root is to be found in the epic narratives of the "former prophets" contained in the Hebrew Bible. The red thread that runs through these texts is blood: the bloody conquest of the Promised Land, blood sacrifices on the altars of the nation, and the blood purity of the "saving remnant." The later prophets had already transmitted God's displeasure with blood religion: "I hate, I despise your feasts," God thundered, "and I take no delight in your solemn assemblies. Even though you offer me your burnt offerings and grain offerings, I will not accept them" (Amos 5:21–22). Rabbinic Judaism and Western Christianity had likewise rejected the old cult of blood sacrifice, albeit for different reasons. But blood religion has been invoked again and again to justify imperialism, state building, and ethnonationalism—and not only by Christians.

It is little wonder that increasing numbers of Americans, confronted with religious nationalism of this kind, now embrace radical secularism. This tradition also has two roots. The first has already been touched upon: libertine liberalism. In the classical liberalism of Hobbes and Locke, freedom is understood as the absence of physical restraints. For the classical liberal, then, we are free if and to the degree that we are not hindered in the pursuit of our desires. In the libertine liberalism that first emerged in the nineteenth century, the classical idea of freedom has been further radicalized. Freedom is now understood as the absence of all restraints on our desires, including moral ones. It is not enough to remove the external restraints; one must also dissolve the internal ones. This is why libertine liberals have such a difficult time with the idea of religious freedom. It seems oxymoronic. Religious belief imposes internal restraints. Thus, emancipation presumes irreligion.

The second root of radical secularism is "total separationism," the claim that the American Constitution mandates a "total separation of religion and politics." Of course, the Constitution itself says no such thing. Rather, it establishes two different and potentially conflicting principles: it prohibited "religious establishments" and guaranteed "free exercise." To be sure, some of the framers did use the word "separation." Madison spoke of a "perfect separation" of church and state, and Jefferson of a "wall of separation" between the two.[14] Both supported an institutional separation of church and state. But neither spoke of a total separation between religion and politics. That is a much more radical demand. What links the two sources of radical secularism is the unspoken conviction that "religion poisons everything" and must therefore be excluded from the public sphere at all costs.

Why should we prefer the ACR to its rivals? For three reasons: internal consistency, historical accuracy, and sociological plausibility. Religious nationalism falls short in all three respects. It is internally inconsistent because it is idolatrous and therefore fundamentally irreligious. In the end, religious nationalism is really nothing but collective self-worship. Religious nationalism is historically inaccurate because it claims that the American Founders were "orthodox Christians" and that the American Constitution is based on "Judeo-Christian values." This is not even half right. The revolutionary generation and the founding documents were both profoundly influenced by the "pagan" ideals of civic republicanism. And insofar as the Constitution was influenced by religious ideals, they were arguably more "Jewish" than "Christian." Third and finally, religious nationalism is sociologically implausible. The cultural and religious unity that religious nationalists yearn for cannot be achieved, at least not peacefully.

Does that mean we should embrace radical secularism instead? Not at all. It, too, falls short in every respect. It is internally inconsistent because it is fundamentally illiberal. It seeks to constrain religious freedom in the name of freedom itself. It substitutes freedom from religion for freedom of religion. It is historically inaccurate insofar as it claims that the United States has a "Godless Constitution" premised on "Enlightenment principles." This, too, is not even half right. For one thing, classical republicanism had a far greater influence on the American Revolution than Enlightenment rationalism did. For another, the radical secularist account omits the nation's second founding document, the Declaration of Independence, which includes not one but four explicit references to God, specifically to "nature's God," the "Creator," "the Supreme Judge," and "divine Providence." This may be an "enlightened" theism, but it is theism nonetheless. Finally, radical secularism is sociologically implausible because the United States remains the most religiously observant nation in the modern West.

Unlike its rivals, the ACR easily passes all three tests. It does not conflate religion and nation, nor does it confuse freedom of religion with freedom from religion. It recognizes the sacred as well as the secular sources of American democracy. As such, it could be affirmed by people of faith—and of no faith. Further, it is elastic enough to encompass an increasingly diverse nation. Whether it is strong enough to contain our increasingly fractious politics remains to be seen.

The Corruption of the Civil Religion

Bellah opened his 1967 essay on the ACR with a close reading of JFK's Inaugural Address. But he could just as easily have chosen speeches by Eisenhower or Johnson or by Teddy or Franklin Roosevelt. For most of the twentieth century, the ACR was a genuinely bipartisan tradition. Democrats made social justice the central imperative of the national covenant. Republicans were more apt to emphasize moral propriety. But these were mostly differences of emphasis.

This began to change after 1968. By the 1980s, the Democratic Party had lost its civil religion. From McGovern through Dukakis, Democratic standard bearers mostly spoke the *langue de bois* of secular liberalism. The Democrats' rejection of civic patriotism made the ACR into the exclusive preserve of the Republican Party. Having monopolized it, they promptly set about corrupting it.

The corrupter-in-chief was Ronald Reagan. The prophetic voice of the ACR had placed the American people under judgment. It commanded them to be a "city on a hill" and a "light unto the nations." Reagan assured Americans of their fundamental goodness and absolved them of their sins. They already were a "city on a hill," more than that, a "*shining city on a hill*."[15] Whatever trouble or darkness they might experience was someone else's fault: the fault of the federal government perhaps or, more likely, the "evil empire." This was Reagan's first civil heresy.

His second was to corrupt the republican tradition that gave his party its name. For Reagan was not a republican at all; he was a liberal. Not a New Deal–style "big government liberal" of course. Rather, a neoclassical liberal who placed his faith in the market and mistook consumption for salvation. He substituted self-interest for civic virtue, and private property for the common wealth. This was Reagan's second civil heresy.

The backup vocals were provided by various leaders of the Christian right. They were usually sung in a minor key. There was much talk of sexual immorality and national decline. But they harmonized surprisingly well with the Reaganesque melody. For James Dobson, Jerry Falwell, and Ralph Reed, too, the source of America's troubles was always somebody else. Not the churches themselves, but "secular humanists" of various sorts.

Then came a brief intermezzo. With his hand on a Bible opened to the beatitudes, George Bush the Elder prefaced his inauguration with this awkward but hopeful prayer: "Use power to help people." If the older Bush was the last act of the noblesse oblige of the northeastern establishment, then the first Clinton (Bill) was the final appearance of the populist Protestantism of the rural South. Quoting fluently from Scripture, Clinton would call the American people to a "new covenant" of social justice and racial inclusion.[16]

The events of 9/11 and the presidency of Bush the Younger marked another key turning point: from a corrupted civil religion to a divisive religious nationalism. Bush, himself, was partly to blame. In the immediate aftermath of the terrorist attacks, he was careful to draw a line between Islam and terrorism. In the run-up to the Second Iraq War, his rhetoric became less cautious. He declared Iraq a nodal point on an "axis of evil" and implied that America could bring an end to evil. He wondered aloud whether a nonbeliever could be a good American, and he told the rest of the world that "you're either with us, or you're with the terrorists."[17] Time and time again, Bush implied that the line between good and evil runs between people and nations rather than through them. That was his great civil heresy.

Of course, others spoke even more recklessly. On Robertson's *700 Club* television show, Jerry Falwell and Pat Robertson insisted that secular humanists were as much to blame for the terrorist attacks as the Islamic terrorists. Meanwhile, secular cheerleaders such as Rush Limbaugh and Sean Hannity were busy untethering American exceptionalism from its religious moorings—thereby preparing the rise of Donald Trump.

The Secularization of Religious Nationalism

Opinion polls suggest that more white evangelicals voted for Donald Trump in 2016 than voted for Mitt Romney in 2012.[18] Why? Why would white evangelicals pull the lever for a man who is the walking antithesis of most everything they claim to stand for—family values, piety, humility, and forgiveness? No doubt, part of the answer is negative polarization and political tribalism. Still, Hillary hatred and party loyalty can't be the whole explanation. The Republican primaries featured a number of candidates with rock-solid evangelical bona fides. And yet a plurality of white evangelicals chose Trump over Jeb Bush and Ted Cruz.

There are various potential interpretations of Trumpism. Reading it as fascism explains its appeal to the white nationalists of the "alt-right." Reading it as populism explains its appeal to a white working class fed up with the "Washington establishment." And reading it as authoritarianism explains its appeal to voters with authoritarian personalities. These interpretations are not necessarily wrong, but they do not explain Trump's appeal to evangelicals qua evangelicals.

So let me propose a different interpretation. On this reading, Trumpism is a *secular form of religious nationalism*. By "secular form of religious nationalism," I mean one that strips religious identity of its ethical content and transcendental reference. In Trumpism, religion functions mainly as a marker of race.

In Trumpism, the age-old rhetoric of blood and apocalypse is secularized, denuded of explicitly religious content. But it is nonetheless full of blood and apocalypse. Consider one particularly revealing—and chilling—example. At his 2016 campaign rallies, Trump often recounted a (debunked) story about General John Pershing. After capturing fifty Muslim terrorists in the Philippines, the story goes, Pershing had fifty bullets dipped in pigs' blood that were then used to execute forty-nine of the prisoners. Pershing then gave the last bullet to the fiftieth man and told him to return to his people. There were no more acts of Islamic terrorism for almost thirty years, Trump would triumphantly conclude.[19] It was one of the biggest applause lines in Trump's stump speech. It evidently spoke to the innermost id of his most fervent supporters.

This same logic underlies Trump's thinking about terrorism and geopolitics more generally. The old strategies of policing and deterrence will not work, he insists. Harder tactics will be necessary. Ultimately, blood will have to be spilled. For Trump, it appears, blood sacrifice has magical powers. Against this background, Trump's remark about blood coming out of Fox newscaster Megyn Kelly's "whatever" sounds more like a Freudian slip than a faux pas.[20]

Trump does not allude to the Tribulation or the Second Coming in the way that old-school religious nationalists like Jerry Falwell or Pat Robertson did. But Trump *does* portray the contemporary world as an apocalyptic hellscape. There are no demons or angels, no monsters or dragons. Just "real Americans" threatened by hordes of Syrian refugees, gangs of Muslim terrorists, and swarms of Mexican rapists. Trump's apocalypse is a secular one.

With Christ out of the picture, the role of Messiah is open again. Trump famously claimed that he and he alone has the power to cast these monstrous minions back into their respective pits, as long as his followers put their faith in him. "Believe me folks," he often says, "I will do it." I will deliver you from evil, I will redeem you from poverty, and I will lift you up again above all races. American will "win" again. In Trumpism, the Second Coming of Christ becomes the First Term of the Donald.

Most of Trump's evangelical supporters are not willing to go this far. They tend to see him as a political rather than spiritual messiah. Some liken him to King David—another adulterous ruler. Others compare him to Cyrus the Great, the Persian emperor who freed the Jews from their Babylonian captivity.[21] In both cases, Trump is presented as an instrument of divine justice.

Reading Trumpism as a secular version of religious nationalism not only explains why so many evangelicals rallied to Trump but also sheds light on *which* evangelicals did so. Not the more pious of the evangelical masses, as it turns out, nor the more theologically astute of its leaders. During the spring of 2016, opinion polls turned up a fascinating finding: an inverse relationship between church attendance and support for Trump. As for Franklin Graham and Jerry Falwell Jr., they are political leaders, not thought leaders.

In short, the affinity is not really between Trump and Christianity—it is between Trumpism and Christianism. By Christianism, I mean Christianity as a political identity denuded of ethical content. Trumpism is a Christianist version of political theology.

Trumpism is often understood as the American equivalent of European neopopulism.²² There is considerable merit to this comparison. Both ideologies have taken root in the same putrid soil of nativist backlash and economic anxiety. Both have appealed to religious conservatives as well.

The advent of Trumpism marks a worrisome turning point in the history of the already worrisome ideology. Loosed from its religious moorings, religious nationalism now floats free of the ethical constraints of Christian ethics and political theology with a would-be messiah clinging to that frayed rope. Secular progressives have often wished for the demise of religious conservatism. They imagined that a reasonable form of secular conservatism would take its place. This now looks like wishful thinking.

Conclusion

Hope is a theological virtue. Perhaps it is a civic virtue as well. I close this chapter with a few signs of hope on the horizon. First, there are the ideological rifts that have opened up within the religious right. One is generational. Since the late 1990s, growing numbers of young evangelicals have become increasingly disenchanted with the narrow agenda of their parents' generation, with its singular focus on the sex and family issues around abortion and homosexuality. While most young evangelicals remain fervently pro-life, fewer and fewer oppose gay marriage and more and more embrace a broader range of issues, from environmental stewardship to human trafficking.²³ The other is gender-based. The leading figures in the older generation of the religious right were all white men. With a few exceptions—one thinks of Phyllis Schlafly, for example—women were relegated to supporting roles. That has changed. Increasing numbers of women have now risen into positions of leadership within the broader evangelical community. Further, as Brad Wilcox and other scholars have shown, the status of women within evangelical households has also been shifting in a more egalitarian direction.²⁴ Race relations are another source of internal division. Let us not mince words here: evangelicalism and racism have often gone hand in hand, particularly in the South. However, a small but growing number of evangelicals have publicly committed themselves to the cause of racial reconciliation, particularly in the South.²⁵

Donald Trump's climate change denialism, blatant misogyny, and flagrant racism have turned these fissures into ruptures. The breakup of the religious right is full of danger. American exceptionalism may devolve still further into white ethnonationalism. But it is also pregnant with possibility, as some segments of the evangelical community become available for new political alliances.

NOTES

1 James E. Campbell, *Polarized: Making Sense of a Divided America* (Princeton, NJ: Princeton University Press, 2016).
2 See, for example, Ruth Braunstein's *Prophets and Patriots: Faith in the Democracy across the Political Divide* (Berkeley: University of California Press, 2017).
3 Thomas E. Mann and Norman J. Ornstein, *It's Even Worse Than It Looks: How the American Constitutional System Collided with the New Politics of Extremism* (New York: Basic Books, 2012).
4 Robert N. Bellah, "Civil Religion in America," *Daedalus* 96 (Winter 1967): 1–21, and *The Broken Covenant: American Civil Religion in Time of Trial* (Boston: Seabury Press, 1975).
5 See Philip Gorski, *American Covenant: A History of Civil Religion from the Puritans to the Present* (Princeton, NJ: Princeton University Press, 2017).
6 See Gorski, *American Covenant*, 40–44.
7 Bernard Bailyn, *The Ideological Origins of the American Revolution* (Cambridge, MA: Harvard University Press, 1967).
8 Gorski, *American Covenant*, 60–66.
9 Bellah, *Broken Covenant*; Gorski, *American Covenant*.
10 Gorski, *American Covenant*, 150–51.
11 Philip Gorski, "Barack Obama and Civil Religion," *Political Power and Social Theory* 22 (2011): 179–214.
12 W. E. B. Du Bois, *Du Bois on Religion*, ed. Phil Zukerman (Walnut Creek, CA: AltaMira Press, 2000).
13 Gorski, *American Covenant*.
14 Lenni Brenner, ed., *Jefferson and Madison on the Separation of Church and State* (Fort Lee, NJ: Barricade Books, 2004).
15 Reagan used the phrase a number of times, including his November 3, 1980, election eve address, his 1988 State of the Union Address, and his January 11, 1989, Farewell Address.
16 Clinton starting using the phrase during his campaign for the Democratic Party presidential nomination in the fall of 1991, then most visibly in his acceptance speech at the 1992 Democratic National Convention.
17 George W. Bush, address to U.S. Congress, September 21, 2001.
18 Jessica Martínez and Gregory A. Smith, "How the Faithful Voted: A Preliminary 2016 Analysis," (Pew Research Center, November 9, 2016), http://pewresearch.org.

See also Philip Gorski, "Why Evangelicals Voted for Trump: A Critical Cultural Sociology," *American Journal of Cultural Sociology* 5, no. 3 (November 2017): 338–54.

19 See Paul A. Kramer, "Trump and the Legend of General Pershing: The Folklore That Emerged from the War on Terror," *Foreign Affairs*, September 11, 2017, www.foreignaffairs.com.

20 Evelyn Rupert, "Trump Offers Belated Defense of Megyn Kelly 'Blood' Comment," *The Hill*, May 6, 2016, https://thehill.com.

21 See reporting on this in Richard Mouw, "The Prophetic Witness of the Christianity Today Editorial," *Religion and Politics*, January 7, 2020, https://religionandpolitics.org; Tara Isabella Burton, "The Biblical Story the Christian Right Uses to Defend Trump: Why Evangelicals Are Calling Trump a 'Modern-Day Cyrus,'" *Vox*, March 5, 2018, www.vox.com.

22 See, for example, Jeremy Ashkenas and Gregor Aisch, "European Populism in the Age of Donald Trump," *New York Times*, December 5, 2016, www.nytimes.com.

23 Jeff Diamant, "Though Still Conservative, Young Evangelicals Are More Liberal Than Their Elders on Some Issues" (Pew Research Center, May 4, 2017), www.pewresearch.org.

24 W. Bradford Wilcox, *Soft Patriarchs, New Men: How Christianity Shapes Fathers and Husbands* (Chicago: University of Chicago Press, 2004).

25 Andrea Smith, *Unreconciled: From Racial Reconciliation to Racial Justice in Christian Evangelicalism* (Durham, NC: Duke University Press, 2019).

2

The Utilitarian Context of American Civil Religion

MARK SILK

Except for citing the chapter on civil religion in Rousseau's *Social Contract*, Robert Bellah's "Civil Religion in America" has nothing to say about the context within which discussion of the role of religion in the state took place in the early American republic. As a result, the essay fails to recognize the extent to which the civil religious language of the Founders expresses a utilitarian understanding of that role, as opposed to a distinctly American faith. By looking at sources that Bellah did not discuss as well as some that he did, this chapter offers a different way of reckoning with the origins of what he identified as the American civil religion.

Religious Legitimation in European Political Theory

Believing Christianity to be fundamentally flawed as a civic institution, Machiavelli was nevertheless convinced that religion was necessary for states to prosper.[1] Over the next several centuries, the only writer of any note who disagreed with him was the seventeenth-century Dutch Calvinist Pierre Bayle, who argued that societies fare as well under atheism as they do under Christianity or idolatry.[2] In the 1730s, the English divine William Warburton contended that a Christian religious establishment is more than adequate to the job of creating a law-abiding, unified, and motivated society—provided it is understood that "the true end for which religion is established is, not to provide for the true faith, but for civil utility."[3] Bayle and Warburton served as the Scylla and Charybdis through which, in 1762, Rousseau sailed to arrive at the end of the *Social Contract* at *la religion civile*—civil religion.

For Rousseau, the Machiavellian conundrum was that, on the one hand, states require religion but that, on the other, Christianity is by its very nature incapable of doing the job.⁴ His way out was not via the kind of elaborate religiosity that, according to the Western republican tradition, had been instituted in ancient Rome by its second king, Numa Pompilius, and his mythical helpmeet, the goddess Egeria. Although "civil theology," as Roman writers called it, effectively bound citizens to the state, it entailed false belief and empty ceremony and ran the risk of making people bloodthirsty and intolerant; moreover, Rousseau believed that no exclusively national religion could be established in his day and age.⁵ So he proposed "a purely civil profession of faith the articles of which it is up to the Sovereign to fix, not precisely as dogmas of Religion but as sentiments of sociability, without which it is impossible to be either a good Citizen or a loyal subject."⁶

Positively, these articles of faith included "the existence of the powerful, intelligent, beneficent, prescient, and provident Divinity, the life to come, the happiness of the just, the punishment of the wicked, the sanctity of the social Contract and the Laws." The sole negative prescription was tolerance of others—or at least tolerance of those who themselves professed tolerance, and whose dogmas contain nothing contrary to the duties of a citizen. Altogether, these "dogmas of the civil religion" were intended to promote a peaceful society of God-fearing citizens who would not fight among themselves over matters of faith or aggressively attack their neighbors. Yet how could they at the same time create strong national identity and purpose? It was that old desideratum of Machiavelli's that preoccupied Rousseau when, in 1772, he returned to the issue of religion and the state in his *Considerations on the Government of Poland*. Unlike the *Social Contract*, this posthumously published work is concerned with much of what these days is treated as civil religion: war memorials, patriotic exercises, founding documents, memorable speeches and poems.

Rousseau wrote the *Considerations* in response to a request for advice from the Confederates of Bar, a faction of the Polish elite that was agitating for political reform and greater independence from Russia. Beginning with a lament on the decline of civilization, Rousseau now claimed that in establishing religious ceremonies, games, spectacles, and plays, all ancient legislators had been guided by the same spirit that had moved Numa, whom he calls the "true founder of Rome." Numa transformed the early Romans into citizens "not so much by means of laws, for which in their rustic poverty they had as yet little need, as by means of mild institutions which attached them one to another and all of them to their soil so that they eventually sanctified their city with these apparently frivolous and superstitious rites, the force and effects of which so few people appreciate."[7] Those apparently frivolous and superstitious rites—Roman religion—had supplied the essential sinews of the Roman state. Rousseau did not go on to propose a reform of Polish religion. Indeed, he says nothing whatever about the actual religions of the population—Roman Catholicism above all, plus Eastern Orthodoxy and Judaism. What he urged, as strongly as possible, was that the distinctiveness of Polish national identity be maintained and enhanced through various forms of patriotic remembrance and ceremony.[8]

In effect, the *Considerations* replaced the *Social Contract*'s generic civil religious sentiments with a set of national exercises designed to weld Poles into the kind of "indissoluble body" that Numa had made of the Romans. The nationalist religious ideology foresworn in the *Social Contract* was now front and center—but, tellingly, with no mention of the supernatural. Rousseau never sought to integrate his two species of civil religion; indeed, one could argue that they are irreconcilable. To what extent did the young American republic engage with either?

American Political Thought at the Framing

The Declaration of Independence is premised on the proposition that "the Laws of Nature and of Nature's God" entitle Americans (along with every other people) to "a separate and equal station" among "the powers of the earth." The Great Seal of the United States, approved in 1782, features the Latin words *Annuit Coeptis*, a phrase adapted from Virgil's *Aeneid* to the effect that "He" (Zeus in Virgil, God in America) "favors [our] undertakings." But the Founders' claim of divine sanction for their new country was limited. John Adams made that clear in the three-volume *Defence of the Constitutions of Government of the United States of America* that he published while serving as minister to England in 1787. "It was the general opinion of ancient nations, that the divinity alone was adequate to the important office of giving laws to men," he writes in the preface. "Among the Romans, Numa was indebted for those laws which procured the prosperity of his country to his conversations with Egeria." As his colleagues back home were preparing to draft a new national constitution, Adams was at pains to inform the world that, unlike other nations past and present, the recently united American states "have exhibited, perhaps, the first example of governments erected on the simple principles of nature." Alluding to the Numa story, he wrote, "It will never be pretended that any persons employed in that service had any interviews with the gods, or were in any degree under the inspiration of heaven, any more than those at work upon ships or houses, or labouring in merchandize or agriculture: it will forever be acknowledged that these governments were contrived merely by the use of reason and the senses."[9]

The following year, James Wilson of Pennsylvania, one of the Constitution's most important drafters, repeated Adams's point in a Fourth of July address. "Did Numa submit his institutions to the good sense and free investigation of Rome?" Wilson asked sarcastically. "They were received in precious communications from the goddess Egeria, with whose presence and regard he was supremely favoured; and they were imposed on the easy faith of the citizens, as the dictates of an inspiration that was divine."[10] Asked why the customary invocation to God was not included in the Constitution's Preamble, Alexander Hamilton reportedly replied, "We forgot it."[11]

Nor was there a sense among many of the American Framers that something like the civil religion of Rousseau's *Social Contract* was required. During the Constitutional Convention, the Maryland delegate Luther Martin reported testily to his state legislature that "a great majority of the convention" had voted, with little discussion, that there be no religious test for holding federal office—although "there were some members so unfashionable as to think, that a belief of the existence of a Deity, and of a state of future rewards and punishments would be some security for the good conduct of our rulers, and that, in a Christian country, it would be at least decent to hold out some distinction between the professors of Christianity and downright infidelity or paganism."[12]

At that moment of high Enlightenment, there were those on both sides of the Atlantic who considered secular values sufficient to maintain good order in society. In the 1790s, François Lanthenas, one of France's leading liberal politicians, did his best to sell his fellow citizens on a revolutionary civil religion that would combine the universal morality of the *Social Contract* with the patriotic purposes of the *Considerations*.[13] Friend and translator of the rationalist Thomas Paine, Lanthenas departed from Rousseau in allowing "nothing spiritual" into his plan. Where ancient legislators had depended on superstition to maintain social cohesion, he expressed confidence that "pure and universal morality" derived from "the contemplation and study of nature, from feeling and reason" would "very well form this cement, this common bond, which is still lacking in republics."[14] In the actual event, the French revolutionaries reinforced their proclamation of liberty, equality, and fraternity with a series of festivals celebrating everything from the Divine Being to the Revolution itself.

In the infant United States, a civil religious enterprise was advanced in various ways. The signing of the Declaration of Independence was marked by annual Fourth of July celebrations. In his 1796 Farewell Address, George Washington asked that the Constitution "may be sacredly maintained."[15] In the third volume of her history of the American Revolution, published in 1805, Mercy Warren wrote that the Declaration of Independence "ought to be frequently read by the rising youth of the American states, as a palladium of which they should never lose sight, so long as they wish to continue a free and independent people."[16] Toward the end of his life, Thomas Jefferson himself embraced the cult of the Declaration, expressing pleasure at the issuance of a facsimile edition because it gave evidence "of reverence for that instrument" and reason to hope that people would "view in it a pledge of adhesion to its principles and of a sacred determination to maintain and perpetuate them"—which he called a "holy purpose." The following year, speaking of the preservation of the desk on which he wrote it (as well as the chair sat in by William Penn), Jefferson wrote, "Small things may, perhaps, like the relics of saints, help to nourish our devotion to this holy bond of Union, and keep it longer alive and warm our affections."[17]

But such expressions of civil religious patriotism from the early years of the republic are few and far between. To explain the paucity, Catherine Albanese, in her extensive examination of civil religion in the revolutionary period, writes, "There was a background awareness; there was a foreground involvement in events and activity which precluded too reflective consideration of the degree of contrivance in what they themselves were creating."[18] This may be true, but given the extensive written record of political reflection among the Founders, I would prefer to say, more simply, that there was little precedent for considering such expressions as being *sub specie religionis*. The Founders did not have Durkheim to read and seem to have been no more familiar with Rousseau's *Considerations* than most students of American civil religion are today.[19] As for the republican tradition of valorizing religion as a buttress to the state, by the late 1780s they had become pretty cavalier about it.

By the mid-1790s, however, the fashion was beginning to change. In 1795, for example, one of the commencement orations at Dickinson College was titled "The Necessity of Religion for the Support of the Civil Government."[20] In the Farewell Address, Washington (with the help of speechwriter Alexander Hamilton) sounded a warning: "Of all the dispositions and habits which lead to political prosperity, Religion and morality are indispensable supports. In vain would that man claim the tribute of Patriotism, who should labour to subvert these great Pillars of human happiness, these firmest props of the duties of Men & citizens." The key sentences come at the end of the paragraph: "And let us with caution indulge the supposition, that morality can be maintained without religion. Whatever may be conceded to the influence of refined education on minds of peculiar structure, reason and experience both forbid us to expect that National morality can prevail in exclusion of religious principle."[21] In his essay, Bellah allows as how "the utilitarian aspect" of this passage "is quite explicit."[22] What it represents, however, is a *return* to the civil religious perspective of classic republicanism, that "religious principle" was necessary for a healthy state.

What was to be done in a country that had radically separated religion from national governance? On the front page of the December 8, 1797, issue of his New York newspaper the *Time Piece*, Philip Freneau, the radical poet of the American Revolution, introduced a translation of several paragraphs from the civil religion chapter of Rousseau's *Social Contract*. "The following judicious sentiments are extracted from one of the most popular works of the celebrated J. J. Rousseau," Freneau wrote, "and it is hoped they will not be unacceptable to our Readers, especially as being in point to many particular circumstances of this country." The sentiments in question had to do with the inability of Christianity to supply the religious underpinnings of the state. Freneau was evidently aware that those who felt otherwise were in the ascendant.[23]

George Washington's emergence as the country's foremost proponent of classic civil religion was locked in by his first biographer, Mason Locke (Parson) Weems: "In this constant disposition to look for national happiness only in national morals, flowing from the *sublime* affections and blessed hopes of religion, Washington agreed with those great legislators of nations, Moses, Lycurgus, and Numa." Some there were who believed that human laws were sufficient to guarantee a nation's well-being, but, exclaimed Weems, "What bloody tragedies have been acted on the poor ones of the earth, by kings and great men, who were *above* the laws, and had no sense of religion to keep them in awe!"[24] It is worth noting that, in striking contrast to the case for civil religion going back to Cicero, Weems (like Luther Martin) saw religion as important to the state as a means of controlling the rulers rather than the ruled. Warren also pointed to Greece and Rome as models for emulation. She saw religion and republicanism going hand in hand—up to the present day. "It may be observed in the character of more modern republics," she wrote, "that religion has been the grand palladium of their institutions." Setting up religion as a palladium alongside the Declaration of Independence must be seen as her reaction to the violent anticlericalism of the French Revolution. Nor was she alone.

In his *Reflections on the Revolution in France*, Edmund Burke became the first in a long line of conservatives to mount a civil religious defense of religion against its secularist opponents.[25] Responding to Burke in *The Rights of Man*, Thomas Paine made a point of singling out Burke's indifference to what kind of religion was employed to undergird the state. "One of the continual choruses of Mr. Burke's book is 'church and state'; he does not mean some one particular church, or some one particular state, but any church and state; and he uses the term as a general figure to hold forth the political doctrine of always uniting the church with the state in every country."[26] No doubt, this passing of the civil religious banner from the likes of Machiavelli and Rousseau to the forces of reaction represented by Edmund Burke was a bit awkward for Americans of the revolutionary generation. When Washington asked, again in the Farewell Address, who could "look with indifference upon attempts to shake the foundation of the fabric" of free government, the foundation he had in mind was religion, and the attempts were those of revolutionary France—though he declined to spell that out.[27] For her part, Warren was at pains to demonstrate that the "skepticism and the late appearance of a total disregard to religious observances in France" had in no way resulted from "the democratic struggles of the nation."[28] The lady might have protested too much.

The most common discussion of the civic utility of religion in the early national period is to be found in the debates over state religious establishments in Massachusetts and elsewhere around New England. One notable example comes from Connecticut, where Oliver Ellsworth, sometime chief justice of the United States and a member of the conference committee that devised the language of the First Amendment, in 1802 headed and wrote the report of a special commission of the legislature that rejected Baptist pleas for the dissolution of the Standing Order. To secure the peace, order, and prosperity of society, Ellsworth wrote, "institutions for the promotion of good morals" are essential. Thus, on the same "principle of general utility" as raising taxes for schools and courts, "the legislature may aid the maintenance of that religion whose benign influence on morals is universally acknowledged."[29] On the basis of language like this, Charles Lippy has argued that Article 3 of the 1780 Massachusetts Constitution, which obliged towns to support religious institutions according to majority vote, established a civil religion.[30] I would prefer to say, instead, that Article 3 and its supporters offered a civil religious rationale for a regime that was designed to support the majority religion. Then, after the Standing Order was abandoned, the rhetoric of civic utility attached itself seamlessly to a nonsectarian Protestant Christianity that was predicated on formal disestablishment.

Toward a "Generalized" Christianity

The earliest proponent of this approach was the Philadelphia physician Benjamin Rush, signer of the Declaration of Independence and a social reformer of strong religious sentiments. Within a few months of Pennsylvania's ratification of the Constitution, Rush proposed that every Christian "sect" send a delegate to what he called "a new species of federal government for the advancement of morals in the United States"—an ecclesiastical convention that would make "men" not "zealous members of any one church" but "good husbands—good fathers—good masters—good servants—and of course good rulers and good citizens"—kind of an Enlightenment-era Promise Keepers.[31] While Rush believed that other religions were capable of promoting "the happiness of society, and the safety and well-being of civil government," his interest was in showing Christianity's ability to do so. "A Christian," he declared, "cannot fail of being a republican."[32] A harder-edged version of this proposal was contemplated by Alexander Hamilton. In April 1802 he wrote to James A. Bayard, a member of Congress from Delaware, suggesting the establishment of a Christian Constitutional Society with the putative objectives of supporting "the Christian Religion" and the Constitution but in fact to elect anti-Jeffersonian candidates—a kind of Federalist Christian Coalition. Bayard thought it was a bad idea, and nothing ever came of it.[33]

By the teens of the nineteenth century Christianity as a general proposition was widely regarded as undergirding the American nation. The "general Principles, on which the Fathers Achieved Independence," John Adams wrote to Thomas Jefferson in 1813, were "the general Principles of Christianity" and "the general Principles of English and American Liberty."[34] Nor was this only talk. Beginning with the *Ruggles* case in New York in 1811, American courts were prepared to find individuals guilty of blasphemy on the theory that Christianity was protected by the common law inherited from England. As the Supreme Court of Pennsylvania put it in the 1824 *Updegraph* case, "Christianity, general Christianity, is, and always has been, a part of the common law of *Pennsylvania*; Christianity, without the spiritual artillery of *European* countries . . . not Christianity with an established church, and tithes, and spiritual courts; but Christianity with liberty of conscience to all men."[35]

Sarah Barringer Gordon has traced how what she calls "the de facto establishment of 'general' Christianity" became embedded in nineteenth-century jurisprudence.[36] I would only underscore this with the following quotation from an 1833 sermon by the Reverend Jasper Adams of Charleston, South Carolina, that was widely circulated and commented upon: "Thus, while all others enjoy full protection in the profession of their opinions and practice, Christianity is the established religion of the nation, its institutions and usages are sustained by legal sanctions, and many of them are incorporated with the fundamental law of the country." Adams did insert a footnote to make clear that he was using "established" in "its usual and not in its legal or technical sense."[37]

That *usual* establishment would last well into the twentieth century. As late as 1931, an associate justice of the U.S. Supreme Court could write, in a majority opinion, "We are a Christian people."[38]

The argument here is that from the early days of the republic, the case for General Christianity—nondenominational Protestantism—was made not on behalf of Christianity per se but because it served the traditional civil religious project of maintaining the social order. Appealing to the precedent of the civilized world past and present, the New York Supreme Court declared in *Ruggles*, "The very idea of jurisprudence with the ancient lawgivers and philosophers, embraced the religion of the country."[39] And in *Updegraph* the court pointed out that the importance ancient lawgivers attached to religion had been described by that famous non-Christian writer Plutarch: "Religion he terms the cement of civil union, and the essential support of legislation."[40]

General Christianity was judged to be the law of the land not because it was true but because it was the prevailing religion of the American people, the religion of this place. And when, in the middle of the twentieth century, the understanding of the religious identity of the American people began to shift, a new formulation was required. In the most famous, or infamous, articulation of American civil religion, Dwight Eisenhower declared shortly before becoming president of the United States, "Our form of government has no sense unless it is founded in a deeply felt religious faith, and I don't care what it is. With us of course it is the Judeo-Christian creed but it must be a religion that all men are created equal."[41] By now we should recognize "and I don't care what it is" as merely a colloquial version of the ancient conviction that any religion might possess comparable civic utility.

I have dealt at length elsewhere with how and why the term "Judeo-Christian" came to be incorporated into American public discourse.[42] Here I simply want to point out that just as the Founders of the new American nation, having at one time embraced a republican ideology indifferent to religion, embraced "General Christianity" on classic civil religious grounds, so their successors turned to a more inclusive concept, again with social utility in mind. This is not to dismiss what Bellah conceptualized in his powerful essay. There are exalted ideals enshrined in the country's founding documents and such subsequent canonical texts as Lincoln's Gettysburg Address and Martin Luther King Jr.'s "I Have a

Dream" speech—ideals that have been lived out by Americans individually and, from time to time, collectively. But in his zeal to glorify the American project at a moment when it seemed to have gone aground in the jungles of Vietnam, Bellah averted his eyes from the traditional utilitarianism of the country's normal civil religious discourse. Instead, he reified the project as an ultimate faith unto itself: "a genuine apprehension of universal and transcendent religious reality as seen in or, one could almost say, as revealed through the experience of the American people." In doing so, he went well beyond what many of his academic readers were prepared to tolerate. But had he not done so, we would not still be discussing the American civil religion more than half a century later.

NOTES

1 "The princes of a republic or of a kingdom should maintain the foundations of the religion they hold; and if this is done, it will be an easy thing for them to maintain their republic religious and, in consequence, good and united. All things that arise in favor of that religion they should favor and magnify, even though they judge them false; and they should do it so much the more as they are more prudent and more knowing of natural things." Machiavelli, *Discourses on Livy*, I.12, translated by Harvey C. Mansfield and Nathan Tarcov (Chicago: University of Chicago Press, 1995), 37.

2 See Pierre Bayle, *Pensées diverses sur la comète*, ed. A. Prat (Paris: E. Droz, 1939), 2 vols., chaps. 113–49 (1:301–50 and 2:5–47).

3 William Warburton, *The Alliance between Church and State* (London, 1811), 287.

4 Jean-Jacques Rousseau, *Du contrat social* IV.8, in *Oeuvres completes*, vol. 3 (Paris: Gallimard, 1964), 460–69; translation from Rousseau, *The Social Contract and Other Later Political Writings*, trans. Victor Gourevitch (Cambridge: Cambridge University Press, 1997), 142–51.

5 Rousseau dismisses a "bizarre" third sort of religion—the double-headed hybrid of church and state such as prevails among the "Lamas," the Japanese, and the Roman Catholics. Dividing people's allegiance between two systems of authority, this form of religion, he says, is not even worthy of discussion, for "everything which destroys social unity is worthless."

6 Rousseau, *Social Contract*, 150. "Il y a donc une profession de foi purement civile dont il appartient au Souverain de fixer les articles, non pas précisément comme dogmes de Religion, mais comme sentimens de sociabilité, sans lesquels il est impossible d'être bon Citoyen ni sujet fidelle." Rousseau, *Du contrat social*, 468.

7 Jean-Jacques Rousseau, *Oeuvres complètes*, 3:957–58; translation from Rousseau, *Social Contract*, 181.

8 "The virtue of Citizens, their patriotic zeal, the distinctive form which its national institutions may give their soul, this is the only rampart that will stand ever ready

to defend it, and which no army could subdue by force. If you see to it that a Pole can never become a Russian, I assure you that Russia will never subjugate Poland." Rousseau, *Social Contract*, 183–85.

9 John Adams, *A Defence of the Constitutions of the Government of the United States of America* (1787), Constitution Society, www.constitution.org.

10 James Wilson, "Oration Delivered on the Four th of July 1788, at the Procession Formed at Philadelphia to Celebrate the Adoption of the Constitution of the United States," in James Wilson, *Collected Works*, vol. 1 (Indianapolis: Liberty Fund, 2007), 287.

11 Douglass Adair and Marvin Harvey, "Was Alexander Hamilton a Christian Statesman?," in *Fame and the Founding Fathers*, ed. Trevor Colbourn (New York: Norton, 1974), 147n8.

12 *Secret Proceedings and Debates of the Convention Assembled at Philadelphia, in the Year 1787, for the Purpose of Forming the Constitution of the United States of America* (Richmond, VA: Wilbur Curtiss, 1839), 89–90. The fashion, at least in the convention, seems to have been to hold religion at arm's length—evidenced by the tabling of Benjamin Franklin's motion to begin every day's session with prayer. James Madison, *The Journal of the Constitutional Convention*, in *The Writings of James Madison*, ed. Gaillard Hunt (New York: G. P. Putnam's Sons, 1902), 3:309–11.

13 For an account of where Lanthenas fits into the world of Jacobinism, see Patrice Higonnet, *Goodness beyond Virtue: Jacobins during the French Revolution* (Cambridge, MA: Harvard University Press, 1998), 117, 207.

14 F. Lanthenas, *Religion civile*, 4th ed. (Paris, 1798), 42–43. Although Lanthenas's fellow Jacobins declined to adopt his program, they pursued a program of civil religion by promoting a seemingly endless series of festivals designed to sanctify national purpose and bind the citizenry together.

15 A little further on, Washington expanded upon the point: "The Constitution which at any time exists, 'till changed by an explicit and authentic act of the whole People, is sacredly obligatory upon all." Washington, "Farewell Address" (Washington Papers, 1796), transcript of final manuscript, 4, 13, http://gwpapers.virginia.edu.

16 Mercy Warren, *History of the Rise, Progress and Termination of the American Revolution* (Boston: Manning and Loring, 1805), 3:308. The palladium was the statue of Pallas Athena that was supposed to guarantee the security of Troy.

17 Quoted in Pauline Maier, *American Scripture: Making the Declaration of Independence* (New York: Vintage, 1998), 186–87.

18 Catherine L. Albanese, *Sons of the Fathers: The Civil Religion of the American Revolution* (Philadelphia: Temple University Press, 1976), 13.

19 The only American author who gives evidence of having read the *Considerations* in the early Republican period is John Adams. See Paul Merrill Spurlin, *Rousseau in America, 1760–1809* (University: University of Alabama Press, 1969), 87.

20 *Kline's Carlisle Weekly Gazette*, October 7, 1795, quoted in David W. Robson, "College Founding in the New Republic, 1776–1800," *History of Education Quarterly* 23 (1983): 335.

21 Washington, "Farewell Address," 20.
22 Robert N. Bellah, "Civil Religion in America," www.robertbellah.com.
23 Freneau makes one significant mistranslation, rendering "Reste donc la religion de l'homme ou le christianisme . . ." as "There remains then only the rational and manly religion of Christianity. . . ." Plainly this was to reassure his pious readers that Rousseau was not anti-Christian.
24 Mason L. Weems, *The Life of Washington*, ed. Marcus Cunliffe (Cambridge, MA: Harvard University Press, 1962), 184–85.
25 See Edmund Burke, *Reflections on the Revolution in France*, ed. J. C. D. Clark (Stanford, CA: Stanford University Press, 2001), 254–69.
26 Thomas Paine, *The Rights of Man Part I* (1791), in Paine, *Political Writings*, ed. Bruce Kuklick (New York: Cambridge University Press, 1989), 95. It took a while for Americans to absorb the antireligious message of the French Revolution. See Gary B. Nash, "The American Clergy and the French Revolution," *William and Mary Quarterly*, 3rd ser., 22, no. 3 (1965): 392–412.
27 Washington, "Farewell Address," 20. Hamilton's original draft of the relevant paragraph reads as follows: "Tis essentially true that virtue or morality is a main and necessary spring of popular or republican Governments. The rule indeed extends with more or less force to all free Governments. Who that is a prudent & sincere friend to them can look with indifference on the ravages which are making in the foundation of the Fabric? Religion? The uncommon means which of late have been directed to this fatal end seem to make it in a particular manner the duty of the Retiring Chief of a nation to warn his country against tasting of the poisonous draught." *The Papers of Alexander Hamilton*, vol. 20 (New York: Columbia University Press, 1974), 280.
28 Warren, *History of the Rise*, 403–4.
29 Oliver Ellsworth, "To The General Assembly of the State of Connecticut, Now in Session," *Hartford Courant*, June 7, 1802.
30 Charles H. Lippy, "The 1780 Massachusetts Constitution: Religious Establishment or Civil Religion," *Journal of Church and State* 20, no. 3 (1978): 533–49.
31 Benjamin Rush, "An Address to the Ministers of the Gospel of Every Denomination in the United States, upon Subjects Interesting to Morals," in *Essays Literary, Moral and Philosophical* (1798; Schenectady, NY: Union College Press, 1988), 72.
32 Benjamin Rush, "Of the Mode of Education Proper in a Republic," in *Essays*, 6.
33 National Archives, "From Alexander Hamilton to James A. Bayard [16–21] April 1802," http://founders.archives.gov; National Archives, "From James A. Bayard to Alexander Hamilton, 23 April," http://founders.archives.gov.
34 The entire quotation reads, "The general Principles, on which the Fathers Achieved Independence, were the only Principles in which that beautiful Assembly of young Gentlemen could Unite, and these Principles only could be intended by them in their Address, or by me in my Answer. And what were these general Principles? I answer, the general Principles of Christianity, in which all those Sects were united: And the general Principles of English and American

Liberty, in which all those young Men United, and which had United all Parties in America, in Majorities sufficient to assert and maintain her Independence. Now I will avow, that I then believed, and now believe, that those general Principles of Christianity, are as eternal and immutable, as the Existence and Attributes of God; and that those Principles of Liberty, are as unalterable as human Nature and our terrestrial, mundane System. I could therefore safely say, consistently with all my then and present Information, that I believed they would never make Discoveries in contradiction to these general Principles. In favour of these general Principles in Phylosophy, Religion and Government, I could fill Sheets of quotations from Frederick of Prussia, from Hume, Gibbon, Bolingbroke, Reausseau and Voltaire, as well as Neuton and Locke: not to mention thousands of Divines and Philosophers of inferiour Fame." John Adams to Thomas Jefferson, June 28, 1813, from Quincy, in *The Adams-Jefferson Letters: The Complete Correspondence between Thomas Jefferson and Abigail and John Adams*, ed. Lester J. Cappon (Chapel Hill: University of North Carolina Press, 1988), 338–40.

35 *Updegraph v. Commonwealth*, 11 Serg. & R. (Pa) 394 (1824). In its decision, the court recognized the general importance of religion to society by appealing to Plutarch: "After reciting that the first and greatest care of the legislators of *Rome, Athens, Lacedaemon*, and *Greece* in general, was by instituting solemn supplications and forms of oaths, to inspire them with a sense of the favour or displeasure of Heaven, that learned historian declares, that we have met with towns unfortified, illiterate, and without the conveniences of habitations; but a people wholly without religion, no traveller hath yet seen; and a city might as well be erected in the air, as a state be made to unite, where no divine worship is attended. Religion he terms the cement of civil union, and the essential support of legislation."

36 Sarah Barringer Gordon, *The Mormon Question: Polygamy and Constitutional Conflict in Nineteenth-Century America* (Chapel Hill: University of North Carolina Press, 2002), 74.

37 Daniel L. Dreisbach, ed., *Religion and Politics in the Early Republic: Jasper Adams and the Church-State Debate* (Lexington: University of Kentucky Press, 1996), 49.

38 *United States v. Macintosh*, 283 U.S. 605 (1931).

39 *People v. Ruggles*, 8 Johns R. 290 N.Y. (1811). The previous sentence reads, "No government among any of the polished nations of antiquity, and none of the institutions of modern *Europe*, (a single and monitory case excepted,) ever hazarded such a bold experiment upon the solidity of the public morals, as to permit with impunity, and under the sanction of their tribunals, the general religion of the community to be openly insulted and defamed."

40 Gordon erroneously presents this not as an indirect quotation from Plutarch but as a direct comment by the court about Christianity: "As the Supreme Court of Pennsylvania put it in 1824, 'General Christianity [is] the cement of civil union, and the essential support of legislation.'" Gordon, *Mormon Question*, 73. The previous two sentences in the court's opinion read, "Amidst the concurrent testimony of political and philosophical writers among the Pagans, in the most absolute

state of democratic freedom, the sentiments of *Plutarch*, on this subject, are too remarkable to be omitted. After reciting that the first and greatest care of the legislators of *Rome, Athens, Lacedaemon*, and *Greece* in general, was by instituting solemn supplications and forms of oaths, to inspire them with a sense of the favour or displeasure of Heaven, that learned historian declares, that we have met with towns unfortified, illiterate, and without the conveniences of habitations; but a people wholly without religion, no traveller hath yet seen; and a city might as well be erected in the air, as a state be made to unite, where no divine worship is attended."

41 Patrick Henry, "'And I Don't Care What It Is': The Tradition-History of a Civil Religion Proof-Text," *Journal of the American Academy of Religion* 49 (1981): 41.
42 Mark Silk, "Notes on the Judeo-Christian Tradition in America," *American Quarterly* 36, no. 1 (1984): 65–85.

3

Sacrifice, Service, and Civil Religion Now

ROSEMARY R. CORBETT

I once asked Robert Bellah, whose writings at times inspired me and at other times confounded me, to describe his relationship with one of the academics who had most influenced him over the course of his life: the scholar of comparative religion Wilfred Cantwell Smith. Bellah was working on his last major treatise at the time, for which he had given considerable thought to that question. He told me what he would later write in *Religion and Human Evolution*: that Smith, along with Talcott Parsons and Paul Tillich, was one of his "three great teachers," whose approach to the study of religion influenced Bellah greatly.[1] This should come as no surprise to those who have followed Bellah's work over the decades. Smith's approach to comparative religion was academically rigorous, often yielding astute observations and theoretical challenges. Yet it was also, and always, a normative project—one meant to diagnose and improve the state of religious people's lives and their dealings with each other.[2] For this reason, Smith ultimately called what he did a kind of public "theology."[3] Although Bellah would go about his work with different methodologies than Smith, he, too, pursued a normative and heavily theological project—particularly when it came to discussing his most contested concept, that of civil religion.

Bellah and Smith had much in common. Both Marxists in their youth, the scholars focused throughout their lives on the relationship between religion and social problems. When Smith offered Bellah a two-year postdoctoral appointment at the Institute of Islamic Studies at McGill University in 1955, Bellah accepted. As Bellah was a former member of the Communist Party, his appointment at Harvard was in jeopardy at that time, and as he put it, he "sought some position in Canada to escape potential persecution."[4] Later, in 1957, Harvard offered Bellah another post. By then, Senator Joseph McCarthy, who had spearheaded Senate interrogations of possible communists during the preceding decade, had died. Bellah accepted the position and stayed at Harvard for ten years, reaching the rank of full professor and sometimes collaborating with Smith at the Center for World Religions there (of which Smith assumed direction in 1963), before moving to the University of California, Berkeley.

As a devout Protestant, Bellah never recovered from the horror of watching American leaders invoke God to persecute those who seemed intent on pursuing the kind of economic justice and concern for the poor that, in Bellah's opinion, Jesus had commanded. Although the political situation and Bellah's personal situation had changed by 1967, his conviction that the United States had strayed from its founding principles remained. This conviction animated his 1967 "Civil Religion in America." American involvement in Vietnam was foremost on Bellah's mind at that time, but commentary on American decadence and the need for social and economic justice—Bellah's concerns since his Marxist college days—would mark much of his writing on the topic in the years that followed.

Bellah's work on civil religion has been subject to debate ever since the publication of his first essay over a half century ago—often, but not always, for good reason. As early as 1968, Bellah was accused of advocating a form of national self-worship and celebration. This was something entirely at odds with his original purpose of calling attention to the nation's fundamental tradition so that, in the midst of the Vietnam War, Americans could correct course by recalling the values by which the country should be judged.[5] Partly because of such accusations and debate, Bellah continued to tinker with his concept of civil religion throughout his life, refining it to take account of criticisms and tailoring it to new political situations.[6] He did so while also trying to convince Americans that civil religion should be less about wartime sacrifices and more about self-sacrificing acts of community service. Although there is still plenty to question in his later diagnoses and correctives, Bellah's insights are worth reckoning with for what they reveal about power dynamics involving religion in the United States. This is the case even if, as with Smith's work, Bellah's normative theological project is not our own.

In what follows, I discuss key moments in Bellah's history of refining the civil religion concept, focusing on the historical circumstances that inspired him to continually grapple with the term and on the corrective insights Bellah gained along the way. Far from suggesting that his initial essay had no merit, however, I also highlight features of that original 1967 piece that are pertinent for conversations about civil religion now. As I will point out, some aspects of what Bellah originally identified as civil religion remain powerful in contemporary discourses about religion and American belonging. This includes the emphases on community service that Bellah first wrote about in 1966—a theme that has recurred over time, not least in President Obama's 2009 argument that national community service projects can unite Americans of all religions.[7]

Importantly, although Bellah's emphasis on the role of service in claiming authentic Americanness was as pertinent in the 1960s as it is today, his earliest essay on the subject of civil religion seriously minimized some of the power dynamics involved in such claims. This is something he began to grapple with only late in his life. For that reason, I reread aspects of the original piece in light of his 2000 essay, "Flaws in the Protestant Code," to draw attention to issues that still haunt those who would claim American belonging by engaging in the civil religion of faith-based community service endeavors. The "flaw" in such endeavors is not, as some critics might argue, that civil religion does not actually exist in the United States. Rather, it is that on the ground, among practitioners, the parameters of such service-based civil religion have been constantly redefined to circumscribe those seeking most earnestly to be included within its frame.

Self-Sacrificing Service to Counter Self-Interest: Bellah's Civil Religion in History

In May 1966, several Vietnamese Buddhists set themselves on fire to protest what they believed was American responsibility in the killing of a member of the South Vietnamese military. Self-immolation, a term that derives from the Latin for "self-sacrifice," was not new in Vietnam.[8] One of the most famous cases during the war had occurred in 1963, when Thich Quang Duc, a Buddhist monk, set himself on fire in Saigon to protest the lack of religious freedom under the South Vietnamese regime with which the United States allied.[9] Not only did this 1963 act gain tremendous media attention in America, it inspired emulation both in the United States and abroad. In 1965, a young Quaker man, Norman Morrison, self-immolated outside the Pentagon office of Defense Secretary Robert McNamara. In 1966, additional nuns and monks set themselves ablaze in Vietnam.[10] The horrors of the Vietnam War and the casualties, American and Vietnamese, were already manifold. Then, in August of that year, former vice president Richard Nixon called for increasing American troops in the country from 287,000 to 500,000—a harbinger of things to come.[11]

Writing his first essay on civil religion in the midst of these events, Bellah could not help but be preoccupied with questions about service, sacrifice, and their relationship to religion. Although his work on civil religion over the course of four decades would involve multiple themes, most of which cannot be fully discussed here, those of sacrifice and service would perennially emerge in his writings on the topic, and Bellah's attempt to shift emphasis away from the sacrifice of military service toward self-sacrificing community and social service formed a leitmotif, of sorts, in his own battle hymn for the republic.

For Bellah, the 1960s had begun with a burst of enthusiasm over the possibilities of greater civil rights for Black Americans. That optimism was soon incinerated by American involvement in East Asia—an area of the world where Bellah had developed his academic specialty after what McNamara has described as the unfolding of American war crimes during World War II.[12] In fact, it was while serving as a Fulbright scholar in Japan in 1960 that Bellah—not a scholar of U.S. culture or history by any means—first broached the topic of religion in America. Forced to secularize their national shrines by an occupying U.S. power, some of Bellah's Japanese interlocutors had asked why Arlington National Cemetery, replete with religious icons, operated under government auspices.[13] Bellah's attempts to reconcile America's professed secularism with its profound religiosity and to locate sacrifice and service in the nation's moral imaginary had begun.

In the opening section of his first essay on civil religion, Bellah quoted inaugural remarks delivered by the recently deceased president, John F. Kennedy, for whom an eternal flame was lit at Arlington, as an illustration of civil religion's existence and applicability to all Americans. Despite Kennedy's Catholicism, Bellah argued, the president echoed the same sentiments as earlier Protestant civil religion luminaries. (This attempt to prove that civil religion, as he conceived of it, transcends Protestantism haunted Bellah's work until the twenty-first century, as we will see.) Kennedy's role in Bellah's essay was not to function merely as a token of diversity, however. Prior to being president, Kennedy had also been a war hero in a conflict generally deemed more just than the one the United States embroiled itself in during the 1960s. And after becoming president, Kennedy redefined the nation's "transcendent goal." Rather than being called to bear arms through military service, Kennedy had argued, Americans were called "to bear the burden of a long twilight struggle . . . against the common enemies of man: tyranny, poverty, disease and war itself."[14] This was, in fact, an animating impulse behind Kennedy's creation of the first overseas civilian service program, the Peace Corps. According to Bellah, Kennedy's evocation of America's calling was "only the most recent statement" of the quintessentially American project of making "God's work" our own.[15]

Continuing with these themes, Bellah turned in the next section of his essay to Benjamin Franklin's call for a kind of public religion that transcends confessional boundaries. Despite his lack of denominational affiliation as an adult, Franklin—as Bellah quotes him—"never doubted . . . the existence of the Deity" or "that the most acceptable service of God was the doing of good to men." These ideas, according to Franklin, are "the essentials of every religion" and were present in all the religions extant in America during his lifetime.[16] With these borrowed words, Bellah underlined the idea that service to humankind is a central tenet of America's pluralistic civil religion (which Bellah insisted again is "neither sectarian nor in any specific sense Christian")[17] and that it has been so since the nation was established.

Bellah turned next to the notion of sacrifice in a section titled "Civil War and Civil Religion." For Bellah, the sacrifices involved in military service were hardly the most authentic expression of God-fearing patriotism (contrary to what prowar politicians argued by conjuring the threat of communist expansion). In fact, Bellah saw the use of military might as a moral failing rather than an authentic ritual of civil religion.[18] While service to others was a tenet of civil religion as old as the republic, for Bellah it was only with Lincoln's assassination that wartime "sacrifice was indelibly written in" to the tradition.[19] Kennedy's assassination only amplified this theme by adding another martyr to America's civil religion pantheon. Crucially, for Bellah, as noted above, Kennedy had also redefined the paradigmatic ritual of civil religion, turning it from the sacrifice wrought through military service back to the self-sacrifice involved in the service of humankind.

In the penultimate and final sections of his first essay, Bellah contrasted the tradition of Franklin and Kennedy with the "Civil Religion Today," in which a "repressive and unstable military dictatorship in South Vietnam becomes 'the free people of South Vietnam and their government'" and America's role as the "New Jerusalem" is to "defend such governments with treasure and eventually with blood."[20] Standing in the biblical prophet Jeremiah's stead, Bellah proclaimed that Americans were in a "third time of trial" not unlike that of the Revolutionary era and the Civil War and stood "at the edge of a chasm the depth of which no man knows."[21] Given this call from the wilderness to return to the nation's founding principles of self-sacrifice in service to humankind and away from the sacrifice wrought through war, it is no wonder that Bellah was bewildered by those who later read his work as a celebration of American nationalism.

For Bellah, war was a powerful crucible for refining the nation's sense of calling and purpose—it was a time in which Americans could reflect on their foundational values and recommit themselves to the right path. While his first essay on civil religion was written largely with this purpose of turning the country back to its rightful aims in the midst of wartime excess, however, Bellah's later works on civil religion more frequently elaborated on the role of religion in the struggle between the forces of corrosive individualism (what he saw as economically inspired self-interest rather than self-sacrifice) and community cohesion. The sacrifice wrought through war remained a persistent, even dominant, theme in discourses of American civil religion, as several scholars have amply shown, but Bellah's work going forward would resist this trend by redefining sacrifice as something that led the nation's citizens to forgo some of their individual interests while serving others as Franklin and Kennedy had intended.[22]

In 1975, Bellah published a long-form jeremiad on the theme of civil religion titled *The Broken Covenant: American Civil Religion in Time of Trial*. In it Bellah was again overt about his prescriptive project. He aimed not to present new data or even to "explain American society in terms of social or economic variables" in that work but to understand and interpret what he took to be "certain central features of the American tradition from the point of view of the problems of late twentieth-century America."[23] In other words, he still sought to find answers in what he saw as the foundational tradition of civil religion for the social issues plaguing the nation. These included the ethical failures of public officials (such as in the spectacular 1972 Watergate scandal), increasing consumerism and materialism, and the perversion of welfare from something that aided the poor to something that aided the military and corporations.[24]

Not long after publishing *The Broken Covenant*, Bellah concluded that his long-form analysis had been incomplete. He thus commenced with a new essay on the subject, which he used to explore in greater detail the problems with American individualism and the need for self-sacrificing service, published in 1978 as "Religion and the Legitimation of the American Republic." The individualism Bellah railed against was something he initially regarded as the legacy of Enlightenment liberalism, although he would later argue that Protestant principles contributed to it too.[25] Community cohesion, on the other hand, came from the social cement provided most frequently by voluntary associations, particularly religious ones. In Bellah's view, such institutions and the values encouraged by them gave rise to the "publick religion" of civic ethics and service that Benjamin Franklin had advocated.[26] And while the public religion could not quite unify the country alone, the sentiments of the churches—which provided, in his view, "the real school of republican virtue in America"—could.[27] At least, they could until the late twentieth century, when "the balance of American religious life [was] slipping away from those denominations that have a historic concern for the common good toward religious groups so privatistic and self-centered that they begin to approach the consumer cafeteria model."[28]

Bellah borrowed from Alexis de Tocqueville in this assessment of the role of religion and religious institutions, as he explained in "Religion and the Legitimation of the American Republic": "Tocqueville saw that naked self-interest is the surest solvent of a republican regime, and he saw the commercial tendencies of the American people as unleashing the possibility of the unrestrained pursuit of self-interest. But he saw religion as the great restraining element that could turn naked self-interest into what he called 'self-interest rightly understood,' that is, a self-interest that was public spirited and capable of self-sacrifice."²⁹ Because Bellah considered this 1978 essay on civil religion "the most theoretically sophisticated defense of the idea that I ever developed," he included it as the "Afterword" to the second edition and later printings of *The Broken Covenant* as well as in his 1980 co-edited book with sociologist Phillip Hammond, *Varieties of Civil Religion*—compiled at a time when Bellah, sick of definitional disputes over the concept, was "ready to drop the term."³⁰

Bellah did stop using the term "civil religion" to a great extent in the years that followed, but he never gave up analyzing the dialectic that civil religion was meant to resolve: the tension between the atomizing forces of self-interest, or individualism, and self-sacrificing communal impulses toward solidarity. Nor did he entirely give up on the concept of civil religion, itself, or his belief that it was best expressed by creating community cohesion, particularly through service. This was an idea that he afforded increasing importance as he saw Ronald Reagan and the "Christian Right" using the language of divine mission to turn away from concerns for social welfare and economic and racial justice and toward what he regarded as ever-greater imperial ambitions—something Bellah addressed in "The Kingdom of God in America," a 1987 talk he delivered at the National Cathedral in Washington, D.C.

In his 1987 talk and the article later derived from it, Bellah contrasted what he saw as self-interested individualism writ large in the form of nationalist imperialism with the idea of the nation as a community covenanted with others (internally and externally) in solidarity for the universal common good. Self-sacrificing service leading to social reform rather than economic self-interest leading to international exploitation and war was central to such a religiously inspired communal covenant, Bellah argued by pulling from Catholic teaching—this time from the National Conference of Catholic Bishops' 1986 statement, "Economic Justice for All." "We have to move from our devotion to independence, through an understanding of interdependence, to a commitment to human solidarity," Bellah quoted. "That challenge must find its realization in the kind of community we build among us. Love implies concern for all—especially the poor."³¹ Elsewhere that year, in another public address that involved quoting from the Bishops' letter, Bellah had elaborated that authentic civil religion (although he did not use that term) involved not imperialistic acquisition but pursuit of the common good through "personal acts of charity by individuals, families, and the church itself" and a reformation of the "economic institutions of society."[32]

Bellah's tendency to refer to or quote from Catholics in his work on civil religion only grew during the decades after he published his first essay in the 1960s. Again, this was not solely because Bellah sought to prove that America's civil religion tradition included and applied to Catholics just as much as it did Protestants—although that was certainly part of it, and Bellah had not mentioned Catholics in what he saw as his most theoretically substantial essay on the topic. In addition to indefatigably insisting on such inclusivity, though, Bellah increasingly came to appreciate Catholic social teaching for the "use of religious language to speak to public concerns."[33] He also admired what he saw as the example of nineteenth-century Catholic immigrants who brought with them to the United States "a clearer understanding of social solidarity and the common good than that of even the most Calvinist of Protestants."[34]

This appreciation for past and present Catholic practices of self-sacrificing service and solidarity stood in stark contrast to the contempt Bellah held for what he believed was the narrow-minded "communal absolutism" and "triumphalist self-righteousness" of the "Christian Right" in the 1980s.[35] (It is perhaps worth noting here that a founding political tenet of the religious right's platform was to oppose the inclusion of Catholics in ecumenical and political coalitions.[36] This may have been a contributing factor in Bellah's decision to co-edit a 1987 volume on Christian-Jewish, Protestant-Catholic, and liberal-conservative tensions called *Uncivil Religion*, in which Bellah appealed for religious communities to find common ground so as to overcome the radical individualism threatening America.)[37] His sometimes romanticized assessment of Catholicism also contrasted with what he saw as the state of most "families and churches or synagogues" in the United States by the 1990s, which he believed were "too colonized by the market" to resist the centrifugal forces of economically inspired self-interest.[38]

In 1999, Pope John Paul II issued an apostolic exhortation to Catholics in the Western Hemisphere titled "Ecclesia in America." In it, the pope railed against the "neoliberalism" promoted across the American continents, which is based in a "purely economic concept of man" and "considers profit and the law of the market as its only parameters."[39] Bellah could not help but take notice. Bellah's increasing fondness for Catholics and Catholic social teaching, his increasing awareness of the persistence of Protestant nativism in the United States, and his disillusionment with what he increasingly viewed as Protestant-derived tendencies to slip into spiritual or economic individualism rather than socially oriented religious observance (the main topic of his 1980s collaborative project, *Habits of the Heart: Individualism and Commitment in American Life*)[40] collectively contributed to one of his greatest intellectual reversals on the topic of civil religion. Whereas Bellah once wrote with certitude that, by the end of World War I, "the Protestant hegemony in American culture had been broken,"[41] he would claim no such thing by the beginning of the twenty-first century. Contrary to his insistence for almost thirty years that the United States had an identifiable and broadly applicable civil religion rooted in self-sacrificing service to others that he, like Benjamin Franklin, believed to be universal, Bellah began the new millennium believing that Protestant dominance exercised more influence over American religious life than he had ever previously acknowledged and that such dominance was a primary reason for the nation's continuing problems.

Protestant Hegemony and the Flaws in Civil Religion

"It is one of the oldest of sociological generalizations that any coherent and viable society rests on a common set of moral understandings about good and bad, right and wrong, in the realm of individual and social action," Bellah wrote in his 1975 preface to the first edition of *The Broken Covenant*. Inspired by Durkheimian theory, he continued, "It is almost as widely held that these common moral understandings must also in turn rest upon a common set of religious understandings.... Such moral and religious understandings produce both a basic cultural legitimation for a society which is viewed at least approximately in accord with them and a standard of judgment for the criticism of a society that is seen as deviating too far from them."[42] So convinced was he of the validity of these statements, Bellah acknowledged, that he would not even try to defend or prove them but would simply accept them as the basis on which to discuss civil religion.

By the late 1990s, Bellah had changed his mind about the nature of societal cultures—particularly national ones. Although he long defended the existence of homogenous elements within each culture despite what might be otherwise abundant examples of heterogeneity, he began to speak less in terms of homogeneity in the 1990s than he did of hegemony. The recognition that overarching power dynamics shaped what he previously took for pluralism was earthshaking for Bellah and for his concept of civil religion, even if he later explained these dynamics in ways that are analytically problematic for scholars who might seek to apply his analysis.

As he reframed it in his 2000 article "Flaws in the Protestant Code: Some Religious Sources of America's Troubles" (the subtitle of which was later changed to "Theological Roots of American Individualism"), "National cultures are still distinctly different from one another, and although not homogenous, are homogenizing: that is, each national society has a culture that, while allowing for difference, nonetheless presses in the direction of a single dominant profile. While the recent emphasis on diversity within nation states has made us aware of long overlooked differences, these differences should not obscure the degree to which national cultures continuously expand their hegemony."[43] For Bellah, the hegemony of self-interested individualism running rampant in American culture was rooted in the centrality of religious dissent to Protestant belief. The insistence among Protestants "on religious freedom," he argued, formed "a seed from which has grown all the extensions of individual rights that have marked our subsequent history."[44]

In the same years that Bellah formulated these thoughts about the homogenizing Protestant nature of American culture, scholars from multiple disciplines questioned the Protestant bias that shaped ideas about the category of religion (questions that should apply equally to invocations of civil religion) and ideas about the ostensible secularity of U.S. society.[45] Despite the attention some of these scholars' analyses received, their work seems not to have been of much interest to Bellah. This is hardly surprising. Historians of American religion had, for years, raised doubts that American society was as pluralistic as it was Protestant-dominated and had amply charted the influence of what some called a kind of Protestant "public power."[46] Bellah seemed to take no notice of them, however, and continued to insist on the almost inherent universality of what he saw as authentic civil religion.[47] Furthermore, for Bellah, the lack of secularity in the United States was not a problem but a possible solution; religion was, and should be, a public resource for reorienting the wayward nation.

Bellah's theological correctives depended on and reinforced his long-held belief in the phenomenological nature of religion and in the reality of U.S. pluralism (the latter of which he defended by pointing to the First Amendment, suggesting quite thinly and unconvincingly that disestablishment translated into social parity among religious groups).[48] These biases may have prevented Bellah from giving credence to many of the debates animating religious studies scholarship in the 1980s and after. When he did finally address Protestant dominance over American religious life, he did so not because of work in the fields of religious studies, anthropology, or sociology but because of the work of a business school colleague at Berkeley who relied on Weber to understand the correlation between economics, environmentalism, and religion. Reading it had led Bellah to an explanation for the malaise he believed he saw afflicting American society: that Protestant tendencies toward individualism triumphed over the collective solidarity promoted within other traditions. In his own words, it led him "to the recognition that there are *cultural codes* embodied in national cultures, and that those cultural codes, however transformed over time, are ultimately derived from religious beliefs."[49]

Positing a slightly more structural take on American society than his emphasis on belief might make it sound, Bellah argued that the "American public sphere was a Protestant invention" through the creation of the First Amendment, "into which Catholics, Jews, and nonbelievers were invited, and later Muslims and Buddhists, as well, and one whose religious form influences its present secular inhabitants."[50] Despite this recognition of how form might influence content, however—and, strangely, for a sociologist who just invoked the formative power of law—Bellah never mentioned or seemed to consider the ways diverse religious institutions, practices, and mores might be shaped by state and federal legislation created in reference to dominant Protestant (Calvinist, then evangelical)[51] understandings of religion, as several religious studies scholars have since done.[52] Rather, Bellah returned to a focus on the effects of faith, arguing in the Weberian tradition that both the religious and economic individualisms troubling America derive from "central Protestant beliefs—ones that have become secularized in many ways" and that he believed were ultimately distorted.[53]

Bellah's solution for such overly individualistic tendencies, be they religious or economic in expression, individual or national in scale, was largely the same in 2000 and later years as it had been decades before: a return to religiously inspired communal solidarity, often involving self-sacrificing acts of service to others. What was different in Bellah's later writings, including his post-2000 works on American empire, was that he no longer labored to prove that America's fundamental religious tradition was anything other than Christian, or, more specifically, Protestant. Positioning himself as Jeremiah again, and citing Paul Tillich (one of his three great teachers, as noted), Bellah called in 2000 for a Catholic corrective to these overly Protestant influences, arguing that it was a "major task of religious individuals . . . to suggest some genetic reengineering of the deep cultural code."[54] Even with such overtly religious analogies, however, his wording revealed his continual indebtedness both to the Marxist debates that he—like Wilfred Cantwell Smith—had immersed himself in as a young man and to the more Hegelian dialectical framework that each scholar had settled on during their later adulthoods.[55] In some ways, this language helps explain why a sociologist could find himself so perpetually fixated on the power of ideals.[56]

Paraphrasing Tillich, Bellah appealed for returning to Catholic concerns with substance (materiality) for the sake of challenging the Protestant principle (ideal/spirit). Observing physical sacraments that reminded Christians of their unity within the one body of Christ—in other words, embodied communion rather than communism—would turn overly individualistic Protestants back to the path of true righteousness, he argued.[57] "The sacrament of communion is the most profound religious expression of the virtue of solidarity as Pope John Paul defines it: 'a firm and persevering determination to commit oneself to the common good, that is to say, the good of all and of each individual.'"[58] Less disillusioned with communism and socialism than Smith (Bellah had been an ardent communist in his youth, whereas Smith had not),[59] Bellah did not stop with promoting individual commitment to the common good. Properly observing the sacrament of communion as all "orthodox Christians" do, he argued, would allow Americans to see that the unrestrained market destroys every social relation and that only a major strengthening of the social control of the market, involving not only national but international controls, will move us in the next decade to recover our connections with each other and the natural world that ultimately make life worth living.[60]

Bellah did not use the term "civil religion" to describe his socioreligious remedy in his 2000 jeremiad or subsequent writings, and, at least to my knowledge, he did not revisit his original essay on the topic after deciding that the religious impulses governing American civic life were fundamentally Protestant rather than pluralistic. "Historically Protestant culture overrides pluralism," Bellah recalls his Berkeley business colleague arguing, perhaps confirming British philosopher G. K. Chesterton's "famous remark that 'in America, even the Catholics are Protestants.'"[61] We may well wonder what Bellah thought of his original essay in hindsight of the new millennium. While we cannot definitively answer that question now, we can speculate on where his later insights leave us. Has some kind of Protestant-influenced civil religion actually existed in the United States, and does it still? If so, what kinds of power dynamics operate in and through this civic form?

One need not adopt Bellah's normative project of theologically interpreting religion in American public life, nor the commitment to dialectical history that fueled his faith in ideals, to recognize that powerful discourses and debates about the rightful role of religion in society have long been part of American culture and politics. Although not always attuned to the way Protestant dominance might shape what he took to be the pluralistic tradition of American civil religion, Bellah did tap into a persistent theme in such discourses—one promoted by those on the right and those on the left for different reasons: community service as the appropriate civic expression of deeply felt faith. Bellah was not wrong to cite Franklin as a believer in the idea that service to humankind is the essence of all authentic religion, nor was he wrong to highlight Kennedy's pivotal role in arguing for religiously inspired community service, rather than military service, as the new civic-religious ritual par excellence. Nevertheless, what Bellah saw in the 1960s as Kennedy's paradigmatic example of pluralist civil religion, he might well have regarded in hindsight as an example of Catholic attempts to struggle for acceptance in terms familiar to Protestants.

Although humanitarianism has a long history with many antecedents (Protestant, Catholic, and otherwise), community service as we know it today is a distinctly twentieth-century invention initially fashioned, as Bellah might have guessed, in the exigencies of war. Far from being the self-evidently universal underpinning of all religion in the United States, it took shape, as I have discussed elsewhere, during World War I in contests between Protestants (mainline and marginalized), Catholics, and Jews over claims to Americanness.[62] It became, and remained through World War II, a powerful way for religious minorities to demonstrate their American belonging at a time when they faced severe progressive Protestant nativism and discrimination. Some early proponents of it, such as editors of the *New York Times*, even considered the main purpose of community service to be assimilating recent immigrants into established (Protestant) American mores.[63]

During and after World War II, narratives about the religious identity of the United States changed markedly. Whereas America's leaders previously lionized it for being a Protestant country, some political and religious elites began to emphasize "Judeo-Christian" commonality and heritage during the 1940s as one way to unite the populace in the fight against fascism.[64] The election of the first Catholic president in 1960 may have appeared from afar as confirmation of the country's comparative pluralism. Kennedy's acceptance was extraordinarily qualified, however, and the notion of an American "Judeo-Christian" tradition is still quite contested. This was nowhere more apparent than in the battles that immediately besieged Kennedy's administration over funding for parochial schools (a century-old issue for Protestant nativists) and over the Peace Corps—Kennedy's overseas civilian service program that was almost entirely derailed by Protestant opposition.[65]

Just as Protestants protested public funding for Catholic schools, they protested public funding or imprimatur for Catholic-organized community service. Catholic Relief Services—an organization that had quietly received state funding for overseas services since World War II—had initially planned to be a primary partner in mobilizing Peace Corps volunteers. By the end of the summer of 1961, which had seen public outcry and threats of congressional rejection of the program, Catholic Relief Services was dropped from involvement. Joining forces with committed secularists, even Protestants otherwise happy to infuse religion into public life insisted on secularism so as to prevent Catholics from gaining what they saw as further entrée into the government.[66] By 1962, the Peace Corps announced that it would not contract with any ecclesiastically controlled organizations, although newspapers reported that Protestant groups, through the National Council of Churches, would help the agency identify projects and determine appropriate ways to support volunteers' *private* religious practices.[67] The next year, Catholic political theorist Francis Canavan lamented what he saw as a major blow to both pluralism and patriotism. True pluralism in America, for Canavan, "permits and encourages private, including religious, institutions of welfare to serve the public as effectively as state institutions do."[68]

Having spent the 1960–61 academic year on a Fulbright in Japan, Bellah surely followed Kennedy's election as closely as possible—although not as closely as he could have stateside. Did he miss some of the virulent Protestant nativism characteristic of those years? Even Kennedy complained that he could not speak sufficiently about real issues during the campaign because he was constantly forced, as a Catholic, to defend his patriotism.[69] Meanwhile, in the midst of Protestant demands for secularism, Bellah's Japanese interlocutors petitioned him to explain how a "secular" country could be so religious. It seems unlikely that Bellah failed to notice Kennedy's trials and tribulations. Yet, as he explained late in his life, he first recognized the extent to which Americans fused religion and state not because of the opposition Protestants showed Kennedy but because of the mourning the entire country engaged in after Kennedy's assassination. "This is not a secular response," he recalled thinking.[70] Perhaps not, but it was certainly one that papered over the antagonism Kennedy had faced on account of his religion.

American Catholics did not cease arguing for the importance of community service and solidarity after Kennedy's death. Those who were most successful in gaining recognition and acceptance, however, were ones who argued for these things in a manner far different than Bellah suggested. Rather than wedding calls for religiously inspired, self-sacrificing service to economic regulation and/or racial justice, some formerly socialist Catholic and Jewish intellectuals of the 1970s wedded them to arguments for market freedom. For these new market liberals (or neoliberals), economic self-interest and religiously inspired community service were two sides of the same coin. Lauding the merits of an almost entirely unregulated market, theologically minded intellectuals at the American Enterprise Institute, for example, simultaneously promoted the strong community bonds and social care practices that they regarded as the product of American religious voluntarism. Only when religious communities take up such care for the poor can the state be relieved of the burden, they argued, and, in turn, allow the market to move freely without fear of deleterious social effects.

The theologians and pundits who began promoting such ideas in the 1970s included Catholic intellectuals such as Michael Novak and Jewish thinkers such as Irving Kristol. As I have discussed elsewhere, they made their arguments at a time when conservative white ethnics (including the descendants of Catholic and Jewish immigrants) railed against President Lyndon Johnson's affirmative action legislation—in part out of some fear that increased standing for Black Americans would translate into decreased standing for other newly respectable minority populations, particularly white ethnic Catholics and Jews.[71] With liberation theology ascendant among Catholics in Latin America and with Jews in the United States still trying to shake off suspicions of communism (ironically, while they were often simultaneously depicted as overly materialistic), some members of these communities used theological justifications for free-market capitalism as, in part, a way of proving their whiteness, their religious authenticity, and their American bona fides. Nevertheless, as mentioned above, conservative Anglo-Saxon Protestants involved in the religious right were still adamant in their exclusions—at least of Catholics.[72]

Ronald Reagan was the first president to flout the concerns of nativist Protestants by creating formal diplomatic alliances with the Vatican (something presidents since Franklin Delano Roosevelt had hoped to do but dared not). The increased political standing of American Catholics under Reagan, however, had as much or more to do with forging late Cold War alliances, opposing domestic social welfare programs, and opposing communism in Latin America than it did with Catholic Americans' attempts to prove their loyalties through community service.[73] Michael Novak, for example, served the Reagan administration in the 1980s, sharing with Reagan a belief in the moral and social supremacy of free-market capitalism and an antipathy to economic regulation. Novak later went on to serve as a mentor to another notable conservative, the formerly Southern Baptist Speaker of the House Newt Gingrich, who converted to Catholicism after his resignation from Congress on ethics violations. Gingrich has since promoted religiously inspired community service as an alternative to what is now a highly racially coded phrase: "the welfare state."[74]

In one of his last essays on the topic of religion in American life, Bellah acknowledged that strong communal ties and social networks did not always coincide with demands for the common good as he understood it. Rather, belief in the necessity of a "strong society, weak state" was a current that ran through American history, inspired by the Enlightenment liberalism and dissenting Protestantism that were both "more comfortable with voluntary associations in the civic sphere and individual entrepreneurship in the economic sphere than with bureaucracy or government direction," and held to fervently by "those who today call themselves conservatives."[75] If pressed, Bellah might have argued that these conservatives included Catholics in America who, under the weight of the nation's hegemonic culture, were becoming "like Protestants." We need not go quite so far as that in understanding the rise of white ethnic neoliberals. We can certainly say, though, that they promoted highly racialized narratives of American exceptionalism (ones reminiscent of earlier progressive Protestants' narratives) as they endeavored to gain acceptance within primarily Anglo-Saxon Protestant power structures from which they were often still excluded. And because of this history, we should be attuned to the power dynamics operating as we again hear community service lauded as the essence of true religion by everyone from the first Black president of the United States to the most marginalized religious population in the United States: American Muslims.

Conclusion: Civil Religion Now

On Saturday, August 30, 2014, numerous Muslim Americans attending the fifty-first annual convention of the Islamic Society of North America (ISNA; the largest Muslim organization on the continent) participated in the organization's Community Service Program. They spent the morning learning about Muslim-led community service endeavors in the city of Detroit and then divided into groups of urban gardeners and teams devoted to urban housing restoration. At the 2014 convention ISNA also held its fifteenth annual Community Service Recognition Luncheon, for which over a thousand conference attendees bought tickets. Despite ISNA's history of emphasizing community service, however, the organization's directors had only recently begun to frame it as a patriotic project rather than a religious obligation undertaken on behalf of coreligionists. This was something spurred equally by personal convictions and political circumstances.

Some of the political circumstances that have inspired Muslim Americans to engage in greater community service efforts include, of course, improving other Americans' impressions of them after the World Trade Center attacks of 1993 and 2001. Yet the emphasis on such activities increased markedly after the first decade of the twenty-first century. This was for two reasons. The first reason was the 2009 launch of President Obama's United We Serve campaign, which Obama created to "make volunteerism and community service part of the daily lives of all Americans" and saw, as mentioned, as a program that could unite Americans of different religions.[76] His initiative gave federal (and formative) weight to the idea that community service is, indeed, America's civil religion. Not long after, ISNA leaders encouraged Muslim Americans to participate in the first National Day of Service, to be held annually on September 11—the anniversary of the 2001 terrorist attacks on the World Trade Center and the Pentagon.[77] The second factor that propelled Muslim Americans to increasingly emphasize community service occurred the very next year: the "Ground Zero Mosque" debate over the appropriateness of building an Islamic community center in Manhattan not far from the former World Trade Center. That controversy brought with it more violence and discrimination toward Muslims than at any point since the days immediately after 9/11 and confirmed in Muslims the impression that they should work harder for acceptance through the avenue recently presented to them.

In 2010, ISNA decided on "Nurturing Compassionate Communities: Connecting Faith and Service" as the theme for its annual conference. Additionally, the organization participated with fourteen other Muslim American leaders and groups in encouraging Muslims across the United States to join the president's community service effort under the banner of "MuslimServe" and to use the Obama administration's website (http://serve.gov) to search for projects in their areas. The goal, according to their "Call to Action," was "to turn the tide of hatred" and "demonstrate our core Islamic values and our dedication to our neighborhoods and our country."[78] Then, between 2013 and 2014, ISNA Development Foundation officials and Founder's Committee members changed the description of their Community Service Recognition Luncheon. Convention materials for 2013 described the lunch as an event where "the nation's Muslim leaders, scholars, and government officials join to honor an individual dedicated to community service within the Muslim community."[79] In contrast, the Annual Convention Program description of the 2014 luncheon omitted that last clause, turning service into a broader national mandate.[80] As Muslim American leaders acknowledged in 2010 and after, a primary goal of such religiously inspired service endeavors was to prove their loyalties. "All eyes will be on us this Eid and on 9/11," the 2010 MuslimServe Call to Action read. "Let's show that we can rise above prejudice and hatred and be the kind of conscientious citizens who give back to our country."[81]

Despite their efforts, and as Catholics found during the 1960s, Muslim Americans are now discovering that the acceptance promised for those who participate in America's civil religion of community service can be quite illusory. Not only did a Pew Research Center poll taken in the summer of 2014 show that Americans regard Muslims less warmly than any other religious minority, but violence and discrimination since then have surpassed even those seen during the controversy over the community center (also meant to be a place of service) in Manhattan.[82] In February 2015, three young Muslim Americans devoted to community service were executed by a white neighbor in their North Carolina apartment complex. Speaking after the funeral to a reporter, one local woman expressed her disillusionment and fear. Muslims were told that they would be safe in America after 9/11 if they had "exemplary character" like that of the victims. The murders of such ideal American Muslim citizens had shredded these hopes for her. "To see that it happened to them means it can happen to anyone."[83] Crucially, these murders occurred even before the rise of Donald J. Trump as the Republican Party's 2016 nominee for president, whose anti-Islamic campaign contributed mightily to increased violence.

In light of these recent events, the 2010 controversy over the Manhattan community center can be seen both as an echo of the Peace Corps controversy fifty years prior and as a dark harbinger of things to come. Rather than accept the developers' arguments that the community center would be a place of service, many American nativists (Protestant and otherwise) insisted that it would further Muslims' surreptitious goal of infiltrating and overthrowing America's government—an accusation Catholics also faced in 1961, despite their years of service to the nation (military and otherwise). In addition to allowing religious minorities to prove their national loyalties by participating in common rituals, it seems, Americans have established a tradition of using the civil religion of community service as a way to exclude those already marginalized. For Muslim Americans, this trend has only escalated.

In 2016, a team from Islamic Relief USA (an organization established in 1993) waded through the murky waters of a flood-ravaged portion of Louisiana to provide residents with aid and shelter. For the first time in the domestic service team's five-year history, they were turned away from a disaster. A local sheriff called the Red Cross center with which Islamic Relief was working and threatened to arrest the team if they did not leave immediately. They pulled out of that area only to be informed by another official that the team would likely face violence if they tried to relocate to a nearby county.[84] While some might argue that such incidents do not represent all of America, the same can be said of anti-Catholic opposition to the Peace Corps civilian service program of the 1960s. The point is not, as some critics of Bellah's might argue, that the civil religion of serving others does not actually exist. It is, as Bellah began to realize late in his life, that such a tradition is less pluralistic and far more a part of nationalist power dynamics than he or others may have initially imagined. Scholars of American religion can now hardly afford not to reckon with the ominous implications of this realization.

NOTES

1 Email communication with Robert N. Bellah, June 4, 2007.
2 I discuss Smith's work in Rosemary R. Hicks, "Comparative Religion and the Cold War Transformation of Indo-Persian Mysticisms into Liberal Islamic Modernity," in *Secularism and Religion-Making*, ed. Markus Dressler and Arvind Mandair (New York: Oxford University Press, 2011), 141–69.
3 See, for example, Wilfred Cantwell Smith, *Towards a World Theology: Faith and the Comparative History of Religion* (Philadelphia: Westminster Press, 1991).
4 Email communication with Robert N. Bellah, June 5, 2007.

5   Robert N. Bellah, introductory note to "Civil Religion in America," in *The Robert Bellah Reader*, ed. Robert N. Bellah and Steven M. Tipton (Durham, NC: Duke University Press, 2006), 225.
6   Among those considered here are Bellah's "Religion and the Legitimation of the American Republic," *Society* 15, no. 4 (1978): 16–23; "The Kingdom of God in America," in *Religion and the Public Good: A Bicentennial Forum* (Macon, GA: Mercer University Press, 1988), 41–61; and "Flaws in the Protestant Code: Some Religious Sources of America's Troubles," *Ethical Perspectives* 7, no. 4 (2000): 288–99; all of which appear in *The Robert Bellah Reader*.
7   Jesse Lee, "The President's Speech in Cairo: A New Beginning" (White House, June 4, 2009), www.whitehouse.gov. The full text of Obama's June 4, 2009, speech is available through the White House website, www.whitehouse.gov.
8   Tammy Castle, "Self-Immolation," in *Religion and Violence: An Encyclopedia of Faith and Conflict from Antiquity to the Present*, ed. Jeffrey Ian Ross (New York: Routledge, 2010), 669–73, 669.
9   Castle, "Self-Immolation," 671.
10 Castle, "Self-Immolation."
11 "Nixon Advocates Use of More G.I.'s," *New York Times*, August 8, 1966.
12 Robert McNamara interview in *The Fog of War: Eleven Lessons from the Life of Robert S. McNamara*, directed by Errol Morris (New York: Sony Classics, 2004).
13 Robert Neelly Bellah, "Introduction to the Second Edition," in *The Broken Covenant: American Civil Religion in Time of Trial* (1975; Chicago: University of Chicago Press, 1992), vii–viii.
14 Bellah, "Civil Religion in America," 229.
15 Bellah, "Civil Religion in America," 229.
16 Bellah, "Civil Religion in America," 230.
17 Bellah, "Civil Religion in America," 233.
18 In "The Kingdom of God in America," for example, Bellah argued that if Americans used the language of faith to talk about national destiny and purpose, "we must be committed, as was Martin Luther King Jr., to the use of nonviolence" (in Bellah and Tipton, *Robert Bellah Reader*, 300).
19 Bellah, "Civil Religion in America," 236.
20 Bellah, "Civil Religion in America," 241.
21 Bellah, "Civil Religion in America," 243.
22 For trenchant analyses of how the theme of sacrifice—particularly in war—infused American ideas about and traditions of civil religion throughout the twentieth century and into the twenty-first, see Raymond J. Haberski Jr., *God and War: American Civil Religion since 1945* (New Brunswick, NJ: Rutgers University Press, 2012); Jonathan H. Ebel, *G.I. Messiahs: Soldiering, War, and American Civil Religion* (New Haven, CT: Yale University Press, 2015); and Andrew Preston, *Sword of the Spirit, Shield of Faith: Religion in American War and Diplomacy* (New York: Anchor, 2012).
23 Bellah, *Broken Covenant*, xiv.

24 Bellah, "Religion and the Legitimation," in Bellah and Tipton, *Robert Bellah Reader*, 261–62.
25 See, for example, Bellah, "Flaws in the Protestant Code: Theological Roots of American Individualism," in Bellah and Tipton, *Robert Bellah Reader*, 333.
26 Bellah, "Religion and the Legitimation," 247n1.
27 Bellah, "Religion and the Legitimation," 258.
28 Bellah, "Religion and the Legitimation," 262.
29 Bellah, "Religion and the Legitimation," 259.
30 Bellah, "Religion and the Legitimation," x.
31 National Conference of Catholic Bishops, "Economic Justice for All: A Pastoral Letter on Catholic Social Teaching and the U.S. Economy" (November 18, 1986), 182–83, quoted in Bellah, "Kingdom of God in America," 301–2.
32 Robert N. Bellah, "Citizenship, Diversity, and the Search for the Common Good," in Bellah and Tipton, *Robert Bellah Reader*, 317–18 (first delivered at a symposium at DePauw University).
33 Bellah, "Kingdom of God in America," 301.
34 Bellah, "Citizenship, Diversity," 312.
35 Bellah, "Citizenship, Diversity," 312.
36 For conservative Protestants' opposition to Catholic inclusion, see Neil J. Young, *We Gather Together: The Religious Right and the Problem of Interfaith Politics* (New York: Oxford University Press, 2015).
37 Robert N. Bellah and Frederick Greenspahn, eds., *Uncivil Religion: Interreligious Hostility in America* (New York: Crossroad, 1987).
38 Robert N. Bellah, "Is There a Common American Culture?," in Bellah and Tipton, *Robert Bellah Reader*, 322 (first delivered as a plenary address to the American Academy of Religion in 1997).
39 John Paul II, *Ecclesia in America* (post-synodal apostolic exhortation on solidarity in America, January 22, 1999), http://w2.vatican.va.
40 Robert N. Bellah, Richard Madsen, William M. Sullivan, Ann Swidler, and Steven M. Tipton, *Habits of the Heart: Individualism and Commitment in American Life* (Berkeley: University of California Press, 1985).
41 Bellah, "Kingdom of God in America," 295–96.
42 Bellah, *Broken Covenant*, xvi.
43 Bellah, "Flaws in the Protestant Code," 333.
44 Bellah, "Flaws in the Protestant Code," 333. This was actually an argument Bellah had begun to make in his 1997 plenary address to the American Academy of Religion, "Is There a Common American Culture?"
45 Among the former were Talal Asad, *Genealogies of Religion: Discipline and Reasons of Power in Christianity and Islam* (Stanford, CA: Stanford University Press, 1993), and Russell McCutcheon, *Manufacturing Religion: The Discourse on Sui Generis Religion and the Politics of Nostalgia* (New York: Oxford University Press, 1997). Among the latter were Janet Jakobsen, Anne Pellegrini, and their collaborators in a special edition of *Social Texts* titled "World Secularisms at the Millen-

nium." See especially Jakobsen and Pellegrini, "Introduction," *Social Text* 18, no. 3 (2000): 1–27, and Robert J. Baird, "Late Secularism," *Social Text* 18, no. 3 (2000): 123–36.

46 Early examples of such work include Catherine Albanese, *America: Religions and Religion* (Belmont, CA: Wadsworth, 1981), and William Hutchison, *Between the Times: The Travail of the Protestant Establishment in America, 1900–1960* (New York: Cambridge University Press, 1989).

47 For a trenchant critique of Bellah on this count, see David Sehat, *The Myth of American Religious Freedom* (New York: Oxford University Press, 2015), 284–85.

48 To those who opposed the use of religious language in public life because of its possibly coercive effects, Bellah responded that the First Amendment prohibited such language from attaining "legally coercive authority" and implied that, short of such legal consequences, "the use of religion in public discourse" was part of a general and often positive "noncoercive discussion that goes on between citizens" ("Kingdom of God in America," 285).

49 Bellah, "Flaws in the Protestant Code," 335.

50 Bellah, "Flaws in the Protestant Code," 339.

51 Bellah's thoughts on which Protestant groups' beliefs most influenced American culture at different points can be found, among other places, in "God and King" in Bellah and Tipton, *Robert Bellah Reader*, 367–69, and in "Flaws in the Protestant Code," 344–45.

52 Among these are Sehat, *Myth of American Religious Freedom*; Winnifred Fallers Sullivan, *The Impossibility of Religious Freedom* (Princeton, NJ: Princeton University Press, 2005); and Tisa Joy Wenger, *We Have a Religion: The 1920s Pueblo Indian Dance Controversy and American Religious Freedom* (Chapel Hill: University of North Carolina Press, 2009). For an overview of some of this work and trends for future research, see Rosemary R. Hicks, "Between Lived and the Law: Power, Empire, and Expansion in Studies of North American Religions," *Religion* 42, no. 3 (2012): 409–24.

53 Bellah, "Flaws in the Protestant Code," 344. To buttress this latter point, Bellah cited Catholic theologian Francis Schüssler Fiorenza on the flaws of the "religious right" (345n24).

54 Bellah, "Flaws in the Protestant Code," 346.

55 On Bellah's enduring commitment to Hegelian historicism and understanding of it as the "deep background" of both Weber and Durkheim's work, see Robert N. Bellah and Steven M. Tipton, "Introduction," in Bellah and Tipton, *Robert Bellah Reader*, 3–7, 3. On Smith's Hegelianism, see Hicks, "Comparative Religion."

56 The tension between idealism and materialism was obviously not the only one in Bellah's work. Influenced greatly by Reinhold Niebuhr, Bellah perpetually struggled to navigate the contradictions between, as Niebuhr saw it, what America was and what it could be. For more on Niebuhr's relevance for civil religion, see Haberski, *God and War*.

57 Bellah, "Flaws in the Protestant Code," 347–48.

58 Bellah, "Flaws in the Protestant Code," 348.
59 On Smith's disillusionment with communism and socialism, see Hicks, "Comparative Religion."
60 Bellah, "Flaws in the Protestant Code," 348.
61 Bellah, "Flaws in the Protestant Code," 336.
62 Rosemary R. Corbett, "For God and Country: Religious Minorities Striving for National Belonging through Community Service," *Religion and American Culture* 26, no. 2 (2016): 227–59.
63 "Community Service" (editorial), *New York Times*, June 1, 1919.
64 For example, see Mark Silk, "Notes on the Judeo-Christian Tradition in America," *American Quarterly* 36, no. 1 (1984): 65–85; Deborah Dash Moore, "Jewish GIs and the Creation of the Judeo-Christian Tradition," *Religion and American Culture* 8 (December 1998): 31–53; and K. Healan Gaston, "Demarcating Democracy: Liberal Catholics, Protestants, and the Discourse of Secularism," in *American Religious Liberalism*, ed. Leigh E. Schmidt and Sally Promey (Bloomington: Indiana University Press, 2012), 337–58.
65 For more on these dynamics, see David Allen, "Religion and Politics in the Kennedy Era, 1953–1965" (MPhil thesis, University of Cambridge, June 2012).
66 See Corbett, "For God and Country."
67 John Wicklein, "Church Council Sets Up Office for Liaison with Peace Corps," *New York Times*, January 5, 1962.
68 Quoted in Kevin M. Schultz, *Tri-Faith America: How Catholic and Jews Held Postwar America to Its Protestant Promise* (New York: Oxford University Press, 2011), 207.
69 John F. Kennedy, "Address of Senator John F. Kennedy to the Greater Houston Ministerial Association" (September 12, 1960), www.jfklibrary.org.
70 Bellah, "God and King," 375.
71 For more on these dynamics and their continuing relevance for contemporary neoliberals (including Newt Gingrich), see Rosemary R. Corbett, *Making Moderate Islam: Sufism, Service, and the "Ground Zero Mosque" Controversy* (Stanford, CA: Stanford University Press, 2016), 26–30.
72 As evangelicals increasingly identified with Israel after the 1967 war, Jews were more often included favorably in Protestant rhetoric and theology, if not actually in all Protestant social circles. See Schultz, *Tri-Faith America*, 199–204, and Thomas Kidd, *American Christians and Islam: Evangelical Culture from the Colonial Period to the Age of Terrorism* (Princeton, NJ: Princeton University Press, 2009).
73 William Inboden, *Religion and American Foreign Policy, 1945–1960: The Soul of Containment* (New York: Cambridge University Press, 2010), 316–17.
74 Corbett, *Making Moderate Islam*, 34.
75 Bellah, "God and King," 369.
76 White House Office of the Press Secretary, "President Obama Unveils 'United We Serve,' Calls on All Americans to Commit to Meaningful Volunteer Service in Their Daily Lives" (June 17, 2009), www.whitehouse.gov.

77 Islamic Society of North America, "ISNA Newsletter" (August 21, 2009).
78 MuslimServe, "A Call to Action: Join Muslim-Serve National Campaign for Service and Understanding on 9/11" (Islamic Circle of North America), www.icna.org.
79 ISNA Development Foundation, "Sponsorship Package" (2013), 1, www.isna.net.
80 ISNA 2014 Annual Convention Program, "Generation Rise: Elevating Muslim American Culture," 8, www.isna.net.
81 MuslimServe, "Call to Action."
82 Pew Research Center, Religion and Public Life Project, "How Americans Feel about Religious Groups" (July 16, 2014), www.pewforum.org.
83 Jonathan M. Katz, "Funeral for Muslims Killed in Chapel Hill Draws Thousands," *New York Times*, February 12, 2015.
84 Islamic Relief USA, "Monthly Newsletter" (March 29, 2016). More information can be found in "Emergency Team Undeterred by Islamophobia in Louisiana Flood Relief" (Islamic Relief USA), http://irusa.org.

4

Regions and Civil Religion(s) in America

ARTHUR REMILLARD

Ira Chernus is right. Scholars need to stop using the phrase "American civil religion." As Chernus sees it, the problem is Robert Bellah's outsized influence in shaping the conversation. In Bellah's infamous 1967 article "Civil Religion in America," he identified the "ethical principles" that he believed held together a diverse America in a post-Protestant age. He would later elaborate that his central aim in using the idea of civil religion "[is] to examine the history of America's religious self-understanding, the myths that have developed to help us interpret who and what we are in America and to inquire whether they may still have power to help us understand our present situation and know how to deal with it." It's the language of "us" and "we" that draws Chernus's contempt. "Whenever 'we' are imagined and supposedly common values are articulated," he charged, "the process is hardly shared in equally by all the inhabitants of the land."[1]

So for Chernus, this thing that scholars call "American civil religion" is actually the product and property of "wealthy, white, male Protestant Christians." A glance at the oft-cited resources deployed by Bellah in developing this category tends to confirm this conclusion. Names like Washington, Jefferson, Adams, and Franklin stand forthrightly alongside the Constitution, the Declaration of Independence, and useful "biblical archetypes" such as Exodus. This ensemble of voices and objects, the argument goes, serve as the binding agent for American society. As for everyone outside of this sphere, they can either adopt this "tradition" or reside in the land of civil religious heresy. It's a formula that Chernus finds troubling enough that he wants nothing to do with this so-called "American civil religion."[2]

Chernus's criticism is nothing new. In 1973 when the civil religion discussion was just under way, Charles Long observed that "various national and ethnic communities" simply have no place in this discussion of "national symbols and meanings."[3] A few decades later, Russell McCutcheon argued that Bellah's article represents "a particular brand of U.S. nationalism."[4] Collectively, these critics assert that "American civil religion" does the work of colonizing the territory of American diversity by planting the flag of sameness, all in the service of constructing a "consensus."

So, yes, "American civil religion" must die. But after some time in the ground, we ought to exhume its bones in order to reanimate the basic idea of this category. Indeed, civil religion offers a way for scholars to examine and interpret the places where religious language and allusions intersect with political identity. "American civil religion" simply has too much baggage to do this at a descriptive level. In its place, then, let us begin the study of "America's civil religions."

Unlike its previous incarnation, this conversation will not pursue questions about what "we" hold in common. Instead, civil religion will be an *analytical tool* used for understanding how different people in different times in different places have developed different ways of creating and maintaining their bonds of affection for each other and their local, regional, and national identities. Hence, civil *religions*—plural—with the possessive "America's," connoting that these discourses exist in many places around America. Guiding this examination of diverse religiopolitical identities will be one important and overriding question: "Whose civil religion am I describing?"[5] How, in other words, do factors such as race, class, gender, ethnicity, and religion influence civil religious discourses? What resources do different populations bring in to this conversation? And how do people ascribe insider/outsider status on their own terms?

Region also complicates and confounds the previous generation's civil religious narratives. "American civil religion" is located almost entirely in Washington, D.C., and the Northeast. In these places, we hear the voices of Puritans and their inheritors echoing off of the highbrow sounds of Enlightenment rationalism. But elsewhere in America, we find ample evidence of civil religious creativity, with an assortment of people drawing on their own resources and histories. An attention to region necessarily decenters the story of America's civil religions, making it uneven, unpredictable, and nonlinear. This messy account is precisely where a new breed of civil religion studies needs to begin.

Decentering Civil Religion

"America may never have been a Christian nation, but its civil religion drew heavily on Judeo-Christian values," explained journalist Yoni Appelbaum in the *Atlantic*. He continued, "Americans long subscribed to the belief, as the sociologist Robert Bellah famously put it, that they shoulder a peculiar 'obligation, both collective and individual, to carry out God's will on earth.' That, Bellah argued, constituted a shared civil religion, one capable of binding together a diverse nation." Appelbaum then compared this to Donald Trump's dystopian vision of America as outlined in the first presidential debate of 2016. "Until now," the author lamented, "the political debate has generally been framed by a set of shared principles, even if they've often been applied to contrary ends." But Trump's meandering bellows signaled a wholesale dismissal of this political heritage. "He didn't ask Americans to make any sacrifices. He didn't tell them what they might achieve together. He didn't affirm that his own actions are subordinate to some higher purpose." What he did do was position himself as the solution to America's supposed woes. In Appelbaum's view, all of this means one important thing: "American civil religion" is dead, and Donald Trump has killed it.[6]

Or did he? To study America's civil religions is to reorient the scholarly gaze away from prescription and toward understanding. So perhaps Trump has given voice to a new breed of civil religious discourse. "Make America Great Again" is a rallying cry. And the candidate's promise of a border wall between the United States and Mexico (paid for by Mexico, of course) has become a symbol of working-class white discontent with immigration and immigrants. What about sacrifice? As Applebaum rightly noted, this was a fundamental piece of Bellah's framing of civil religion. "I think I've made a lot of sacrifices," Trump responded to a reporter, arguing that his selflessness is evidenced by the thousands of people he has employed and the "millions of dollars" he has raised for veterans.[7] One might doubt the authenticity of this claim. But that does not account for the fact that Donald Trump too could use the language of sacrifice to his own ends. "Trumpism," in other words, is doing real civil religious work.[8] The billionaire's words and deeds became the "shared principles" of the millions who call themselves his supporters.

To study civil religion is to confront pronouncements that run afoul of the scholar's refined moral sensibilities. Martin Luther King Jr.'s "I Have a Dream" speech has an abundance of civil religious substance. So too does George Wallace's "Segregation Now, Segregation Forever" speech. Both were prophetic. Both were saturated with "Judeo-Christian" references. And both claimed to have the ultimate purpose and destiny of the nation as a central concern.[9] Yet only one figures into the conversation of "American civil religion." This, no doubt, is a by-product of Bellah's influence.[10] Bellah made no secret that he was trying to describe "American civil religion" "at its best." In doing so, he arguably ascribed a degree of concreteness to the category, as if it existed "out there" in reality. And because it has structure, there are those who belong and those who do not. We see this logic repeated through the likes of George Marsden, who speculated that "American civil religion" celebrates soldiers who make "the supreme sacrifice" by fighting and dying in war. Quakers, Mennonites, Amish, and Moravians, he continued, represent the "major exceptions." For "refusing to fight in a good cause," these communities have historically earned reputations as traitors.[11]

But are these pacifists truly civil religious "exceptions"? Or is it more accurate to say that they have a *different*, albeit controversial, civil religious discourse wherein peace is an uncontestable "good cause"?[12] "Man has not yet learned to forgive his enemies," exclaimed one Mennonite author in 1889. "He prefers to let the wound of animosity fester, rather than heal it with the balm of peace." Echoing the social gospel rhetoric of the time, the author imagined an America where an ethic of charitable forgiveness set the groundwork for an "absolute peace."[13] Bellah made war a centerpiece of his 1967 article, and Marsden was obviously drawing from this theme. More than that, though, both scholars arguably projected out into reality an "American civil religion" that has distinct parameters. This, then, opens the door for judgments about who belongs and who does not. But when civil religion remains as an analytical tool, we begin to discover that certain pockets of the American population have resisted the dominant narratives and created their own.[14]

In moving from prescription to description, then, it is important to state that an effort to understand a civil religious discourse is not an endorsement of it. Rather, understanding requires a degree of empathy for the purpose of better discerning why people do what they do.[15]

It's a methodological position that requires a bracketing out of judgment, a willingness to suppress normative binaries such as "true" and "untrue," and "good" and "bad." As Robert Orsi stated, "It is the challenge of the discipline of religious studies not to stop at the border of human practices done in the name of the gods that we scholars find disturbing dangerous, or even morally repugnant, but rather to enter into the otherness of religious practices in search of an understanding of their human ground."[16] To study religion—or civil religion for that matter—is not to create a hierarchy of preferred practices, elevating some and denigrating others. The point is to understand and contextualize these expressions on their own terms. This often means recognizing that civil religion is a discourse of power. As Michel Foucault explained, power is not just the property of the privileged few. Instead, "power must be understood in the first instance as the multiplicity of force relations immanent in the sphere in which they operate and which constitute their own organization."[17] Power is everywhere, influencing everyone and transforming people at all ends of the social spectrum. Power both pushes and pulls, advances and resists. To study the power dynamics of one group, then, we must also understand those whom they oppose and vice versa. The advocates of a martial strain of civil religious discourse have as their counterpoint a handful of Anabaptists. Both find ways to gather power to their advantage, and both define themselves in contrast to the other.

With this in mind, we begin to understand that civil religious discourses are the product of people of all ranks, colors, and creeds. Power is an animating force behind these discourses, as individuals and groups seek to assert their complex agendas in public spaces. Statements of social values and shared beliefs alternatively include as they exclude. Following these narratives is the scholar's challenge. Determining whose civil religion is *the* civil religion is not.

So if we are to bury "American civil religion," we must also add Bellah's 1967 essay and subsequent writings on the topic. After all, the sociologist was neither the first nor the last to ponder the idea of civil religion. As Mark Silk has shown, the substance of civil religion has long been part of Western thinking, even though the term first appeared during the European Enlightenment. Silk notes how philosophers often made reference to Numa Pompilius when thinking of the role of religion and political organization. Numa was the legendary second king of Rome who succeeded the warmonger, King Romulus. Accounts of Numa cast him as a peaceful sage who united the disparate kingdom and brought prosperity to the land. The king's success, the stories have suggested, resulted from his "civil theology," which comprised a religious calendar, the cults of Mars and Jupiter, the vestal virgins, and the temple of Janus.[18]

French Enlightenment philosopher Jean-Jacques Rousseau was a deep admirer of Numa's "Roman religion." With Numa serving as a backdrop, Rousseau coined the term "civil religion" in his 1762 *Social Contract*. Rousseau had no use for organized religion, viewing it as an incubator for intolerance and ignorance. Still, he viewed the moral function of religion as essential for society. Guided by a minimum set of beliefs, or "positive dogmas," Rousseau's concept of "civil religion" sought to eliminate intolerance and enhance personal liberty for the sake of creating a productive, peaceful, and stable society.[19]

By the time Bellah recovered the idea of civil religion, the concept had undergone a series of iterations. Neither exclusively Christian nor American in its early stages, the idea of civil religion was a place for philosophical consideration about politics, religion, and their ongoing interplay. Significantly, the philosophical observers treated civil religion as a social invention used to project a sense of uniformity onto a fragmented world. The constructed nature of civil religion arguably faded in Bellah's treatment of the category. But there have been sociologists and others who have tried to reorient the conversation in this direction. Foremost among them is N. J. Demerath III and Rhys Williams's influential article "Civil Religion in an Uncivil Society." The authors draw a critical aim at the common understanding of civil religion "as a cohesive force, a common canopy of values that helps foster social and cultural integration." The "complex reality," countered Demerath and Williams, is that "[civil religious] discourse has become a tool for legitimizing social movements and interest-group politics." With this in mind, Demerath and Williams called for future studies that account for "the contexts and uses of civil-religious language and symbols, noting how specific groups and subcultures use versions of civil religion to frame, articulate, and legitimate their own particular political or moral visions."[20]

Demerath and Williams's reconceiving of civil religion did manage to attract the attention of some scholars. For example, Rita Kirk Whillock examined American political discourse and portrayed civil religion in terms of "declarations of principles from competing groups seeking to define what America is and the values that should prevail."[21] But for the most part, scholars have been content to allow Bellah to be the sine qua non of civil religion theory.[22] A 2014 book on the topic lists Bellah on the first and final pages of the text, a suitable emblem of the status of "American civil religion."[23] When it comes to this category, the sociologist's writings offer the first, last, and too-often dominant words on the topic.

As we have seen from Mark Silk, though, the idea of civil religion predates Bellah by centuries. And while the philosophers pondered the ways in which well-positioned political figures invented a civil religious discourse for the purpose of manufacturing unity, this basic insight can bend in a Foucauldian direction. In other words, a decentered understanding of civil religion destabilizes the dominant themes that compose "American civil religion," democratizing understandings of where civil religion is at work. Since the 1960s, this discussion has concentrated on a handful of moments, people, and places, assuming that this combination of social forces has generated unity for all. In contrast, the study of America's civil religions seeks out the stories of everyone else. The wealthy and well-positioned did not create their civil religious worldviews in isolation. They too contended with the power dynamics of a variety of other groups, large and small, threatening and safe. Moreover, throughout America's history, the marginalized, the alienated, and the persecuted have possessed the will and imagination necessary to define on their own terms what their local, national, and international communities *ought* to look like. While there is no denying that some voices are louder and more influential than others, the scholar's task is not to determine the winners and losers.

To imagine America's civil religions, then, is to imagine a category with no center or periphery. Any civil religious discourse is a mash of competing forces and mutual opposition. Location matters in this conversation. Civil religion happens everywhere, not just in Washington, D.C., and the urban Northeast, voiced by Puritans and Enlightenment rationalists. When we look outside of these places, we find new stories that reflect the diverse ways that people have conceived of their corporate identities.

One Nation, Civil Religiously Divided

In 1832, city leaders in Boston held a public celebration to commemorate the centennial of George Washington's birth. The event began as the Massachusetts governor and legislators processed from the State House to Old South Church, while cannons boomed and church bells rang. At the service, the musical score featured Handel's "Hallelujah Chorus" and scripture readings came from Psalms, Ecclesiasticus, and 1 Maccabees. Francis Gray then stepped to the stage to give the featured address. Born in Salem, Gray was a Harvard-educated lawyer, politician, philanthropist, and writer. He was also a Federalist who had a deep reverence for the Constitution and the central government. Accordingly, when it came to George Washington, Gray had little difficulty heaping praise on the "founding father," calling him a "special instrument of divine providence." While careful not to betray his rationalist leanings, the speaker nonetheless spent two hours painting Washington—the "Apostle of Liberty"—with a semidivine gloss.[24]

If there was a checklist for the 1967 version of "American civil religion," this would hit every single box. With George Washington at the center and Christian symbols adorning the edges, America's "myth of origin" was on full display. Each ritual, each image, and each word reinforced a towering structure of American unity and exceptionalism. But hidden in the shadow of this structure, we find many hands busily constructing this edifice. These are, of course, the hands of northern, white, wealthy Protestants. This was their civil religious production, which served their interests in their specific time and place.

If we shift our gaze to other sections of the country, we find alternative "myths of origin" speaking for different populations. In the same year that Francis Gray waxed nostalgic about Washington, city leaders in Santa Fe hosted a public celebration that focused on their own history of independence and heroics. The independence, in this case, was from another European power, Spain. And the hero was Padre Jose Miguel Hidalgo y Costilla, often considered the father of the Mexican nation. Twelve years had passed since independence in New Mexico, and life there had changed very little as a result. Poverty and political instability produced an air of insecurity in the region. But Santa Fe had the advantage of being a trade crossroads, with merchants and businesspeople developing strong economic ties to the United States in particular. With this as a context, their Independence Day celebration in 1832 was a time for hope in the future. Artillery blasts, dancing, and processions were all preludes to the central event of the day, a mass celebrated by Padre Antonio Jose Martinez. An influential political and religious leader, Martinez was known for his deep commitment to independence and sincere reverence for his fellow priest Miguel Hidalgo. As the audience sat in the brown adobe church, they heard Martinez compare Hidalgo "to the liberator of the world, to Jesus Christ." He continued, "Hidalgo, following in these footsteps, preached the doctrine of his decisions, attacked the tyrants, gave us his example and finally died at the [hands] of the same [tyrants], for the good of his country." The speaker portrayed Hidalgo not as Christ but as someone who at that historical moment had Christ working through him.[25]

This fundamentally Catholic and southwestern origin narrative does not fit neatly into the standard accounts of "American civil religion." But New Mexico and its Catholic inhabitants would officially become part of the United States in 1848, as would their stories of independence and heroics. As Randi Jones Walker has argued, scholars need be more attentive to these differences. "The society of the United States," she emphasized, "is too complex to be understood in terms of a single myth of origin, no matter how dominant." The twin myths of Washington and Hidalgo tell us, in other words, that America's civil religions take on new shapes and forms when we look to new people and places.[26]

A focus on regional distinctiveness is one way that scholars can begin to decenter civil religion. When Mark Silk and Andrew Walsh completed their eight-volume book series "Religion by Region," they summarized their conclusions in *One Nation, Divisible: How Regional Religious Differences Shape American Politics*. "The American story," they stressed, has never been told by one voice. No one region or population can ever hope to speak for everyone."[27]

And yet the enterprise of "American civil religion" has tried to do just that, especially when considering the foundational myths of the nation. A "myth of origin" is particularly useful in studying civil religion. As Bellah noted, such myths serve as "a strategic point of departure because the comparative study of religion has found that where a people conceives itself to have started reveals much about its most basic self-conceptions."[28] But while myths have a veneer of objective certainty, they are unstable precisely because they are the product of a human effort to advance political agendas. This was a fact duly noted by Plato. As he contemplated the nature of the "good society" in *The Republic*, the philosopher proposed a "single bold flight of invention" called the "myth of the metals." The myth dictated that each person was born with bronze, silver, or gold in their blood. The individual's station in life, he supposed, would be determined by their metal. He further suspected that, over time, the myth would become ensconced in the social imagination, ensuring greater stability and encouraging people to "care more for the commonwealth and for one another."[29]

Myths, then, translate nostalgic sentiments into a sense of unity. But as Bruce Lincoln has noted, societies are fluid entities and so are their myths. As people become estranged from some groups and attracted to others, they engage in a "strategic tinkering with the past" in order to make a new myth for their present.[30] The result is a plurality of mythical constructs, each competing for broader social space. To look through the regions and subregions that make up America, we see no shortage of "strategic tinkering" at work in the many myths of these places.

Consider the American South. As Charles Reagan Wilson has shown, in the decades after the Civil War and Reconstruction, defeated white southerners went about developing a civil religious discourse that was rooted in the Lost Cause. From Virginia to Texas, monuments devoted to Confederate heroes such as Stonewall Jackson, Robert E. Lee, and Jefferson Davis led to a unique, regionally defined myth of origin.[31] Wilson effectively redirected attention southward, showing how historical events in Dixie generated civil religious activity that differed profoundly from northern expressions. But even within the South there were variations.

Soon after his death in 1899, Pensacola, Florida, citizens erected a monument to William Chipley, which read, "Soldier—Statesman—Public Benefactor. On the battlefield he was without fear and without reproach; in the council of state he was wise and sagacious; and in his public and private benefactions he was ever alert and tireless. The history of his life is the history of the upbuilding [sic] of West Florida; and its every material advancement, for two decades, bears the impress of his genius and his labor."[32] While certainly containing hints of the Lost

Cause, this monument spoke more to the progressive elements of the "New South"—the same elements that fueled the ire and discontent of the Lost Cause. In 1886, newsman Henry Grady delivered his infamous "New South" speech in New York, assuring audience members that the South had "wiped out the line where the Mason Dixon's line used to be." The South of the future would be urbane, industrial, and prosperous.[33] At the heart of the New South's developing identity, then, was an optimistic story about the end of Reconstruction. Political redemption, for New South advocates, also signaled a broader social redemption. Now freed from the bonds of northern "intrusion," a rising industrialist class could rebuild the South as only southerners could.

William Chipley was a man of the New South, an embodiment of its origin myth. A Civil War veteran who witnessed the political tensions of Reconstruction firsthand, he became known as "Mr. Railroad of West Florida" in his postwar professional life. His trans-panhandle line enabled the mass transport of commerce and travelers in and out of West Florida. Alongside his railway, sawmills gave way to a new lumber and turpentine industry. Additionally, he brought a Chautauqua to the region. This institution, which was born in the North through the efforts of liberal Protestants, seemed profoundly out of place in the former Confederacy. For Chipley, though, the Chautauqua was yet another way to lure wealthy travelers southward on his railroads.[34]

Chipley would go on to find a career in politics all the while becoming even more legendary in West Florida. Along the way, his life and afterlife connected to an origin story of southern progressivism. Monuments were one way that white southerners chose to venerate his memory. But commentators were keen on applying lofty language to railroads, buildings, and other markers of industrial development. Railroads did not just move people and goods. And bricks did not just build new structures. These were the raw materials of a new civilization, of a society that would be prosperous, stable, and free.[35]

Of course, the civil religious discourses of white southerners—Lost Causers and progressives alike—existed in tension with many other rising social ideologies. For example, the newly freed Black population had a profoundly different experience of war and Reconstruction. For this population, an origin story emerged that looked with hope and longing at the promise of Emancipation. Conversely, the end of Reconstruction spelled only doom and disaster. In 1877, two Black politicians were murdered in central Florida while they were traveling to an assembly of Black Republicans in Tallahassee.[36] In response, Rev. W. G. Stewart of Tallahassee's AME Church sent a letter to a local newspaper denouncing the murders and calling the victims "martyrs." Political redemption and the end of Reconstruction, the minister announced, had "ruined" the hopes of Blacks in the region that they might ever enjoy "future prosperity." The newspaper's editor published his own response, ridiculing Stewart's "religio-political blast." Admitting that the murders were "horrible [crimes]," the editor added, "it is not just to attribute that murder to a Democratic victory or to cite it as proof that the rights of the negro are less secure than formerly."[37]

Fueling Steward's rhetoric was an origin story that interpreted emancipation and Reconstruction as delivering a promise of equality and freedom to freed Blacks. The end of northern oversight in the region, however, promised only danger and disorder. Conversely, white southerners upheld an alternative usable past, one that looked dimly on the events of Reconstruction. They recalled it as a time of chaos that ended only when southern whites returned to power. In the Jim Crow South, this myth funneled into a sense that any threat to the racial status quo was also a threat to social order.[38] As Donald Mathews has shown, lynching was one way that white southerners asserted and sanctified their need for racial supremacy—this violent spectacle, in other words, was a civil religious ritual.[39]

An emphasis on the South after the Civil War sheds light on the ways that race has fueled competing origin stories. Ethnicity is another category around which differences form, as evidenced by the midwestern account of the Kensington Runestone. In 1898 near Kensington, Minnesota, a Swedish American farmer unearthed a rock with strange writing scrawled on it. A translation of the stone revealed the account of Nordic explorers—Vikings—who had suffered a bloody Indian attack in 1362. In 1908, the stone was procured by Hjalmar Holand, a Norwegian immigrant who had been commissioned to tell the story of Norwegians in the Midwest. He used the stone as a prologue to his collection of stories, all of which told of Norwegians making great sacrifices to settle the frontier. In addition to relaying an unconventional history of America's founding, then, the stone also fed into a foundational account of Christian warriors dying for a larger cause. This myth of origin came with inflections of Norwegian history and culture.[40]

In the coming decades, Holand made it his life's work to advance this midwestern mythology. Norwegians, he stressed, were the "true Americans" who had made their claim to the land long before Columbus. Pageants, parades, images, and even a monument helped to make this narrative more and more concrete. Some Catholics also found meaning in the stone. In 1909, Archbishop John Ireland of Saint Paul attended a meeting of the Minnesota Historical Society where the stone was the centerpiece of conversation. Drawing his attention was the segment of the inscription that read "AVM save [us] from evil." The archbishop saw this as a reference to Ave Virgo Maria. Thus, he and others reasoned that the first prayer to the Blessed Mother would have emerged from Minnesota.[41] In an era when anti-Catholicism was on the rise, symbolic moves toward reconciling Rome and America did the work of battling nativist bigotry.

By the Cold War era, divisions within Christianity faded and in their place stood the idea of a "Christian America." With "In God We Trust" appearing on the coinage and "under God" inserted into the pledge, the national government launched into a rhetorical crusade against "godless communism." All of this localized in western Minnesota around the stone, as Indians in the story became a proxy for the Soviets, while the Vikings assumed the role of Christian defenders of truth and goodness. At the same time, though, the veracity of the stone had been called into considerable question. Experts gathered sufficient evidence to prove that the stone was a hoax. In response, runestone enthusiasts fought back, tethering together the stone and Cold War Christian nationalism. To question the authenticity of the Kensington Runestone, in other words, was to question the authenticity of Christian America.[42]

The story of the runestone shows how one object's myth of origin and meaning change over time, adapting to the present needs of the people who create and sustain them. Of course, any one region can also have numerous myths at work. In the Northeast, for example, John Winthrop's name evokes an Anglo-Protestant myth of origin that was a favorite of the likes of Ronald Reagan. This thoroughly male story has a curious counterpoint in the figure of Anne Hutchinson, the woman whom Winthrop called "the American Jezebel." Bellah also commented negatively on Hutchinson, casting her as an emblem of the supposedly deleterious effects of "religious individualism." But feminists and proponents of religious liberty have come to view the myth of Anne Hutchinson differently, depicting her as a noteworthy "founding mother." In 1923, a statue to Hutchinson was erected in Boston, with an inscription heralding her as a "courageous exponent of civil liberty and religious toleration."[43] The designation of "founder" is also influenced by region. In California, a monument to Junípero Serra tells of yet another "founding father." The myth of origin connected to him is one of missions, Spanish Catholicism, and colonial power. Its meaning and purpose continue to adapt in the present, as the missionary's ultimate legacy became a source of debate when Pope Francis named Serra a saint.[44]

From place to place and over time, the civil religious myths of America have taken on multiple forms. The task of the scholar of civil religion is not simply to write all of these stories into one narrative. It is instead to honor their distinctions and rest with the uneasy reality that America and its regions mean many things to many people.

Beyond Bellah

Because of its decentered framework and focus on understanding, a study of America's civil religions has limitless possibilities. For example, scholars might begin challenging the ways in which "American civil religion" has been inextricably linked to "Judeo-Christian" resources.[45] To be sure, civil religious discourse in America—all over America—often has an unmistakable Christian tilt. But this is not a necessary condition for scholars to consider a word, act, or deed in a civil religious context. Making this point clear is Anne Blankenship's examination of the civil religious dissent of Japanese Americans who were incarcerated during World War II. Distraught and displaced, the incarcerees—the majority of whom were of Buddhist persuasions—developed a unique civil religious discourse of resistance through participating in ordinary "American" celebrations such as Christmas. Homemade cards, decorations, and images of Uncle Sam and Santa Claus created scenes of Christmas contentment. But each of these items carried a hidden transcript, as a simple card might juxtapose a bucolic image of snow and reindeers with a sketch of the camp's grim dwelling places. With gloom and celebration in close proximity, the creators of these objects, Blankenship summarizes, "used civil religious traditions for their own ends, simultaneously demonstrating their patriotism and dissent."[46]

A study like this is a healthy reminder that the idea of civil religion is not just a "Judeo-Christian" construct. Also, the resources that go toward making political identities sacred are not always "religious" in a conventional way. Arguably, even an atheist can advance a civil religious agenda. In 1865, Charles Chilton Moore, the grandson of revivalist and reformer Barton W. Stone, left his Kentucky pulpit and announced that he was an atheist. In Lexington, he became a noted newsman and "infidel editor" who published the notorious *Blue Grass Blade*, where he criticized and mocked organized religion in ways that often upset the status quo. When federal authorities tried to censor Moore, he blasted, "No citizen, no institution, no paper or periodical, in America can be, or ought to be, discriminated against because of its anti-religious or anti-Christian utterances, as the Constitutional guarantee of religious liberty includes the right to express a non-belief in god as it does to express a belief in god." For Moore, America was exceptional precisely because it allowed the freethinker to think freely. Moore's journalistic career was an exercise in resisting Protestant civil religious discourses. In doing so, he generated his own set of social values, where unbelief was tolerated and censorship was not. Freethinking failed to gain a wide audience in the South, but Moore forced his voice into the region's complex civil religious fabric.[47]

Civil religion can be a useful analytical tool—if scholars allow it to be. If, however, this category remains a playground for scholarly conjecture about American "consensus," the critics will have sufficient ground to continue denouncing its merit. For the idea of civil religion to truly have a new phase, scholars must finally move "beyond Bellah." Fields like American religious history have long stopped citing Sydney Ahlstrom and others from this generation in their studies, and for good reason. Scholars of civil religion must do the same. Their questions were the product of their generation. While the field owes them a debt, today's scholars must also continue pursuing new questions.[48]

As a final thought, the argument presented in this essay is not offered as an exercise in ivory tower detachment. Neither is it cynical. Instead, I contend that acknowledging difference and diversity is both honest and humane. As a parallel, consider Stephen Prothero's book, *God Is Not One*. In it, he takes aim at the notion popularized by the likes of Huston Smith and Karen Armstrong that all of the world's religions amount to different paths up the same mountain. A closer look at these traditions, however, shows that the questions and answers that these faiths deal with are profoundly different. "We pretend these differences are trivial because it makes us feel safer, or more moral," posits Prothero. But the world remains dangerous and unstable. So if "tolerance" and "respect" are truly virtues, Prothero suggests that we make sense of these differences rather than piling everyone into the same bucket.[49]

In a similar way, I advance an understanding of civil religion that opens the door to many, listening closely to those who have been heard and those who have to shout for mere recognition. Individuals and groups have always lingered in the margins, cast aside and treated as insignificant. It is not my job to give these groups any more status than they had. But it is also not my job to continue to marginalize them in my treatments of America's civil religions. Instead, I can recover their histories. I can catalog their cultural resources. And I can situate their civil religious discourses within broader conversations, as an exchange between the influential and the insignificant, the heroic and the loathsome, and the insider and the outsider. This is the way that the category of civil religion can be both rigorous and affirming, including all of the familiar faces alongside those who have been left out, ignored, or dismissed.

NOTES

1 Ira Chernus, "We Need to Stop Using the Phrase 'American Civil Religion,'" *History News Network*, June 18, 2012, http://historynewsnetwork.org; Robert N. Bellah, "Civil Religion in America," *Daedalus* 96 (Winter 1967): 1–21; Robert N. Bellah, *The Broken Covenant: American Civil Religion in Time of Trial* (1975; Chicago: University of Chicago Press, 1992), 2.

2 Chernus, "We Need to Stop." See also Ira Chernus, "Civil Religion," in *The Blackwell Companion to Religion in America*, ed. Philip Goff (Malden, MA: Wiley-Blackwell, 2010).

3 Charles H. Long, "A New Look at American Religion," in *The Writing of American Religious History*, ed. Martin E. Marty (New York: K. G. Saur, 1992), 87. Reprinted from *Anglican Theological Review* 55 (1973): 117–25.

4 Russell T. McCutcheon, *The Discipline of Religion: Structure, Meaning, Rhetoric* (New York: Routledge, 2003), 280. For a comprehensive overview of the critics, see Marcella Cristi, *From Civil Religion to Political Religion: The Intersection of*

Culture, Religion and Politics (Waterloo, ON, Canada: Wilfrid Laurier University Press, 2001).

5   I take my lead here from Bruce Lincoln, "Theses on Method," in *The Insider/Outsider Problem in the Study of Religion*, ed. Russell T. McCutcheon (New York: Cassell, 1999). "The same destabilizing and irreverent questions one might ask of any speech act ought be posed of religious discourse. The first of these is 'Who speaks here?,' i.e., what person, group, or institution is responsible for a text, whatever its putative or apparent author. Beyond that, 'To what audience? In what immediate and broader context? Through what system of mediations? With what interests?' And further, 'Of what would the speaker(s) persuade the audience? What are the consequences if this project of persuasion should happen to succeed? Who wins what, and how much? Who, conversely, loses?'" (396).

6   Yoni Appelbaum, "America's First Post-Christian Debate," *Atlantic*, September 27, 2016, www.theatlantic.com.

7   "Trump Says He's 'Made a lot of Sacrifices,'" *CNBC*, July 30, 2016, www.cnbc.com.

8   Peter Manseau, "Is Trumpism Its Own Religion?," *Los Angeles Times*, June 21, 2016, www.latimes.com.

9   Andrew M. Manis, *Southern Civil Religions in Conflict: Black and White Baptists and Civil Rights, 1947–1957* (1987; Athens: University of Georgia Press, 2002).

10 See Peter Gardella, *American Civil Religion: What Americans Hold Sacred* (New York: Oxford University Press, 2014), 306–7.

11 George M. Marsden, *Religion and American Culture*, 2nd ed. (New York: Harcourt, 2001), 53.

12 See also James A. Christenson and Ronald C. Wimberly, "Who Is Civil Religious?," *Sociological Analysis* 39 (1978).

13 Harvey G. Allebach, "Charity of To-Day," *The Mennonite*, November 1889. See also Theron F. Schlabach, *Peace, Faith, Nation: Mennonites and Amish in Nineteenth-Century America* (Eugene, OR: Wipf & Stock, 2007), 164.

14 Raymond Haberski Jr., *God and War: American Civil Religion since 1945* (New Brunswick, NJ: Rutgers University Press, 2012).

15 See Kathryn Lofton, "Understanding Is Dangerous," *The Point*, November 2016, https://thepointmag.com.

16 Robert A. Orsi, *Between Heaven and Earth: The Religious Worlds People Make and the Scholars Who Study Them* (Princeton, NJ: Princeton University Press, 2005), 188, 191–92.

17 Michel Foucault, *The History of Sexuality: An Introduction*, trans. Robert Hurley (1978; New York: Penguin, 1990), 92.

18 Mark Silk, "Numa Pompilius and the Idea of Civil Religion in the West," *Journal of the American Academy of Religion* 72, no. 4 (December 2004): 890.

19 Jean Jacques Rousseau, *The Social Contract* (1762), www.constitution.org. For commentary on Rousseau and civil religion, see Cristi, *From Civil Religion to Political Religion*, 17–30.

20 N. J. Demerath III and Rhys H. Williams, "Civil Religion in an Uncivil Society," *Annals of the American Academy* 480 (July 1985): 154, 156, 166, 165. See also Cristi, *From Civil Religion to Political Religion*; Michael W. Hughey, *Civil Religion and Moral Order: Theoretical and Historical Dimensions* (Westport, CT: Greenwood, 1983).
21 Rita Kirk Whillock, "Dream Believers: The Unifying Visions and Competing Values of Adherents to American Civil Religion," *Presidential Studies Quarterly* 24, no. 2 (1994): 375.
22 John E. Semonche, *Keeping the Faith: A Cultural History of the U.S. Supreme Court* (Lanham, MD: Rowman & Littlefield, 1998); Jeffrey F. Meyer, *Myths in Stone: Religious Dimensions of Washington D.C.* (Berkeley: University of California Press, 2001); Craig R. Smith, *Daniel Webster and the Oratory of Civil Religion* (Columbia: University of Missouri Press, 2004).
23 Gardella, *American Civil Religion*. See also Alexander T. Riley, *Angel Patriots: The Crash of Flight 93 and the Myth of America* (New York: New York University Press, 2015), 8–11; Luis D. Leon, *The Political Spirituality of Cesar Chavez* (Berkeley: University of California Press, 2015), 22; John D. Wilsey, *American Exceptionalism and Civil Religion: Reassessing the History of an Idea* (Downers Grove, IL: IVP Academic, 2015), 20–22.
24 Randi Jones Walker, "Liberators for Colonial Anáhauc: A Rumination on North American Civil Religions," *Religion & American Culture* 9, no. 2 (July 1999): 193.
25 Walker, "Liberators for Colonial Anáhauc," 192–93.
26 Walker, "Liberators for Colonial Anáhauc," 184.
27 Mark Silk and Andrew Walsh, *One Nation, Divisible: How Regional Religious Differences Shape American Politics* (Lanham, MD: Rowman & Littlefield, 2008).
28 Bellah, *Broken Covenant*, 3.
29 Plato, *The Republic*, trans. Francis Cornford (New York: Oxford University Press, 1945), 106, 107.
30 Bruce Lincoln, *Discourse and the Construction of Society: Comparative Studies of Myth, Ritual, and Classification* (New York: Oxford University Press, 1989), 20, 21.
31 Charles Reagan Wilson, *Baptized in Blood: The Religion of the Lost Cause, 1865–1920* (Athens: University of Georgia Press, 1980).
32 Quoted in Lillian D. Champion, *Giant Tracking: William Dudley Chipley and Other Giants of Men* (Columbus, GA: Quill, 1985), 1–2.
33 Henry Grady, "The New South," in *The New South: Writings and Speeches of Henry Grady*, ed. Mills Lane (1886; Savannah, GA: Beehive Press, 1971), 13.
34 Arthur Remillard, *Southern Civil Religions: Imagining the Good Society in the Post-Reconstruction Era* (Athens: University of Georgia Press, 2011), 33–37.
35 Remillard, *Southern Civil Religions*, 31–42.
36 Edward C. Williamson, *Florida Politics in the Gilded Age, 1877–1893* (Gainesville: University Press of Florida, 1976), 36–37.
37 "The Tallahassee District," *Weekly Floridian*, November 20, 1877.
38 Remillard, *Southern Civil Religions*, 45–77.

39 Donald G. Mathews, "Lynching Is Part of the Religion of Our People: Faith in the Christian South," in *Religion in the American South: Protestants and Others in History and Culture*, ed. Beth Barton Schweiger and Donald G. Mathews (Chapel Hill: University of North Carolina Press, 2004). See also Remillard, *Southern Civil Religions*, 45–77, 106–62.

40 David Krueger, *Myths of the Runestone: Viking Martyrs and the Birthplace of America* (Minneapolis: University of Minnesota Press, 2015), 15–40.

41 Krueger, *Myths of the Runestone*, 96.

42 Krueger, *Myths of the Runestone*, 130–31.

43 Robert N. Bellah, Richard Madsen, William M. Sullivan, Ann Swidler, and Steven M. Tipton, *Habits of the Heart: Individualism and Commitment in American Life* (Berkeley: University of California Press, 1985), 233; Eve LePlante, *American Jezebel: The Uncommon Life of Anne Hutchinson, the Woman Who Defied the Puritans* (New York: HarperCollins, 2010).

44 Steven W. Hackel, *Junipero Serra: California's Founding Father* (New York: Farrar, Straus and Giroux, 2013).

45 See Robert Wuthnow, *The Restructuring of American Religion* (Princeton, NJ: Princeton University Press, 1988). This bundling is forthrightly asserted as Wuthnow writes, "Civil religion consists of Judeo-Christian symbols and values that relate the nation to a divine order of things, thus giving it a sense of origin and direction. The utilitarian ideology, emanating from Enlightenment political philosophy, provides the nation with a sense of proper governmental procedure, as well as fundamental guiding values such as life, liberty, and the pursuit of happiness" (244).

46 Anne M. Blankenship, "Civil Religious Dissent: Patriotism and Resistance in a Japanese American Incarceration Camp," *Material Religion* 10, no. 3 (2014): 288.

47 Charles C. Moore, "Religious Liberty Threatened," *Blue Grass Blade*, May 31, 1908. See also John Sparks, *Kentucky's Most Hated Man: Charles Chilton Moore and the Blue Grass Blade* (Nicholasville, KY: Wind, 2009).

48 Catherine L. Albanese, "American Religious History: A Bibliographical Essay," in *Currents in American Scholarship Series* (Washington, DC: U.S. Department of State, 2003).

49 Stephen Prothero, *God Is Not One: The Eight Rival Religions That Run the World—and Why Their Differences Matter* (New York: HarperCollins, 2010), 15.

5

Seeing Bellah's Civil Religion through a Black Feminist Lens

KORIE LITTLE EDWARDS

There is a problem with framing America's dominant and institutionalized cultural beliefs, practices, values, and experiences as "American civil religion." To explore dimensions of this problem, I draw upon Black feminist theory and critical whiteness theory to provide a different and relevant framework for understanding how we ought to view Bellah's American civil religion.[1] The Black feminist perspective proposes that social locations in the world, especially those most responsible for structuring everyday lives and life courses, critically inform and constrain scholarship and how it makes sense of social phenomena. Thus, when we conduct our scholarship or examine others' scholarship, we need to recognize that our intersecting social locations, or our standpoints, matter. The critical whiteness theoretical perspective is similar to the Black feminist perspective in that it problematizes dominant structures and the ideologies that support them. Importantly, critical whiteness theory focuses specifically on how society is organized around the unspoken normativity of whiteness. The dominant social position of whites and the norms, ideologies, and values that reinforce this social position are taken for granted. Bellah's work on civil religion suggests that he too presumed the normativity of whiteness, a presumption surely rooted in his own standpoint.

It is worth noting that Bellah modified his view and definition of American civil religion since the publication of his 1967 piece. This is particularly clear in his book *The Broken Covenant: American Civil Religion in Time of Trial*. Bellah expanded on the idea proposed in his first essay that throughout America's history there have been tests to its civil religion.[2] A perpetual test facing white Americans, from the early waves of European conquest and settlement through to the civil rights movement era, is how they would engage the people already here, the American Indians, and those who were or descended from West Africans who were kidnapped, transported across the Atlantic, and enslaved on what came to be known as American soil.

Nevertheless, Bellah's refinements of his concept never really got any intellectual traction in the academic circles adopting his idea.[3] The original ideas outlined by Bellah remain at the center of the American civil religion debate (see chapter 4 by Remillard in this volume). This is true whether the responders were supporters or critics, as both affirmation and engaged criticism resulted in a similar reproduction of ideas. By the time *Habits of the Heart* was published in 1985, Bellah perhaps recognized that the academy was not so much interested in the need for diversity, openness, inclusion, and making amends as he trumpeted throughout *The Broken Covenant*.[4] *Habits*, by design, was a study of white, middle-class Americans, authored by the same, and presented as a portrait of "American" culture. Like those of his *Daedalus* essay, the ideas of the later book were rather easily and widely embraced, or at least legitimated with ardent critical engagement. In that regard, different standpoints and theoretical approaches have as much to do with the broader scholarly community's understanding of civil religion as it does with Bellah's formulations. The near immediate engagement and reproduction of his original ideas on American civil religion reveals the academy's investment in certain frames and perspectives, and its discounting of others.

The promise of Bellah's civil religion, a system of beliefs and behaviors that unifies Americans around a common identity and purpose and yet continues to urge the nation to be better than it is, is attractive. While I question the conceptualization of a civil religion based upon the ideas and articulations of privileged, powerful leaders, I am very sympathetic to the impulse of scholars of civil religion (several of whom are in this volume, although I do not consider myself one) who hope that a Bellah-esque "religion" is possible. Admittedly, in my own work on multiracial and multiethnic religious communities there is a similar current of hope. In this chapter I examine if and how diverse religious communities can be forged and sustained. Toward the end of the chapter, I draw upon lessons learned from my work to inform how we might think about developing a system of beliefs and behaviors that integrates and elevates humans. However, carefully interrogating the implications of Bellah's conceptualization of American civil religion reveals what we gain and lose from such a perspective of our social world.

Bellah's American Civil Religion

In his *Daedalus* essay, Bellah reviews the public language of select key American figures beginning with those from the American Revolution and up to President Lyndon B. Johnson. His analysis focuses on American presidents, although he includes the public language (via a biography) of Benjamin Franklin. The reason for this, he claims, is because "the president's obligation extends to the higher criterion."[5] Presidents are often charged with speaking for and to the body politic and are regularly thought to represent the best of the nation's ideals (and hence such contention surrounding public language used by Donald Trump and the dismay of many Americans when Barack Obama, a Black man, was in the presidency).

How does a religion exist without a deity of some sort? Core to the idea of the American civil religion is its God. Bellah notices, emerging first with the "Founding Fathers," a pattern. They consistently referenced God or some form of a deity in their public speech. According to Bellah, the God of American civil religion is not specifically Christian but "unitarian," less interested in "salvation and love" than in the right order of things, and judging and holding society accountable. But then perhaps most importantly, the God of American civil religion is "actively interested and involved in history, with a special concern for America."[6] America epitomizes God's idea of an exemplary social order, one that is to be used as the standard against which other nations should measure their own societies. Emerging from these foundational beliefs about God is a "collection of beliefs, symbols, and rituals with respect to sacred things and institutionalized in a collectivity," that is, a civil religion.[7] Ultimately, the American civil religion is "concerned that America be a society as perfectly in accord with the will of God as men can make it, and a light to all the nations."[8] The "motivating spirit" of American civil religion is an "obligation . . . to carry out God's will on earth."[9]

Bellah admits that America's faith in its civil religion has been greatly "tested." These tests plague Bellah, so much so that he spends considerable time in the essay assessing America's success in facing those tests.

There is the Revolutionary War, of course. The country passed this test, which was one of independence, although, Bellah argues, this had less to do with America's strength and resolve and more to do with Britain's military distractions and allied support, in the form of French ships and Dutch funders. Less than a century after the Revolutionary War, America faced its first real test—the Civil War. Now, Bellah explains, "The Civil War raised the deepest questions of national meaning. The man who not only formulated but in his own person embodied its meaning for Americans was Abraham Lincoln. For him the issue was not in the first instance slavery but 'whether that nation, or any nation so conceived, and so dedicated, can long endure.'" Nevertheless, "the issue of slavery as the deeper cause of the conflict had to be faced" and was addressed by Lincoln in his second Inaugural Address.[10] It represented a reoccurring challenge for America, ensuring the "full institutionalization of democracy."[11]

The final trial Bellah highlights in his *Daedalus* piece is the U.S. response to "a revolutionary world" where other societies and groups aim to "attain many of the things, material and spiritual, that we have already attained."[12] Will the country hold true to its civil religious ideals or succumb to tyrannical impulses? The United States would do well, Bellah seems to argue, to remember the biblical edict "to whom much is given, much is required."

Bellah's *The Broken Covenant* offers an honest interrogation of his American civil religion concept. Throughout this volume he seems to be asking whether America is up to the task of fulfilling the expectations of its deity.

Bellah's American Civil Religion Expanded

The Broken Covenant expands on the trials Bellah introduced in his 1967 article. This volume from the beginning assumes a different tone in that it is not hopeful in the promise of America. It laments the social problems plaguing the United States of the late twentieth century, a country that has perhaps been given too much. Throughout the volume, Bellah is concerned with America's capacity to become a tyrannical government. He argues that the erosion of the country's moral and religious substructure made it susceptible to such an outcome.

Several trials are highlighted in *The Broken Covenant*, but I focus on what Bellah views as the most persistent problem facing America: racial and ethnic exclusion and oppression. As he explains, "The problem of exclusion and inclusion has been especially acute with respect to racial groups."[13] He had, in fact, already acknowledged this in 1967, stating, "The civil religion has exercised long-term pressure for the humane solution of our greatest domestic problem, the treatment of the Negro American."[14] It seems this pressure never succeeded in freeing people of color.

Bellah drew a good deal upon the assimilation and pluralism theory of Milton Gordon to organize his thoughts on this matter. He agreed, to a large extent, that despite the common assertion that America was open to all, Anglo-Saxons were understood to be the ideal European group by which to establish the standard for the American republic. Other European immigrants had to find their way within this dominant cultural and structural framework. Nevertheless, over time, most European immigrants were afforded a path toward integration and upward mobility. They came to assimilate and integrate into American society.

The path was continually blocked, though, for American Indians and Black Americans. Bellah was keenly aware of this. He argued that from the country's inception, a "double crime" took place. American Indians had, in his words, experienced "expropriation and extermination," and Blacks experienced "forcible transportation" and "enslavement."[15] In this, America never lived up to its identity as a place that is welcoming and open to all, offering anybody a chance to make one's way. In practice, of course, "anybody" meant those of Northern and Western European descent.

Perhaps learning a bit from reactions to his *Daedalus* piece, in *Broken Covenant* Bellah incorporated, albeit in limited doses, the ideas and experiences of Black American intellectuals including Malcom X, W. E. B. Du Bois, and Harold Cruse. In the cases of Malcolm X and Du Bois, he mainly points to their stories as evidence of American exclusion, although he later referenced Du Bois's thoughts on how Black and white Americans might reconcile to the extent that they recognize their complementary culture. Bellah proclaims Cruse, a Black studies scholar, to be the "most thoughtful of contemporary Black intellectuals," citing Cruse's views on the fiction of American pluralism.[16] One implication of this statement is that for Bellah there really were few Black, as well as Indian and Chicano, modern intellectuals.[17]

In the end, though, *The Broken Covenant* is about reasserting the relevance of American civil religion. The era in which the book was written was one of incredible social and political disillusionment. Bellah writes, "Today the American civil religion is an empty and broken shell" and "has been betrayed by its most responsible servants."[18] We see, then, that the oppression and exclusion of Blacks and American Indians was a grievous disregard of America's civil religion. The abduction, sale, genocide, segregation, and institutionalized discrimination and racism experienced by Blacks and American Indians were unfortunate outcomes of white people not living up to their own civil religious ideals. But Bellah repeatedly claims that the experiences of groups of color in America are unfortunate exceptions to this broader story. Their oppression is of a "special" nature. The solution to the brokenness of American civil religion and the country's eroded moral and religious substructure is to "reaffirm the outward or external covenant and that includes the civil religion in its most classical form."[19] Put another way, people of color and their experiences are not central to the story of American civil religion; their inclusion is to be valued, but their exclusion does not damn the entire enterprise.

Consequently, *The Broken Covenant*, although well intended, does not take seriously the ideas and experiences of American Indians and Black groups and individuals. These experiences and ideas do not stand on their own, nor are they respected as a valid and theoretically necessary contradistinction to the ideas and experiences of whites in America. So, despite his earnest lamenting about the failure of America to fully incorporate Blacks and American Indians, Bellah didn't question the reality of an American civil religion or reconceptualize what he observed as such. If anything, he doubled down even more on the efficacy and appropriateness of his idea of American civil religion. For Bellah, the problem was not with the construct but that America has failed to live up to the ideals of its own civil religion, repeatedly so.

Moreover, Bellah frames the experiences of people of color and women as trials, in other words, as problems or barriers that American civil religion must overcome. In some strange way, this framing implicitly objectifies people of color and women. The objectification might seem subtle at first read, but the implications can be read as treating people of color and women, and the subordination and oppression that they have experienced and continue to experience throughout American history, as primarily an opportunity to refine and actualize Bellah's American civil religion—which remains a set of beliefs, values, and rituals developed and perpetuated by elite white men. People of color and women serve to move America toward its civil religious ideals but remain on the margins of the national story.

But to treat race and gender in this manner is a grave error. Race and gender are structures that organize every segment of social life in America. They are indeed constitutive of and implicated in all its institutions, including politics and religion. And while perhaps it ought to be obvious, it is worth noting that race and gender organize the lives of white men just as much as they do Black women or Black men or white women. To frame the ideas, values, practices, and experiences of one racialized and gendered group as reflective of and relevant to all, when groups' experiences are so obviously and fundamentally different, represents a blindness not only intellectual but moral. Suffice to say, Bellah does not intellectually engage with the high probability that groups of color and women have their own rituals, practices, values, and beliefs, ones born out of their experiences as subordinates in a racist and patriarchal society. This is also a moral blindness because no group's human experience ought to be understood to exist for the sole benefit of improving that of another group. Does Bellah say this explicitly? Again, no. However, it is one reading of his original piece, and despite his intent to address the perpetual oppression and exclusion of people of color, neither he nor the academy can seem to let go of his position that American civil religion itself, as he constructs it, is not what needs to be changed.

The Underbelly of Bellah's American Civil Religion

It is difficult to read Bellah's conceptualization of American civil religion and not see it as another frame deployed to extol the values, ideologies, and virtues of America of and for privileged white men. And from the perspective of someone who belongs to groups (people of color and women) that did not participate in the formation and then perpetuation of Bellah's American civil religion but rather suffered from it, American civil religion is but a more contemporary and palatable mid-twentieth-century repackaging of manifest destiny. That is, Bellah's conceptualization of civil religion affirms the initiation and persistence of a social structure where certain groups are subordinated and others, namely elite white males, are elevated, for the sake of reaching and securing that pinnacle of societal evolution—America. I understand this is a strong statement. And I am not suggesting that Bellah aimed to do this. Indeed, he stated specifically that civil religion was not to be understood as sacralizing the status quo,[20] and recognized the potential of civil religion for doing harm, conceding that "civil religion has not always been invoked in favor of worthy causes."[21] And yet, it is a common interpretation of the civil religion idea. There is no shortage of examples of how American religion and ideologies have been used toward such ends.

Manifest destiny, for example, purported that America's spread across the North American continent was rooted in the presumed superiority of the nation and the divine purpose of the nation. That the nation was white America was assumed. It was a long-standing explanation for racial stratification in America and the social structures that perpetuated it. In the United States, this perspective, at least in part, originated with a view that the subordinated racial group and its members in some way deserved to be oppressed because they were not Christian. Of course, this ideology soon enough subsumed a belief that people of color were not just spiritually inferior but biologically inferior to whites or incapable of certain capacities as well. Thus, they could not be trusted with the bounty that is America. American slavery and other systematic acts of racial oppression, such as the genocide of American Indian tribes, were perpetrated based on a belief that people who were not white were morally and intellectually inferior to those who were white, that it was God's will that whites buy, sell, and exploit the minds, souls, and bodies of people of color for profit. People of color were excluded from freedom, citizenship, and rights because of their supposed innate moral and intellectual inferiority.

After the Civil War, these religiously informed beliefs about the biological and cultural inferiority of people of color were supplanted by a belief in eugenics—a theory that claimed certain groups occupied higher statuses in society because of their genetic superiority. This movement gained steam in the United States at the turn of the twentieth century and continued to fuel the belief that certain behaviors were biologically determined. People supposedly possessed certain group-specific genes that significantly increased or decreased their capacities, capabilities, and chances in life.

It is perhaps no coincidence that the increased popularity of eugenics paralleled immigration reforms in the United States that barred entire people groups from entrance into the country, beginning with the Chinese Exclusion Act of 1882. This law prohibited the entrance of Chinese immigrants to the United States. It was the only law up to that point that specifically targeted and blocked immigration of a particular racial or ethnic group. But thirty-five years later, Congress and President Woodrow Wilson expanded this law to exclude the immigration of anyone from the continent of Asia with the Asiatic Barred Zone Act of 1917. Then, in 1924, the Johnson–Reed Act drastically reduced the immigration of people from Southern and Eastern Europe, while also retaining a complete ban on people from Asia. Support for eugenics precipitously declined during the mid-twentieth century as global political pressure mounted against Nazi Germany, which used this pseudo-scientific ideology to encamp and kill people of Jewish descent and others thought to be racially inferior.

Back in the United States, while racist immigration laws determined who could and could not enter the country, racial segregation, commonly known as Jim Crow, was institutionalized in states across the South (and often elsewhere too). The civil rights movement of the late 1950s and 1960s seemingly woke the United States up to its ideological and institutional contradictions. The federal government responded, overturning and passing laws to eliminate barriers to full civic inclusion. This included outlawing Jim Crow laws. It also included repealing the immigration laws of the first part of the twentieth century and replacing them with more open ones.

This is admittedly a sweeping overview of how American religious, civic, and political ideologies subverted the values and virtues of Bellah's American civil religion and how they have been advanced only through extraordinary effort. Similar historical reviews could be done for gender and other social minorities. America in the 1960s aimed to make amends in some way for its crimes, in Bellah's words. Nevertheless, despite landmark legislation of that decade, racial, gendered, and other forms of institutionalized social subordination have continued to today and remain central organizing structures of the American social landscape. Considering racial stratification, in particular, one has to look only at the rate of mass incarceration of Blacks and Latinx people as evidence of persistent and pernicious racial inequality. And still whites in America remain the most advantaged on a vast majority of social, cultural, and economic indicators.

Bellah, a religious man himself, wanted America to be a better country. He wanted America to repent of its sins and adhere to its own ideals. I can almost hear Bellah imploring America and its leaders to do so. So I find myself empathizing with him and his longing for his country to do and be better. And yet it remains that his view is limited. He can see and understand only that which is accessible to him. It is no fault of Bellah's that his view is limited. This is altogether human, as we are finite beings. However, that he does not own his limitations and that the academy does not expect him to account for his limitations, and thus the limitations of his broad claims, does fall on him and us. A proper corrective and framing to this failure can be found in Black feminist thought and critical whiteness theory.

Take Another Look: The Lenses of Black Feminist Thought and Critical Whiteness Theory

Black feminist thought and critical whiteness theory are both critical social theories. Patricia Hill Collins's Black feminist thought is a response to the ways in which those who control the institutional power centers have used their power to oppress others.[22] Modes of oppression have no limits. But Collins addresses how violence, exclusion, racism and sexism, and production of knowledge and images support and reproduce white male hegemonic structures. She focuses on Black women of course, but the theoretical frame is general and can apply to any group in the hierarchical system.

Central to Black feminist thought is the idea of standpoint. A qualitative methodological epistemology would say that we account for ourselves as instruments. This approaches what is meant by our "standpoint." By knowing, owning, accounting for, and deploying our standpoints in our scholarship, we are more than calibrating ourselves as research instruments. We are performing a humble recognition that we cannot fully understand any social phenomenon we study. Our standpoints are strengths, uniquely equipping us to understand the social world in ways that people situated in other social locations cannot. But at the same time, they limit our view of the social world. We are capable of seeing only that which is within our field of vision.

Race, gender, and class together situate people in particular social locations, standpoints, that allow them to see and understand the world in particular and distinct ways. They also provide groups' greater or lesser proximity to institutional power centers. Western society gives white educated men, particularly those who are heterosexual, the most power. The more different groups are from these intersecting statuses, the less power they have.

When explicating a Black feminist epistemology, Collins focuses her attention on power centers that control the production of knowledge. She writes, "Because elite White men control Western structures of knowledge validation, their interests pervade the themes, paradigms, and epistemologies of traditional scholarship."[23] Collins delineates the different components of the knowledge production process. However, she is particularly interested in how epistemology can be inherently biased and contribute to oppression. "Epistemology," she writes, "constitutes an overarching theory of knowledge. It investigates . . . why we believe what we believe to be true. Far from being the apolitical study of truth, epistemology points to the ways in which power relations shape who is believed and why."[24] And "the level of epistemology is important because it determines which questions merit investigation, which interpretative frameworks will be used to analyze findings, and to what use any ensuing knowledge." She further asserts, "Although designed to represent and protect the interests of powerful White men, neither . . . social institutions nor the actual epistemologies that they promote need be managed by White men themselves. [Others] may be enlisted to enforce these connections between power relations and what counts for truth."[25] Consequently, Western epistemologies are a hegemonic enterprise, supported and affirmed by those people who are neither elite nor white nor men.

What does Black feminist thought have to do with Bellah's American civil religion? Maybe everything. Bellah's American civil religion is squarely situated in Western epistemology. He exclusively draws upon the ideas of elite white men to develop his concept in his original article. It is as if the only people on the continent with relevant views and perspectives about what organizes and guides what has come to be American society were people from this powerful group. Yet are we to believe that the ideas of the elite white women were not pertinent, or those of any white women for that matter? How about the millions of American Indians on the continent, whose land white people illegitimately claimed as their own? Or how about the views, ideas, and perspectives of Blacks, who composed over 15 percent of the U.S. population in 1800?

Admittedly, in *The Broken Covenant* Bellah notes the views and experiences of a few African Americans, including W. E. B. Du Bois and Malcom X. However, he is quite selective in how he draws upon these views and experiences, and these selections are used in service of his argument. Bellah is selective in two ways. One way is in whom he references. Not only does he draw upon the ideas and stories of African American *men*, but these men are all "intellectuals" in the dominant definition of that term. This is further illustrated in a brief statement in a discussion on Anglo-Saxon intellectuals. He writes, "A qualification has to be made, as usual, with Blacks and even more to groups like the Indians and Chicanos whose social situation has virtually prevented the emergence of intellectuals in the modern sense."[26] By accepting that definition, Bellah helps to reproduce the notion that subaltern groups did not have their own conceptions of the nation or their own sense of whom Americans were. Of course, Blacks, Indians, and Chicanos had an abundance of people who could insightfully deconstruct the social circumstances of America, its cultural practices, values, beliefs, and structures. Slave narratives would have been a wonderful place to start. Bellah simply possessed a Western epistemological view on whose ideas, stories, and frames count.

Critical whiteness theory (CWT) would say that Bellah's understanding of whose ideas, stories, and frames count is predictable. CWT is an extension of critical race theory (CRT). CRT scholarship originated among law professors, but scholars in other areas, sociology and education in particular, have also been important contributors to this body of work.[27] CRT emerged as a response to the work of scholars, such as William Julius Wilson, that came out in the late seventies that was interpreted to suggest that race was no longer or at least less central to the organization of people's lives, particularly people of color.[28] CRT asserts how race has structured and continues to structure the Western world. But the impact of race cannot be explained away by class indicators. CRT reasserts the centrality of institutional racism and discrimination to the American way of life and the systematic way in which the racial hierarchy continues to be reproduced and sustained, despite the elimination of explicitly racist and discriminatory laws and practices.

A good deal of scholarship, even with the emergence of CRT, still focuses on people of color, problematizing them (us) and their (our) experiences. Too often, it seems, racism and discrimination involve no oppressor. Consequently, there is an extensive body of work on racial inequality that avoids or ignores the reality of a racial hierarchy that is systemic and consequential for people's lives. CWT is a response to the overwhelming emphasis on people of color in the social stratification literature.[29]

CWT argues that whiteness is foundational to the American racialized structure.[30] Ian Haney-Lopez calls it the "lynchpin."[31] Consequently, we can never undo institutional racism and discrimination by spotlighting the challenges and persistent social problems experienced by people of color. Rather, if we are to deconstruct a racist society, we need to place in the spotlight the ideologies, values, behaviors, and experiences of whites and how these sustain and reproduce a society that privileges them.

"Whiteness consists of three constitutive, interdependent dimensions that work together to create and sustain white hegemony":[32] white structural advantage, white normativity, and white transparency.[33] White structural advantage simply means that society is organized to give whites a systematic advantage across all institutions (perhaps save religion in the United States). Consequently, whites do not have to do anything to get resources. Social and cultural structures (e.g., norms, networks, belief systems, etc.) deliver privileges to them without any individual effort. White normativity is the process by which the cultural practices, understandings, and ideologies of whites, and their location atop the social hierarchy, are perceived and accepted as just how things are. They are, therefore, unquestioned. Finally, white transparency is the systemic tendency of white persons to have a total lack of racial consciousness. In other words, they do not see themselves as raced beings and consequently are blind to the advantages the structure and normalization of whiteness affords them.

Perhaps it could go without saying, but Robert Bellah was one of those elite white men that Collins's work points to, even if not as an individual. It is important to name this because it has implications for the conceptualization of American civil religion. Bellah, as a white person in a white supremacist society and a male in a patriarchal one, was situated in a position of powerful privilege. Following CWT (and gender theory as well), his intersecting statuses situated him (and others like him) in a social position where his ideas, values, and practices, even his very being, are presumed relevant and worthy of consideration simply because he proposed them or because he is present and worthy of being seen. And then, more importantly, when those ideas, values, and practices affirm the overarching white supremacist and patriarchal belief systems, it is all the more likely they will be embraced. Bellah and his ideas, values, practices, and very being are given power because they are taken for granted. The advantages afforded Bellah and other elite white men along with their culture and structural dominance are just how things are. Their ideologies, paradigms, and epistemologies are normative because they are presumed to be superior. Both those who are dominant and those who are subordinate consent to this system. As an elite white man, Bellah lived a life where he had the freedom to ignore how the institutionalization of race and male privilege structured his life. His Christian status and elite class as an adult made this all the more true as elite white Christian males are situated at the epicenter of American society.

All intersecting social statuses come with blind spots. No one is exempt from them, no matter where one is situated within the social structure. That Bellah did not interrogate or express in his scholarship how his intersecting social statuses affected his scholarship is not surprising, but should in fact be expected, not just of him but of all of us. It takes tremendous psychological awareness and self-conscious effort to deconstruct the world in which one lives, especially when that world is so very kind to one. This world taught Bellah, others like him, and everyone subjected to it that his scholarship could (perhaps even should) ignore the perspectives, values, ideologies, and experiences of people for whom their race and gender or sex identify them as other or not normative. Bellah could sideline race and gender and focus exclusively on the perspectives of elite white men as sources for developing the concept of civil religion. And this is why the academy embraced a conceptualization presented as encompassing American culture and structure that was based exclusively on the perspectives, values, ideologies, and experiences of elite white men.

Imagine for a moment that Bellah submitted an article presenting a concept called *American* civil religion based exclusively on the perspectives, values, ideologies, and experiences of poor Black women or even all Black people. Let's expand that even further to include all people of color. Do we imagine the academy would embrace a concept of American civil religion with this level of diversity? Or how about if the sources came from an even greater pool, one that included all people of color and white women as well? In other words, do we imagine that the academy's epistemology and paradigm would have been flexible enough, especially in 1967, to embrace and reproduce a conceptualization of American civil religion that did not take into account the perspectives, values, ideologies, and experiences of any white men? I believe it is safe to say the answer to these questions is no.

One more point. Bellah wrote briefly, and basically positively, about the civil religious themes that he saw in the speeches of Barack Obama.[34] While he was particularly pleased with Obama's use of the nation's history to focus on its unmet promise, a clear implication was the potential for this national understanding to have universal acceptance. Obama's speeches indeed had a familiar civil religious ring to them (see chapter 1 by Gorski in this volume). Laced with hope in the purpose and promise of America, they too referenced God, the proper moral order of things, and where America excelled and where it was still found wanting. It is tempting to say that because it was a Black president who spoke these words, Bellah's American civil religion is inclusive and crosscuts race and gender distinctions. But this does not erase Bellah's focus on the public language of elite white men and the civil religious practices of white people (and Bellah's essay lauds Obama for his knowledge of the Western philosophical tradition) or that the academy embraced American civil religion even though it was based upon sources from a small and distinct group of people.

Moreover, Obama crafted this public message in some contradistinction with more critical ideas about the American racial order. This became evident in the 2008 controversy about the Reverend Jeremiah Wright of Chicago's Trinity United Church of Christ. Obama was a member there, and Wright officiated at his wedding. Having visited a worship service of this church in the early 2000s for a research project I was involved with at the time, what stood out to me most was its clear identification with an Afrocentric blackness. The church's slogan, "unashamedly Black and unapologetically Christian," was placed in very visible spots in the building. Wright's sermons revealed an ideology and theology that did not raise up America as a divine standard for the world but named how America, at its core, was quite oppositional to the Bible's message.[35]

It is possible that Obama attended Trinity for twenty years and yet still held to ideological understandings similar to those of Bellah's American civil religion. But when Reverend Wright's message became the focus of media reports and political controversy during this 2008 campaign, Obama was caught in a clear dilemma. He seemed genuinely loath to cut ties with Wright, someone he considered a mentor, although he eventually did and partially renounced some of Wright's more critical positions. I suggest that Obama's deployment of ideas consistent with Bellah's American civil religion reveals the hegemony of white dominant culture, a set of ideas and practices that includes references to a God who favors and thinks of America as special and that also reproduces a racialized and patriarchal society. Obama's shot at the White House depended upon him extolling these ideals and shunning anything that contradicted them.

Becoming Diverse or Becoming Just

A primary theme of Bellah's *Broken Covenant* is that America, from its inception, was composed of many different groups, not only white Anglos. He pays particular attention, as already noted, to Blacks and American Indians. Throughout the book, he expresses sorrow for the oppression they experienced at the hand of America. He also notes that America has always been diverse. Referencing mainly European immigrants, he highlights their eventual inclusion as they experience assimilation into the dominant culture. This gives Bellah some hope.

He ponders at one point, "Perhaps . . . encouragement of a broad range of experiments with cultural symbols and styles of community may be essential."[36]

Bellah's hope for a diverse yet inclusive America is a common one. It is rare, especially in today's America, for organizations and institutions to not at least state they want to be "diverse and inclusive." For nearly two decades, I have studied how diverse and inclusive communities in America are developed and sustained in multiracial religious organizations. *The Elusive Dream: The Power of Race in Interracial Churches* tells the story of Crosstown Community Church and how it became and worked to sustain a racially diverse congregation. It highlights the challenges leadership faced in this endeavor and how and why different constituent groups in the church facilitated those aims at times and undermined them at others. I drew upon the National Congregations Study to provide supplemental quantitative analysis of my findings that demonstrated patterns consistent with what emerged in the case study. The barrier that repeatedly hindered Crosstown was one that all American institutions must scale if they want to be racially integrated and just, and that is whiteness. The story of Crosstown showed that whiteness is a tricky and elusive system, yet amazingly good at reproducing itself even in the seemingly most amenable and affirming contexts.

More recently, I have turned my attention to head clergy of racially diverse churches in America with the Religious Leadership and Diversity Project (RLDP). The RLDP is a multimethod study. Central to the study are interviews with head clergy of racially and ethnically diverse congregations and surveys and focus groups with congregants of the churches of participating clergy. There are interviews with denominational leaders as well.

The RLDP has been a fascinating study of how leaders do diversity. There are rays of hope in the stories and experiences of the head clergy. That hope lies in the commitment of people, both the leaders and congregants, to keep working toward building racially and ethnically diverse communities in a highly racialized society. But make no mistake about it—doing diversity is hard in this American context, one that is highly racialized and often xenophobic. Challenges range from making decisions about worship elements, such as what statues to have in the sanctuary or music to sing during services, to how to tackle racially and politically divisive issues, such as Black Lives Matter and the nomination and election of Donald Trump, in a way that is satisfying to groups in their congregations with completely different ideas, desires, and needs.

Religious contexts might seem to offer great hope for actualizing Bellah's vision, in part because American civil religion, Bellah's protests aside, is heavily influenced by a Christian ethos (see chapter 3 by Corbett in this volume). Yet a large majority of religious organizations are in fact hyper-racially segregated. The institutionalized hyper-racial segregation of religion combined with the racialization and racial segregation that exists in nearly all other institutions makes creating and sustaining racially diverse communities, religious or otherwise, a difficult endeavor. All head clergy have to deal with conflict and challenges, but head clergy of racially and ethnically diverse churches have the added challenge of creating and sustaining a racially and ethnically diverse community in a social environment that works against it at practically every turn. American society pushes people toward racial segregation not racial integration, let alone racially integrated communities where equality, justice, and mutuality are what bind people.

Bellah was, in some ways, aware of this. His repeated references to the oppression of people of color in America suggest as much. And yet Bellah did not have the theoretical frame for making sense of why racial harmony never developed. Nor was he willing to question the ideological roots of America, which are, at least in part, the roots of his American civil religion. Even after outlining how America repeatedly failed to live out his American civil religion in *The Broken Covenant*, Bellah remained steadfastly committed to a belief in its reality and, if practiced righteously, its redemptive power. He simply would not, perhaps he could not, given his standpoint, entertain the notion that America's stubborn incapacity to live up to its ideals of equality and inclusivity was because those ideals were not what America truly aspired to be.

An ideal America would be one that is culturally open and inclusive, one that has rejected and atoned for its systemically oppressive ways, as Bellah hoped. America, though, is far from ideal, especially for people of color. Scholarship on race and religion has repeatedly shown just how challenging achieving Bellah's possible solution can be, especially for people of color.[37] Does this suggest we should not aspire to achieve the ideal? No. Rather, it suggests that America's capacity to make it happen cannot be found in its ideological foundations, as Bellah continued to believe. The answer must be sought elsewhere. More than anything, it perhaps suggests that it is in fact America's ideological foundations that are the problem. These must first be deconstructed before the country can move forward toward achieving a just and collaborative humanity.

Some Concluding Thoughts

American civil religion is an intriguing concept. That America, a country that is simultaneously deeply religious and very secular, would have a civil religion is altogether plausible. Founded by elite white men who supported ideals of the Enlightenment and others who wanted to freely practice their religion, America, it seems, would have some kind of a religion, in the true sense of the word, and secular and modern. And this religion would integrate society with the gifts that only religion can offer: a moral foundation, the attention of God or gods, communal ties, purpose and identity. Yet, it would, ideally, temper pursuing the promises of modernity, which encourage us to set our sights on human advancement and control, without restraint.

Still, Bellah's choice to use the idea of religion to conceptualize the social phenomenon he observed is only one of the ways in which he could have framed it. Why not "American civic system" or "American civic culture," for example? Or how about "American civil philosophy"? A philosophy has all the qualities of a religion, save the mandate and moral absoluteness of the sacred. Since Bellah's civil religion was not meant to exclude the irreligious or unbelieving, would not philosophy be more inclusive? Admittedly, civic system, civic culture, and civic philosophy do not have the same appeal as American civil "religion." But one could argue that they are more reflective of what Bellah actually observed. Bellah's intentions for choosing "religion" to conceptualize what he observed are irrelevant. What is relevant is that language matters. Words are limiting and saddled with meanings that go beyond the intent of the user. Once Bellah chose to use the word "religion" to frame a set of dominant ideologies, values, and practices, it was out there, so to speak, ready to be manipulated and influenced in all the ways that the established meaning allows. Naming it a civil "religion" provided Bellah's concept with a political and cultural legitimacy.

Additionally, Herbert Richardson's essay "Civil Religion in Theological Perspective" provides a theological basis to wonder about the consequences of referring to a social phenomenon as a "religion." He notes that when religion is used as a descriptor "we ascribe to that thing some ultimate value or transcendent meaning" and "we conceive ultimate reality as if it resembled [that aspect of life]."[38] In other words, the civic and political world is then attributed with transcendent goals and aims and is seen as a reflection of an ultimate reality, including who God is and how God relates to humans. Consequently, Richardson says that when we connect the civil and political world to religion, it suggests that this world is "true." "Whenever we seek to relate American politics to God's sovereignty, we are also relating God's sovereignty to American politics."[39] Ultimately, Richardson's theological critique questions both the appropriateness and the efficacy of trying to assign a civic and political power structure, which is by definition very human and which suffers from the inevitable inadequacies, contradictions, and limitations associated with humanity, a value that is equated with the sovereignty of God.

Taken further, the concept of religion immediately conjures up a notion of the sacred; that whatever the social phenomenon, with its body of beliefs, values, practices, and experiences that compose and reinforce it, it is something to be revered, taken seriously, even protected. It should be beyond criticism because religion should not be questioned but believed. Moreover, as a religion, it is promoted as ubiquitous, affecting directly or indirectly all institutions. It is what gives institutions and the people who are a part of these institutions meaning and purpose, direction, and a sense of identity. Taken together, religion provides sacred, unchallengeable answers for why and how the social world is governed as it is.

This is all the more true when we place "civil" in front of the word "religion." What "civil religion" suggests, then, is that the civil world, or more specifically civic and political society, is founded on a set of beliefs, values, norms, and experiences that are sacrosanct. Civic and political society, which arguably is the cornerstone of any society, is beyond reproach, not to be contested. Turning to the American context, what are we to do with this country's long history of imperialist, racist, sexist, genocidal, and exclusionary tendencies? Arguably, it is these tendencies that most define America, not its religious or modernist values or Enlightenment ideals. It is because of this reality that the concept of an American civil religion is a careless, if not frightful, one. Was Bellah intending to be careless or frightful? I highly doubt it. Rather, I believe his standpoint socialized him to see, value, and highly regard the ideas of elite white males.

Depending on our standpoint, we might be tempted to see the collection of beliefs, values, experiences, and behaviors of Bellah's American civil religion as a useful conceptualization or a problematic one. I find it problematic. I find there to be troubling aspects of how American civil religion was conceptualized, how it was developed, and the implications of the process by which this concept was canonized for our scholarship. Nevertheless, I suggest that we take a cue from feminist scholarship and put such dichotomous thinking aside, even though it may be a challenge. Given the effectiveness of the global Western imperialist project, we have all been either wholly or partially socialized to adopt a Western worldview, one that is elite white male centered and constructs the world in opposing dichotomies. I suggest that we see the gray. We have to be willing to bury those ideologies that have sustained a racist and patriarchal America. We also have to be willing to retain those that move us toward a community that affirms and gives dignity to everyone's humanness. Along the way, let's discard language like "religion," which conjures up notions of the sacred and protects America's dominant sociopolitical and civic values, ideologies, and practices. Let us replace American civil religion with a complex, integrated, and diverse view of America and language that signifies our common humanness, not a belief in American greatness. This, I believe, is an important first step to ultimately achieving Robert Bellah's vision.

NOTES

1 Robert N. Bellah, "Civil Religion in America," *Daedalus* 96, no. 1 (Winter 1967): 1–21.
2 Robert N. Bellah, *The Broken Covenant: American Civil Religion in Time of Trial* (Chicago: University of Chicago Press, 1975).
3 Matteo Bortolini, "The Trap of Intellectual Success: Robert N. Bellah, the American Civil Religion Debate and the Sociology of Knowledge," *Theory and Society* 41 (2012): 187–210.
4 Robert N. Bellah, Richard Madsen, William M. Sullivan, Ann Swidler, and Steven M. Tipton, *Habits of the Heart: Individualism and Commitment in American Life* (Berkeley: University of California Press, 1985).

5 Bellah, "Civil Religion in America," 4.
6 Bellah, "Civil Religion in America," 7.
7 Bellah, "Civil Religion in America," 8.
8 Bellah, "Civil Religion in America," 18.
9 Bellah, "Civil Religion in America," 5.
10 Bellah, "Civil Religion in America," 9.
11 Bellah, "Civil Religion in America," 16.
12 Bellah, "Civil Religion in America," 16.
13 Bellah, *Broken Covenant*, 88.
14 Bellah, "Civil Religion in America," 15.
15 Bellah, *Broken Covenant*, 37.
16 Bellah, *Broken Covenant*, 93.
17 Bellah, *Broken Covenant*, 98.
18 Bellah, *Broken Covenant*, 142.
19 Bellah, *Broken Covenant*, 151.
20 Robert N. Bellah, "American Civil Religion in the 1970s," in *American Civil Religion*, ed. R. Richey and D. Jones (New York: Harper, 1974), 255–72.
21 Bellah, "Civil Religion in America," 14.
22 Patricia Hill Collins, *Black Feminist Thought: Knowledge, Consciousness, and the Politics of Empowerment* (New York: Taylor & Francis, 1999).
23 Collins, *Black Feminist Thought*, 251.
24 Collins, *Black Feminist Thought*, 252.
25 Collins, *Black Feminist Thought*, 253.
26 Bellah *Broken Covenant*, 98.
27 Richard Delgado and Jean Stefancic, *Critical Race Theory: An Introduction* (New York: New York University Press, 2017).
28 William Julius Wilson, *The Declining Significance of Race: Blacks and Changing American Institutions* (Chicago: University of Chicago Press, 1978).
29 W. E. B. Du Bois highlighted the centrality of white people in the racialized structure at the beginning of the twentieth century.
30 For a review of critical whiteness theory and its origins, see Delgado and Stefancic, *Critical Race Theory* and Ashley W. Doane and Eduardo Bonilla-Silva, eds., *White Out: The Continuing Significance of Race* (New York: Routledge, 1993).
31 Ian F. Haney-Lopez, *White by Law: The Legal Construction of Race* (New York: New York University Press, 1996).
32 Korie L. Edwards, *The Elusive Dream: The Power of Race in Interracial Churches* (New York: Oxford University Press, 2008), 10.
33 See Barbara Flagg, *Was Blind, but Now I See: White Race Consciousness and the Requirement of Discriminatory Intent* (New York: New York University Press, 1993) and Ashley Doane, "Rethinking Whiteness Studies," in Doane and Bonilla-Silva, *White Out*, 3–20, for more on these dimensions.
34 Robert N. Bellah, "This Is Our Moment, This Is Our Time," *Immanent Frame*, January 12, 2009, https://tif.ssrc.org.

35 For a description of this series of events, see Rhys H. Williams, "Civil Religion and the Cultural Politics of National Identity in Obama's America," *Journal for the Scientific Study of Religion* 52 (June 2013): 239–57.
36 Bellah, *Broken Covenant*, 110.
37 See Edwards, *Elusive Dream*; Brad Christerson, Korie L. Edwards, and Michael O. Emerson, *Against All Odds: The Struggle for Racial Integration in Religious Organizations* (New York: New York University Press, 2005). For a review, see Korie L. Edwards, Brad Christerson, and Michael O. Emerson, "Race, Religious Organizations and Integration," *Annual Review of Sociology* 39 (2013): 211–28.
38 Herbert Richardson, "Civil Religion in Theological Perspective," in *American Civil Religion*, ed. Russell E. Richey and Donald G. Jones (New York: Harper & Row, 1974), 161.
39 Richardson, "Civil Religion in Theological Perspective," 164.

6

Civil Religion and the Problem of Origins

WENDY L. WALL

Between September 1947 and January 1949, Americans engaged in what many scholars would consider a remarkable performance of civil religion: a red, white, and blue locomotive dubbed the Spirit of 1776 pulled a traveling exhibit known as the Freedom Train through 322 cities in all forty-eight states. The contents included many documents and artifacts on loan from the National Archives: Thomas Jefferson's rough draft of the Declaration of Independence, George Washington's annotated copy of the Constitution, the original copies of the Bill of Rights and "The Star-Spangled Banner," Abraham Lincoln's draft of the Emancipation Proclamation, the congressional resolution proposing a women's suffrage amendment, and the flag that U.S. troops had planted at Iwo Jima in February 1945. An estimated three and a half million Americans boarded the Freedom Train. Millions more encountered its message of national unity and shared values through a nationwide media blitz. Newspapers, newsreels, and national magazines gave the traveling exhibit extensive coverage. Its journey was hailed in outdoor advertising and on radio shows ranging from the *Cavalcade of America* to *Fibber McGee and Molly*. Chambers of commerce, schools, and community organizations passed out pamphlets, study guides, and other train-related materials, including millions of copies of the handbook *Good Citizen* and the comic book *Captain Marvel and the Freedom Train!* Many who preferred to spend their time in bars heard Bing Crosby and the Andrews Sisters performing Irving Berlin's new song "Freedom Train" on the jukebox.[1]

As the Freedom Train circled the nation over the course of sixteen months, civic and religious messages intertwined. Both the onboard exhibit and accompanying pamphlets and media materials suggested that Americans' deepest common belief was the sanctity of the individual, a belief they traced to a shared Judeo-Christian consensus. "The cornerstone of our republic," the handbook *Good Citizen* explained, "is a religious concept: that *'every human being is endowed with a soul that is sacred in the eyes of a Sovereign God and with the power to distinguish right and wrong; that the judgment expressed by a majority of such divinely created human beings is likely to be closest to God's will for all of them; and that every mortal soul is endowed by its Creator with certain natural inalienable rights that no human agency whatever can justly invade.'"[2] *Good Citizen* was the work of a Jewish advertising executive, but preachers and laymen of diverse faiths echoed its themes. Rabbis, priests, and ministers appeared together in Freedom Train ads, on radio talk shows, and on train welcoming committees, stressing "how closely related are our religious ideals and the American form of freedom." Towns along the train's route held Rededication Weeks featuring parades, pageants, rallies, Freedom of Religion Days, and mass recitations of a Freedom Pledge and a Rededication Prayer.[3] Those coordinating the extravaganza dubbed these local celebrations "revival meetings for democracy" and frequently referred to the train's contents as "American scriptures." Winthrop Aldrich, the chairman of both Chase National Bank and the foundation that organized the Freedom Train, compared the entire project to a "pilgrimage":

> It is a different kind of pilgrimage from the ones that took our ancestors to the Holy Land or Chaucer's wayfarers to Canterbury. For this time, because of the vastness of the country, we are taking the shrine to the people, instead of the people to the shrine.
>
> But the spirit and purpose are the same. It is a means of paying our profound respect to the ideas in which all Americans believe. It is a means of renewing our faith.[4]

As I suggested at the beginning of this essay, the story of the Freedom Train speaks directly to the issue this volume considers: civil religion. That term, at least in the American context, has proven notoriously slippery since Robert Bellah popularized the concept in 1967. Borrowing a phrase first coined by Jean-Jacques Rousseau, Bellah defined civil religion as a "set of beliefs, symbols, and rituals with respect to sacred things" that was "institutionalized in [the] collectivity" of the nation beginning in the earliest years of the republic. While Bellah's civil religion was nonsectarian, it provided "a grounding for the rights of man" and "a transcendent goal for the political process."[5] Subsequent scholars have used the term to refer to nondenominational "god talk" in the public arena; the sacralization of the nation's Founders, national holidays, patriotic symbols, and key documents; and an array of beliefs and cultural practices that instill in Americans a sense of shared unity and purpose. A search of both the scholarly and the popular press shows that the term "civil religion" has been applied in recent years to everything from McGuffey Readers and Marvel Comics to environmentalism and the "Church of Baseball."[6] (A Duke public policy professor recently suggested that basketball, not baseball, was North Carolina's "civil religion.")[7]

By just about any definition of civil religion, the story of the Freedom Train and the accompanying American Heritage campaign would seem to fit. The episode involved the sacralization of "America's heritage," the deployment of nonsectarian religious language, and repeated invocations of both God and "the ideas in which all Americans believe." Yet in telling the Freedom Train story in my 2008 book *Inventing the "American Way,"* I used Bellah's term only once and put it in scare quotes.[8] In fact, that was my only reference to "civil religion" in the entire book. I avoided the term despite the fact that the volume explored the origins, permutations, and political implications of the "American Way," a phrase that the religious sociologist Will Herberg famously used to denote civil religion.[9]

I am not alone. Over the past two decades there has been an explosion of interest on the part of twentieth-century U.S. historians in what Bellah once called the "religious dimension in political life."[10] For decades, historians of modern America either ignored the role of religion entirely or treated it as, in Jon Butler's words, a kind of "jack-in-the-box faith": religion might "pop up colorfully on occasion"—in nods to Billy Sunday, the Scopes Monkey Trial, or the Moral Majority—but religion was rarely seen as connected to "larger enduring patterns in American life."[11] Much has changed since Butler wrote those words in 2004. A host of modern U.S. historians have shown that we can't understand topics like the labor, civil rights, and antiwar movements; the political role of corporate America; Cold War militarism or diplomacy; or the rise of the new right without reference to religion.¹² Yet the term "civil religion" rarely appears in these works, with the notable exception of those focused on foreign policy. Jonathan Herzog's *The Spiritual-Industrial Complex* recounts the efforts of secular leaders during the early Cold War to sacralize American values and institutions, yet he uses the term "civil religion" only twice in the text.¹³ In *One Nation Under God*, Kevin Kruse traces the origins of many rituals and rhetorical practices that Bellah certainly considered to be part of America's "civil religion"; yet Kruse prefers the terms "religious nationalism" and "public religion."¹⁴

Why is this? In the fifty years since Bellah published his famous article, sociologists, religious and American studies scholars, and others have elaborated, revised, updated, and deployed Bellah's concept. Why have *historians* of modern American political culture been slow to follow suit? One issue is undoubtedly the term's definitional fuzziness. How much explanatory power can "civil religion" have if, as Herzog warns, "every ritual, every mention of God, and every parade becomes part of this expansive concept"?¹⁵

For me—and, I suspect, for many others—this is only part of the problem. At least in the American context, "civil religion" has never been able entirely to break free of its origins, both chronological and disciplinary. Bellah published his landmark article at the end of a historical era when Americans were unusually focused on defining their common ground, and the term still implies a widespread consensus. (This is why the reference to baseball as America's "civil religion" makes intuitive sense to many people.) Moreover, Bellah was a Durkheimian sociologist, more concerned with exploring broad societal patterns than with the human actors behind the drama. Not all subsequent scholars have followed his lead. Still, scholarship on "civil religion" too often directs our attention toward supposedly "common" beliefs, symbols, and practices and away from the government officials, corporate elites, political activists, and others who have sought to shape American culture and values for particular ends. It is those human actors—and the messy agendas, conflicts, and compromises that often lurk beneath apparent consensus—that are of most interest to me and to many of my fellow historians.

In what follows, I expand on these two points, drawing heavily on my own work. While most of this chapter focuses on civil religion as an *analytical* category, I switch hats at the end and briefly discuss its *pre-*

scriptive dimensions. As a historian, I am wary of using the term "civil religion." But as a concerned citizen who has watched the deepening divides between "red" and "blue" America, as well as the rise of racial and religious nationalism in the United States and other parts of the world, I am deeply concerned about the fraying of our nation's social fabric. As a citizen, I yearn for civil religion—not perhaps for Bellah's version, but for a variant updated to our times.

* * *

In early 1967, Robert Bellah's publication of "Civil Religion in America" pointed scholars toward a new way of thinking about the relationship between religion and American public life. Bellah cast his essay as a reflection on cultural patterns that stretched back to the nation's founding, but he wrote it at the end of a historical moment marked by what I have called the "politics of consensus."[16] This era began in the late 1930s, when domestic and international pressures converged to give questions of national identity and cohesion unusual salience. The Depression intensified class and ethnocultural divisions in the United States, while calling into question many of the assumptions that had long guided American society and policy making. The New Deal united millions of Americans in a sweeping reform coalition, but it also triggered fierce ideological debates about the proper contours of the nation's political economy. In the lead-up to World War II, strains or open hostility between the ancestral homes of millions of American citizens amplified group tensions in the United States. Finally, the challenge posed by the "alien" ideologies of fascism and communism intensified Americans' sense of unease. Many liberals and leftists saw in rising nativism, red baiting, union busting, and particularly anti-Semitism the seeds of a domestic fascism. Economic conservatives, meanwhile, worried that the New Deal and the amorphous left-wing movement that supported it foretold the U.S. arrival of "state socialism." Both fears proved greatly exaggerated, but to many at the time they seemed real indeed.

Driven by such concerns, individuals and organizations across the political spectrum launched an array of competing, and sometimes collaborative, efforts to define for Americans their common ground. Intellectuals, New Dealers, business and advertising executives, interfaith activists, and other elites took part in such campaigns, propelled by anxieties about social fragmentation and the spread of "un-American" creeds. Their efforts also drew urgency from another source that cut across ideological divides: the need to defend America against fascism and communism without succumbing to the evils of those "totalitarian" states. Enforced uniformity was widely considered to be a hallmark of totalitarianism, so American writers and speakers repeatedly emphasized the diversity that distinguished U.S. society. But diversity alone, many opinion molders believed, could breed chaos and intolerance, as it apparently had in much of the rest of the world. (Many read the unexpected fall of France in 1940 as foreshadowing the fate of nations that remained internally divided.) To be an attribute, rather than a danger, diversity needed to be circumscribed and solidly embedded in common ground. Thus, celebrations of American pluralism in the late 1930s and early 1940s were almost always linked to invocations of consensus. At the same time, many of the paeans to America's unifying ideals in this period were intended not simply as descriptions of the nation but as prescriptions for the United States and the world. By *declaring* that Americans of diverse ethnic, religious, regional, racial, and class backgrounds shared deeply rooted civic values, American elites sought to call such a consensus into being—to create a nation that was at once diverse and harmonious.

The "cultural conversation" thus launched in the late 1930s lasted nearly three decades, spawning short films, comic strips, movies, radio shows, advertising blitzes, reading lists, and civic education campaigns like the Freedom Train. Those who spearheaded such efforts seized on the notion of a unifying and distinctive "American Way"—a term that exploded into popular use only in the late 1930s—and sought to define it in ways that furthered their own political and social agendas. They did not always agree on the specific values and attributes their fellow citizens shared: some hailed economic security, while others emphasized free enterprise, religious tolerance, or cultural pluralism. At the same time, all had a strong interest in cementing national cohesion. Many took pains to hide their differences in public and to suppress grassroots evidence of open dissent. The compromises they made and the alliances they forged did much to produce the consensus culture that marked the public arena during the postwar years.

The politics of consensus that shaped the immediate postwar decades also transformed the relationship between religion and American public life. Despite the nation's stated commitment to religious freedom, no form of nativism was more widespread or virulent in the United States in the late nineteenth and early twentieth centuries than anti-Catholicism. Anti-Semitism, too, surged after the turn of the century, assuming particularly venomous forms during the Great Depression. Yet during and after World War II, the long-standing equation in public discourse of "Americanism" with Protestantism gave way rapidly, if incompletely, to the notion that the United States was a Judeo-Christian nation. Countless public forums in the 1940s, 1950s, and early 1960s featured a priest, a minister, and a rabbi, or secular representatives of the three faiths. And as the story of the Freedom Train suggests, many American elites argued that the nation's unifying creed rested on a vague, but shared, monotheistic belief. While demographic changes reinforced this shift, they were not the sole catalyst. To elites who were trying to define the nation through a contrast with fascist or communist enemies, the notion that Americans were united "under God" proved particularly useful. Both fascists and communists were said to embrace coercive homogeneity and to reject any religion other than that of the state. In this context, ecumenical religion could serve simultaneously as a powerful symbol of American pluralism and American consensus.[17]

The notion that America was a broadly Judeo-Christian nation—that Protestantism, Catholicism, and Judaism were diverse representations of spiritual ideals and moral values that all Americans shared—served the interests of some groups at the forefront of promoting a consensual political culture. Assimilated American Jews and some Catholics advanced the idea in an effort to reposition their groups as part of the American "mainstream."[18] Many in the business community sought to legitimate their vision of the nation's political economy by arguing that the "sanctity of the individual" was *the* core American value and then rooting this belief in Americans' shared belief in God.

Given this postwar emphasis on both American religiosity and national consensus, it is hardly surprising that the 1950s and 1960s produced two of the first, and most influential, formulations of American civil religion. Will Herberg did not use Rousseau's term in his seminal 1955 work *Protestant-Catholic-Jew*. Yet he argued that Americans shared a unifying creedal system, a "civic religion" or "common faith," which "coexisted" alongside "the historic faiths of the American people." Christianity and Judaism, Herberg wrote, "tend to be prized because they help promote ideals and standards that all American are expected to share. Insofar as any reference is made to the God in whom all Americans 'believe' and of whom the 'official' religions speak, it is primarily as sanction and underpinning for the supreme values of [this] faith." Herberg argued that the nation's "civic religion" dated back to the Puritans. Nevertheless, the fact that he called it the "American Way of Life"—together with his emphatic declaration that Protestantism, Catholicism, and Judaism were America's "three great faiths"—suggests how much his analysis owed to the consensus-seeking political culture of his era.[19]

Twelve years after Herberg called attention to Americans' "common faith," Bellah popularized the term "civil religion" in his famed *Daedalus* essay. Herberg was centrally concerned with positioning Jews and Catholics as part of the American mainstream; Bellah, by contrast, saw civil religion as a "universal and transcendent religious reality" that could be used to advance civil rights or critique the nation's involvement in Vietnam. Despite these differences, he, like Herberg, rooted civil religion in consensus. Throughout his essay, Bellah insistently used the singular, referring to "*the* American civil religion." He also dismissed both Christian defenders of slavery and the "overt religiosity of the radical right" because "their relationship to the civil religious consensus is tenuous."[20]

That Bellah could dismiss a group—the religious right—that historians now see as central to the story of late twentieth-century American politics suggests one of the problems with his vision of civil religion. In recent decades, scholars have questioned whether Americans indeed share a common moral framework (or ever have) and have emphasized the many who—because of their politics, religion, class, or race—are left out of Bellah's vision. Some scholars have dealt with this problem by arguing that the United States has not one but two or more civil religions. In his influential work, *The Restructuring of American Religion*, sociologist Robert Wuthnow argues that America has two competing civil religions, one conservative and one liberal, "that seem to have very little of substance in common."[21] Religious studies scholar Arthur Remillard has suggested that, in the post-Reconstruction South, "Blacks, whites, men, women, northerners, southerners, Democrats, Republicans, Catholics, Protestants, and Jews" often had different visions of the "good society," visions that Remillard calls civil religions.[22]

Many historians have been slow to follow this lead, which brings me to a second "origins problem": the one of disciplinary approaches. Both Herberg and Bellah were Durkheimian sociologists, and this perspective shaped their understanding of civil religion. Herberg's "American Way of Life" may have evolved since Puritan days, but it wasn't molded by human actors. Bellah acknowledged that Abraham Lincoln helped reformulate America's civil religion, introducing new themes of death, sacrifice, and rebirth. Still, Bellah's essay was replete with passive constructions, and "the civil religion" itself was the central protagonist. To give but one example, Bellah wrote that "the civil religion serves to mobilize support for the attainment of national goals."[23] Bellah was referring here to President Johnson's 1965 speech asking Congress to pass a voting rights bill. Yet civil religion, not Johnson, was the primary agent in the passage, and Bellah never questioned either who defined the "national goals" or how widely embraced they were.

This tendency to focus on symbolic systems of meaning rather than on the human actors behind them permeates many more recent works on civil religion, even those that question the existence of a single overarching consensus. Wuthnow, for instance, describes a conservative version of civil religion that emphasizes the biblical principles that supposedly guided the nation's Founders and claims divine sanction for American-style capitalism and a militant foreign policy. He sees this as operating alongside a liberal version of civil religion focused "less on the nation as such, and more on humanity in general." According to Wuthnow, the liberal variation is prophetic and speaks of America's responsibility to promote peace, justice, human rights, and ecology both at home and abroad.[24] Wuthnow brilliantly outlines these competing discourses, but he barely mentions the people behind them. Tellingly, his book has an extensive topical index, but one that indexes no individual names.[25]

This general approach to civil religion has not deterred historians whose primary focus is foreign affairs. In his monumental 2012 study of the influence of religion on U.S. foreign relations, Andrew Preston repeatedly invokes "*the* American civil religion." In *God and War*, published the same year, Ray Haberski explores the refashioning of American civil religion against the backdrop of America's various military conflicts since 1945. There are many reasons why diplomatic historians might find the term "civil religion" more useful than do other historians of the modern United States. International crises tend to unify the nation—or at least to produce a public rhetoric of unity. The key actor in diplomatic dramas has traditionally been seen as the "state."[26] Finally, in foreign affairs, more than in most other arenas, a single individual plays an inordinately large role. As Preston notes, the president is not only the nation's chief executive and commander in chief but also its head of state. "There is no official hierarchy in the American civil religion," he writes, but "the president has acted as its de facto pope."[27]

For historians of domestic political culture, this emphasis on a single authoritative voice—whether that of the president or that of the state—is more problematic. I and my colleagues are intensely aware that civil religion does not simply settle like a "sacred canopy" over the land.[28] If there is such a thing as "civil religion," it is shaped and deployed by human actors for particular ends—to encourage support for war, to curb certain forms of prejudice, to shore up support for the existing corporate order, and to mobilize Americans on behalf of civil rights, among other things. It is also true, and essential to remember, that some Americans have more power than others in shaping public discourse.

To illustrate this, let me briefly return to my story of the Freedom Train, focusing less on what the public saw and more on what they did not. Although both the train and the media barrage were ostensibly designed to *remind* Americans of their "shared" heritage and values, comments made by the project's organizers reveal that it was designed to *instill*, rather than simply reflect, common mores. Even organizers did not have precisely the same goals. Attorney General Tom Clark, whose office originated the idea, argued that "indoctrination in democracy is the essential catalytic agent needed to blend our varying groups into one American family." Paramount Pictures president Barney Balaban, the son of Russian Jewish immigrants and the man who helped transform the Freedom Train into a major extravaganza, saw in it "a wonderful vehicle for creating good will among various racial and religious groups." Thomas D'Arcy Brophy, the advertising executive who ultimately orchestrated the entire project, hoped to defuse class tensions and head off "state socialism" in the United States by "re-selling Americanism to Americans." Winthrop Aldrich, the Chase National Bank chairman quoted above, had a similar goal.[29]

Each of these individuals had a different agenda, and they were not the only ones shaping the project. Indeed, the façade of consensus surrounding the Freedom Train concealed an ongoing contest involving many different groups: corporate and advertising executives, Truman administration officials, civil servants with New Deal loyalties, communists, pacifists, ardent segregationists, and southern Blacks fighting to end Jim Crow. Behind the scenes, and occasionally in public, these groups and others vied to control the message and meaning of the train.

Long before the Freedom Train left the station, controversy erupted over which documents should be sacralized through inclusion in the exhibit and over the interpretation ascribed to each. Were the Fourteenth and Fifteenth Amendments to the Constitution—those guaranteeing "due process" and the right to vote—really the *"common heritage of all Americans"*? (National Archive staffers had proposed these documents, but the corporate lawyers and executives who made the final cut decided that they were not.) Were pictures of immigrants, artifacts documenting the rise of the labor movement, or President Franklin Delano Roosevelt's 1940 speech declaring America to be the "arsenal of democracy" sufficiently noncontroversial to be displayed aboard the Freedom Train? How much attention should be paid to Alexander Hamilton, a favorite of economic conservatives, as compared to Thomas Jefferson, the Founding Father beloved by New Deal Democrats? In this charged environment, even a word as seemingly central to America's national identity—and its civil religion—as "democracy" was ultimately deemed too controversial to be used in slogans and press materials. Under the banner of "freedom," American elites with divergent interests used the Freedom Train to reinforce the corporate order, shore up support for the cold war, and campaign for interfaith unity and intergroup tolerance.[30]

The Freedom Train's organizers, however, did not operate in a vacuum, and as the train circled the country on its thirty-seven-thousand-mile journey other Americans interpreted its message in their own ways. The U.S. Communist Party decried the "reactionary" purposes of the campaign's corporate organizers and called on "prominent progressives" to lead tours of the train linking its contents to ongoing struggles over civil liberties, labor issues, and civil rights. Supporters of conscientious objectors, some of whom were still in prison or had lost the right to vote, noted that the train carried the Bill of Rights, "whose spirit surely stands for freedom of conscience." "What meaning has this document," Margretta Lawler wrote in a letter to the *St. Louis Globe-Democrat*, "if our government fails to give these men still in prison their freedom and full citizenship?" Mrs. R. Raney of Bridgewater, New Jersey, proposed returning the train to Washington in the hopes that a close look at its contents would convince members of Congress to end support for European governments at a time when "we lack funds to aid our veterans, the aged, the poor." The train arrived in Binghamton, New York, just as a controversy erupted over whether an African American veteran and his family should be allowed to move into federally subsidized veteran housing. Several locals invoked the Freedom Train in letters to the editor applauding the ultimate decision of city officials to allow the move.[31]

For the elites behind the Freedom Train, preaching a message of unity and national consensus proved particularly tricky when the train headed into the South. Segregation was still the law of the land below the Mason-Dixon line, and few southern cities wanted to allow white and Black citizens to board the train and view its exhibits together. Freedom Train organizers initially hoped to duck the issue by suggesting that they had no responsibility for local viewing arrangements. But this approach drew the ire of both local Black activists and national figures like the acclaimed poet Langston Hughes. As Hughes wrote in a poem that appeared in both the *New Republic* and the Black picture magazine *Our World*,

> If my children ask me, *Daddy, please explain*
> *Why There's Jim Crow stations for the Freedom Train*,
> What shall I tell my children? . . . *You* tell me—
> 'Cause freedom ain't freedom when a man ain't free.

Ultimately, these African American protests, combined with the intransigence of white city officials, prompted the Freedom Train's organizers to cancel the train's stops in Memphis, Tennessee, and Birmingham, Alabama. The cancellations garnered headlines across the nation; other southern cities scrambled to integrate their viewing lines; and even the communist *Daily Worker* called the Freedom Train's southern journey "a spectacular victory over the Jimcrow system."[32]

To be sure, some of those protesting the train in different contexts used language that foreshadowed Bellah's two decades later. Members of the Fellowship of Reconciliation (FOR), a radical pacifist group, picketed the Freedom Train in New York City in late September 1947. "Is our American Heritage a past to worship? . . . Or the challenge of an Unfinished Task," a leaflet distributed by the FOR asked. If the former, "then the documents on the Freedom Train are shrines where we bow, paying our respects to what we might have been," the leaflets declared. "In that case we are stuck with many miserable contradictions of the spirit and meaning of these symbols," including segregation and disfranchisement and "legal" violations of the Bill of Rights. FOR urged a different interpretation of the train's cargo: The documents "ARE plans for the future," the leaflet declared. "They provide for correcting mistakes in them." The organization urged Americans to "live out the creed set forth in the Freedom Train."[33]

The language used by the FOR protesters, like that deployed by Winthrop Aldrich and other organizers of the train, could be considered evidence of an American civil religion. But was there one civil religion here or even two? Certainly, there was overlap—if not absolute agreement—in the documents, historical events, and keywords hailed as central by different parties. But to view the Freedom Train through the lens of civil religion—to ignore human actors and agendas and to focus instead on what Wuthnow calls a "legitimating creed"—seems to obscure as much as it reveals.[34]

In my own work, I have found it more useful to adopt the approach taken by intellectual and cultural historian Daniel T. Rodgers in his pioneering volume *Contested Truths*. Americans, he reminds us, have long shared a rich political language and a common set of motifs and historical references. "Vying for control of a common vocabulary, stealing each other's terms in hopes of investing them with radically altered meanings, political opponents have often left behind an illusion of consensus," he writes.[35] That to me seems the best way to describe Americans' ongoing discussion of their common values, including the interaction between the sacred and the secular in the public sphere.

* * *

For most of this chapter, I have talked about civil religion as an analytical category, but it is also—and often—prescriptive. Both Herberg and Bellah had unspoken prescriptive agendas: respectively, to speed the incorporation of Jews and Catholics and to provide moral leverage for opposition to the Vietnam War. Many who study the subject argue passionately not only for the existence of an American civil religion, but for the *need* for one.[36] And I have a confession to make. As a concerned citizen, I agree with them. I believe *some* common ground is necessary in a pluralist democracy—that some level of consensus or solidarity is the precondition for intergroup harmony and the achievement of something approaching the "common good." I believe that what Bellah called "American civil religion" has at times helped to extend a canopy of inclusion over more of this nation's diverse people. (The postwar notion that America was "one nation under God," for instance, not only promoted "Christian libertarianism" but also opened a door for Catholics and Jews.) And I understand the powerful lever that an appeal to supposedly transcendent "American" values can give to prophetic outsiders who invoke it on behalf of social change. Would Martin Luther King Jr.'s "I Have a Dream" speech have been so powerful—or had the resonance it has today—if it had not been cast in the form of a jeremiad?

The historian in me is exquisitely aware of the obverse of all these claims: that what appears to be consensual is often hegemonic; that civil religion excludes some, even as it includes others; and that even as some versions of civil religion can be used to promote racial and economic justice, others can be used to legitimate war, cultural imperialism, and economic oppression. For more than a decade, such concerns made me at best an agnostic on the question of our need for civil religion; however, recent trends have begun to convert me. Culture wars and a yawning economic chasm between haves and have-nots have produced a politics of partisanship unrivaled since the Civil War. A resurgence of racial and religious nationalism in the United States and around the globe now threatens pluralist democracies worldwide. Americans have always debated the meanings and the implementation of any "shared" national values. Now, however, large groups of Americans inhabit such different cognitive frameworks that they no longer seem able to engage in a common "cultural conversation."[37] In this context, I feel a new sense of kinship with the intellectuals of the late 1930s and early 1940s who looked out on a fractious nation and fractured world and balanced yearning against despair. "One cannot counter the religious faith of fascism unless one possesses a faith equally strong, equally capable of fostering devotion and loyalty and commanding sacrifice," the left-liberal intellectual Lewis Mumford wrote in 1940. A few months later, the conservative historian James Truslow Adams asked, "Are we a nation with a common background and, despite our political battles a continuing national ideal?"[38]

That question, or a version of it, seems as relevant today as it was in 1940. Yet much has changed in the decades since Adams posed it or since Bellah responded by defining an American civil religion that drew heavily on Old and New Testament themes. Between 1947 (when pollsters first started asking about religious affiliation) and the end of the 1960s, more than 95 percent of Americans identified themselves as Protestant, Catholic, or Jewish.[39] That is no longer true. The Immigration Act of 1965 opened the door to millions of Muslims, Buddhists, Hindus, and members of other non-Judeo-Christian faiths, and these religious traditions have also been swelled by converts.[40] Meanwhile, the percentage of Americans who describe themselves as having no religious affiliation has surged in recent years. Bellah also saw American civil religion as forged by three great "trials" in U.S. history: the Revolution, the Civil War, and the Cold War. Our understanding of all three has changed over time.

Is there a version of civil religion that could encompass all, or nearly all, Americans today? If so, it would likely look different from the version outlined by Bellah a half century ago. In his famous *Daedalus* essay, Bellah emphasized both God talk and a series of Hebraic and Christian archetypes: "Exodus, Chosen People, Promised Land, New Jerusalem, Sacrificial Death and Rebirth."[41] A revised civil religion might place less emphasis on biblical motifs and more on hallowed political texts and transcendent secular values like equality and freedom. A revamped civil religion might recognize that almost all Americans are spiritual (even if they are not overtly religious), while also acknowledging that a pluralist democracy cannot long survive if its "congregants" are not engaged in— and bound by—a fact-based conversation about shared values.

In her 2014 book *Our Declaration: A Reading of the Declaration of Independence in Defense of Equality*, political theorist Danielle Allen gestures in this direction. In this book, Allen parses the 1,337 words of the Declaration with a kind of intensity and reverence usually reserved for religious texts. She finds in the document a "cogent philosophical case" for what might be considered a transcendent value, political equality. "The point of political equality," she writes, "is not merely to secure spaces free from domination but also to engage all members of a community equally in the work of creating and constantly re-creating that community." One does not have to be a theist to accept the Declaration's argument, Allen asserts. One must simply "hold sacred the flourishing of others."[42]

Allen came to this reading by working through the Declaration with her night students at the University of Chicago. These harried adults often had no jobs, two jobs, or "dead-end part-time jobs," which they juggled with "children's school schedules, undependable daycare arrangements, and a snarled city bus service." Allen does not tell us her students' races or religions, but she notes that they lived in a world of "gunshots and overdoses and chronic disease and battery." Yet they "metabolized" the argument of the Declaration and experienced a "personal metamorphosis": They developed a political "consciousness" and "built a foundation from which to assess the state of their political world," Allen writes. "They gained a vocabulary and rhetorical techniques for arguing about it."[43] What Allen doesn't say, but certainly implies, is that her students shared that sacred vocabulary. They shared it with their teacher, and with all other Americans, with everyone who can claim the Declaration as "ours." Should a civil religion do anything more?

NOTES

1. The story of the Freedom Train recounted in this essay draws heavily on Wendy L. Wall, *Inventing the "American Way": The Politics of Consensus from the New Deal to the Civil Rights Movement* (Oxford: Oxford University Press, 2008), 201–40.
2. *Good Citizen: The Rights and Duties of an American* (New York: American Heritage Foundation, 1948), 61.
3. "The First Two Years: A Progress Report to the Board of Trustees of the American Heritage Foundation," Records of the American Heritage Foundation, National Archives and Records Administration II, College Park, MD, box 17.
4. "Remarks by Winthrop W. Aldrich in Connection with the Inauguration of the Freedom Train, Grand Central Terminal, New York, Wednesday, September 24, 1947," in Winthrop W. Aldrich Collection, Baker Library, Harvard Business School, Boston, "American Heritage Foundation, September 1947" folder, box 19.
5. Robert N. Bellah, "Civil Religion in America," *Daedalus* 96 (Winter 1967): 1–21, 8, 4.
6. See, for example, Jason Fredrick Earle, "The McGuffey Readers and Civil Religion, 1918–1963" (PhD diss., University of Minnesota, 1995); Maaheen Ahmed and Martin Lund, "'We're All Avengers Now': Community-Building, Civil Religion and Nominal Multiculturalism in Marvel Comics' Fear Itself," *European Journal of*

American Culture 35 (2016): 77–95; Jeremy Bites, "Captain America: Civil Religion (and Why Donald Trump Thinks He's Batman)," *Religion Dispatches*, May 20, 2016, http://religiondispatches.org; J. Ronald Engel, "Sacred Sands: The Civil Religion of the Indiana Dunes," *Landscape* 25, no. 1 (1981): 1; Sallie McFague, "Toward a New Cascadian Civil Religion of Nature," in *Cascadia: The Elusive Utopia*, ed. Douglas Todd (Vancouver: Ronsdale Press, 2008), 157–72; Douglas Todd, "Environmentalism: The New Civil Religion," *Vancouver Sun*, March 3, 2007; Christopher H. Evans and William R. Herzog II, eds., *The Faith of 50 Million: Baseball, Religion and American Culture* (Louisville, KY: Westminster John Knox Press, 2002), 13–34; Craig A. Forney, *The Holy Trinity of American Sports: Civil Religion in Football, Baseball and Basketball* (Macon, GA: Mercer University Press, 2007).

7 Prof. Mac McCorkle is quoted in "NCAA Turns Up Pressure on North Carolina over Bathroom Law," *Charlotte Observer*, September 13, 2016.

8 Wall, *Inventing the "American Way,"* 224.

9 Will Herberg, "America's Civil Religion: What It Is and Whence It Came," in *American Civil Religion*, ed. Russell E. Richey and Donald G. Jones (New York: Harper & Row, 1974), 77.

10 Bellah, "Civil Religion in America," 4.

11 Jon Butler, "Jack-in-the-Box Faith: The Religion Problem in Modern American History," *Journal of American History* 90 (March 2004): 1359.

12 See, for example, Doug Rossinow, *The Politics of Authenticity: Liberalism, Christianity, and the New Left in America* (New York: Columbia University Press, 1998); Mary Lethert Wingerd, *Claiming the City: Politics, Faith, and the Power of Place in St. Paul* (Ithaca, NY: Cornell University Press, 2001); Evelyn Savidge Sterne, *Ballots and Bibles: Ethnic Politics and the Catholic Church in Providence* (Ithaca, NY: Cornell University Press, 2003); David L. Chappell, *A Stone of Hope: Prophetic Religion and the Death of Jim Crow* (Chapel Hill: University of North Carolina Press, 2003); Seth Jacobs, *America's Miracle Man in Vietnam: Ngo Dinh Diem, Religion, Race, and U.S. Intervention in Southeast Asia, 1950–1957* (Durham, NC: Duke University Press, 2004); William Inboden III, *Religion and American Foreign Policy, 1945–1960: The Soul of Containment* (New York: Cambridge University Press, 2008); Bethany Moreton, *To Serve God and Wal-Mart: The Making of Christian Free Enterprise* (Cambridge, MA: Harvard University Press, 2009); Darren Dochuk, *From Bible Belt to Sunbelt: Plain Folk Religion, Grassroots Politics, and the Rise of Evangelical Conservatism* (New York: Norton, 2010); Andrew Preston, *Sword of the Spirit, Shield of Faith: Religion in American War and Diplomacy* (New York: Knopf, 2012); and Elizabeth Fones-Wolf and Ken Fones-Wolf, *Struggle for the Soul of the Postwar South: White Evangelical Protestants and Operation Dixie* (Urbana: University of Illinois Press, 2015).

13 Jonathan P. Herzog, *The Spiritual-Industrial Complex: America's Religious Battle Against Communism in the Early Cold War* (Oxford: Oxford University Press, 2011), 32, 179. Herzog's second reference is also in scare quotes.

14 Kevin M. Kruse, *One Nation Under God: How Corporate America Invented Christian America* (New York: Basic Books, 2015). Kruse argues that conservative corporate leaders, seeking to roll back what they saw as the "creeping state socialism" of the New Deal, promoted an ideology of "Christian libertarianism."
15 Herzog, *Spiritual-Industrial Complex*, 226.
16 The following discussion of this epoch draws heavily from my book *Inventing the "American Way."*
17 I develop this argument further in Wendy L. Wall, "Symbol of Unity, Symbol of Pluralism": The 'Interfaith Idea' in Wartime and Cold War America," in *Making the American Century: Essays on the Political Culture of Twentieth Century America*, ed. Bruce J. Schulman (New York: Oxford University Press, 2014), 171–87.
18 For a detailed account of the role Catholics and Jews played in creating a "Protestant-Catholic-Jewish" America, see Kevin M. Schultz, *Tri-Faith America: How Catholics and Jews Held Postwar America to Its Protestant Promise* (New York: Oxford University Press, 2013).
19 Will Herberg, *Protestant-Catholic-Jew: An Essay in American Religious Sociology*, rev. ed. (1955; Garden City, NY: Anchor Books, 1960), 72–98, esp. 81–82. Although Herberg did not use the term "civil religion" in his 1955 book, he did employ it in his 1974 essay "America's Civil Religion: What It Is and Whence It Comes."
20 Bellah, "Civil Religion in America," 12, 14. For an insightful discussion of the differences between Herberg and Bellah, see Ronit Y. Stahl, "A Jewish America and a Protestant Civil Religion: Will Herberg, Robert Bellah, and Religious Identity in Mid-Twentieth Century America," *Religions* 6, no. 2 (2015): 434–50.
21 Robert Wuthnow, *The Restructuring of American Religion: Society and Faith since World War II* (Princeton, NJ: Princeton University Press, 1988), 244.
22 Arthur Remillard, *Southern Civil Religions: Imagining the Good Society in the Post-Reconstruction Era* (Athens: University of Georgia Press, 2011), 1.
23 Bellah, "Civil Religion in America," 13.
24 Wuthnow, *Restructuring of American Religion*, 241–67.
25 I owe this observation to George Marsden, "The Great Divide," *Reviews in American History*, (June 1989): 286.
26 This has started to change in recent years. As the field of diplomatic history has evolved into the field of "the United States and the world," practitioners have begun to pay increasing attention to non-state actors.
27 Preston, *Sword of the Spirit*, 14; Raymond Haberski Jr., *God and War: American Civil Religion since 1945* (New Brunswick, NJ: Rutgers University Press, 2012). William Inboden III also uses the term repeatedly in *Religion and American Foreign Policy*.
28 The phrase "sacred canopy" comes from Peter L. Berger, *The Sacred Canopy: Elements of a Sociological Theory of Religion* (Garden City, NY: Doubleday, 1967), but it has been used by many scholars to describe civil religion.
29 Wall, *Inventing the "American Way,"* 3–4.
30 Wall, *Inventing the "American Way,"* 209–16.

31 Wall, *Inventing the "American Way,"* 216–17; Margretta S. Lawler's letter to the editor, *St. Louis Globe-Democrat*, June 13, 1948; Mrs. R. Raney's letter to the editor, *Courier-News* (Bridgewater, NJ), November 20, 1947; letter to the editor of the *Press and Sun-Bulletin* (Binghamton, NY) by "American," November 10, 1947; Pastor Wheaton Phelps Webb's letter to the editor, *Press and Sun-Bulletin*, November 12, 1947.
32 Wall, *Inventing the "American Way,"* 227–39.
33 Wall, *Inventing the "American Way,"* 217–18.
34 Wuthnow, *Restructuring of American Religion*, 241.
35 Daniel T. Rodgers, *Contested Truths: Keywords in American Politics since Independence* (New York: Basic Books, 1987), 8.
36 For a recent example of this, see Philip Gorski, *American Covenant: A History of Civil Religion from the Puritans to the Present* (Princeton, NJ: Princeton University Press, 2017).
37 I have borrowed the term "cultural conversation" from R. W. B. Lewis, who used it in *The American Adam: Innocence, Tragedy and Tradition in the Nineteenth Century* (Chicago: University of Chicago Press, 1955), 2–3. "A culture," Lewis wrote, "achieves identity not so much through the ascendancy of one particular set of convictions as through the emergence of its peculiar and distinctive dialogue."
38 Lewis Mumford Jones quoted in Richard Pells, *Radical Visions and American Dreams: Culture and Social Thought in the Depression Years* (New York: Harper & Row, 1973); James Truslow Adams, "The Ideas That Make Us a Nation," *New York Times Magazine*, November 24, 1940, 3.
39 Claude S. Fischer and Michael Hout, *Century of Difference: How America Changed in the Last One Hundred Years* (New York: Russell Sage Foundation, 2006), 193–94.
40 Both Adams and Bellah wrote during what historian David Hollinger has called "the great immigration interregnum" that followed the adoption of draconian immigration restrictions in the 1920s. During that period the proportion of Americans born abroad declined precipitously. The Immigration Act of 1965, which ended this interregnum, did not take effect until June 30, 1968.
41 Bellah, "Civil Religion in America," 18.
42 Danielle Allen, *Our Declaration: A Reading of the Declaration of Independence in Defense of Equality* (New York: Liveright, 2014), 34, 138.
43 Allen, *Our Declaration*, 31–32, 35.

7

Uncle Sam, the Statue of Liberty, and Images of National Identity

RHYS H. WILLIAMS

There are many ways in which the concept of "civil religion" and the debates around it are about national identity. The interesting question is not "does a civil religion exist?" but rather "what kind of society is the United States?" If the nation has a special relationship to the Divine, what is required, in terms of collective action, by this faith? To what extent is this a "Christian nation"? And if so—or if not—how can it best realize its special status in domestic and foreign policy?

It is also true, and no surprise, that in the United States the politics of immigration—both historically and currently—are also largely a debate about American national identity.[1] Who should be allowed to come here? Who has the potential to become an "American"? While the basis of national belonging in the American popular imagination has often varied among such statuses as religion, race, national origin, and skin color, the fundamental question of "who belongs" has been central to political contention about immigration and immigrants, whether in the 1850s, the 1920s, or the 2000s.

Thus, it is interesting that in Robert Bellah's original article on civil religion, and in the many articles and books developing, disputing, emending, and extending the concept, consideration of immigration and its place in national discourse and political contention rarely occurs.[2] It is perhaps not surprising that Bellah's article itself did not engage immigration in any particular fashion. His piece was published in 1967, so he was writing at the very end of the longest period of low immigration in the nation's history. In the early 1920s, several pieces of legislation, culminating in the National Origins Act of 1924, drastically curtailed immigration to the United States compared to the half century before. The legislation was designed to limit the number of immigrants coming to the United States from Southern and Eastern Europe and from Asia (most of which had been curtailed prior to 1920) and to promote, if anything, migrants from Northern and Western Europe. Due to the barring of people who wanted to come to the United States and favoring those who were less interested in immigrating, immigration numbers dropped dramatically. They did not pick up again until after the 1965 passage of the Hart-Celler Act (officially the Immigration and Nationality Act of 1965) that removed the national quota system. Immigration to the United States since 1970 has both increased significantly and shifted in region of origin from Europe to Asia and Latin America.

Rather than a focus on immigration, the mid- to late 1960s political scene in which Bellah originally wrote was roiled by the civil rights movement and its very active segregationist opponents and the Vietnam War and its opposition. Moreover, the nation had elected its first Roman Catholic president a few years earlier, on the heels of Will Herberg's ode to a convergent American unity, *Protestant-Catholic-Jew*.[3] It was not unusual or particularly unreasonable to think that religious prejudice, which had animated so much nativist politics in the late nineteenth and early twentieth centuries, was declining in the United States, and thus not the most pressing of national concerns.

However, the first decade and a half of the twenty-first century is a different period. Contention about immigration has again arisen, as have dramatic increases in religious and ethnic diversity. Immigrants from Asia, Africa, and the Middle East have brought numbers of Muslims, Hindus, and Buddhists heretofore unknown in the United States. And the politics have changed. Whereas immigration used to be thought of as a political issue marked by "cross-cutting cleavages" (i.e., attitudes toward immigration policy did not align cleanly with partisan political identity, with both Republicans and Democrats having both pro- and anti-immigration factions), in the past few years the polarization that has been so evident in other political issues has also reshaped immigrant debates.[4] Statements about immigration and immigrants made by Republican presidents Ronald Reagan and George H. W. Bush are now often used by Democrats to show how much the GOP has changed its orientation. Whether this counts as hypocrisy by Republicans is open to dispute, but it is indisputable that one would not hear Reagan's or Bush's statements welcoming immigrants in a Republican primary campaign now. Alongside the continuing saliency of political conflicts that have their roots in the cultural contention of the 1960s and 1970s, immigration is now a hot-button issue.

Interestingly, the political polarization many call a "culture war" may well be the reason for a resurgence of interest in the civil religion concept—scholars wonder what bases of national cohesion might remain in a national political culture that seems utterly contentious. That contention leads many scholars to question the existence of civil religion. If civil religion is conceptualized as a unifying force that brings a shared sense of the sacred to the nation, but we live in a country so divided by race, religion, gender, and politics, does a civil religion really exist?

There is very little documentation for *a* civil religion in the way Bellah and many of those following him implied. However, there is "civil religious discourse" in American political culture and depictions of national identity.[5] That is, there are ways of talking about American national history, identity, and destiny that link the nation to a sense of the sacred, and these representations imbue the nation with a special status in the world and often require special responsibilities as well. These are what many have called the "legitimating myths" of the American nation; indeed, Bellah himself claimed that understanding America's sacred legitimating myths was his true interest in 1967, not the naming of another "religion" per se.[6]

These discursive myths, however, can offer radically different portrayals of what the nation is and should be and how it should live up to its status as providentially blessed. Here I contrast two legitimating myths—two stories of the American nation that Americans themselves use while proclaiming the United States an "exceptional" nation. I do so by focusing on the deployment of two icons of U.S. identity, Uncle Sam and the Statue of Liberty, to show how differently they represent the nation and how differently they are used when they are employed to express ideas about immigration and national identity.

Political Contention about Immigration in 2006

This chapter uses political cartoons to illustrate these two national myths, specifically cartoons that were published around the political contention over immigration in 2006. The Border Protection, Antiterrorism, and Illegal Immigration Control Act of 2005 (HR 4437) was passed by the Republican-controlled House of Representatives in December 2005 (basically along party lines); it became known as the Sensenbrenner Bill after its major sponsor in the House, James Sensenbrenner (R-WI). Two features of the bill were notable. First was that the bill was overwhelmingly oriented toward curtailing, apprehending, and punishing "illegal" immigration—that is, those immigrants in the United States without documented legal authority. Second, along with items such as a border fence, the bill included significant legal penalties, including some felonies, for anyone aiding undocumented persons while they are in this country.

The Senate never passed the bill, President George W. Bush was tepid in his response to it, and it never became law. But it sparked an outpouring of protest in the spring of 2006 and elevated immigration to the center of national political contention. Of course, this controversy was not brand new; issues regarding immigration, particularly undocumented immigration, had been gaining attention for a while, with several attempts by Republican administrations to control it (such as the 1986 Immigration Reform and Control Act). In 1994, Californians passed Proposition 187, which denied public services such as schooling and health care to undocumented immigrants and made immigration issues increasingly visible.[7]

These rising political tensions really flared after the House passed the Sensenbrenner Bill and the publicity surrounding it. There were major protest marches against the bill in Chicago, Los Angeles, and Dallas on March 10, March 25, and April 10, 2006. In response to this mobilization, many immigrant advocacy groups declared May 1, 2006, a "day without an immigrant" and encouraged undocumented immigrants and those who supported them to abstain from buying anything and to skip work or school. The intention was both to show the American public that their economy is helped by immigrants, including the undocumented, and to demonstrate general opposition to punitive immigration reform efforts. The protest marches on May 1 involved well over one million people in major cities including Los Angeles, New York, Chicago, and Dallas, along with smaller events in most states, most prominently in Pennsylvania, Virginia, and North Carolina. Crowds in Los Angeles were estimated at six hundred thousand, and in Chicago an estimated four hundred thousand attended. Not all the organizations in the immigrant rights movement supported the boycott/strike, and the effect the day had on the economy is largely unknown. But the events sparked a real uptick in immigration controversy as a political issue and helped contribute to the increasing polarization of the issue.

I use this short period of highly public political contention on immigration as a way to explore important national myths that explain why the United States is a definable, distinct, and morally admirable society. Within immigration discourse are representations of two distinct civil religious discourses—two approaches to American national identity and two approaches to thinking about the good society that inform our national self-understanding. The point is what the subtext of immigration rhetoric says about Americans' assumptions about what it takes for the nation to be a "good society," and thus how immigration is a dimension of our civil religion.

Using Imagery in Understanding Civil Religion

This chapter draws on public political claims made after the passage of the Sensenbrenner Bill in December 2005 until just after the two main immigrant rights protest events, in March and May 2006. All the cartoons presented here were syndicated and distributed in U.S. newspapers during that period. I treat the cartoons as rhetoric in the classic sense that they are forms of language—symbolic expression—meant to persuade others. In trying to persuade others, the cartoonists use language and pictorial symbols that they expect to be understood and to be persuasive to others. They assume a certain amount of "resonance" between the images they employ and the audiences for their claims.[8] It may be true that the arguments, claims, and symbols used by an advocate fall upon deaf ears and are not particularly persuasive to anyone. Whether the rhetorics illustrated here actually work in persuasion is an empirical question, not addressed here. The point is that public claims by political actors are believed to be fairly easily understood and thus potentially persuasive.

Because of my concern with depictions of American national identity and its connections to immigration politics, I specifically chose cartoons that employed either Uncle Sam or the Statue of Liberty. Many other cartoons from this period referenced immigration, and it is easy to find political cartoons that use Uncle Sam or Lady Liberty regarding many social issues. These cartoons do both because the cartoonists were using those two symbols as representations of the nation, and how those figures were portrayed relative to the issue at hand was a way of commenting on the relative "Americanness" of the political stances they represent. The cartoonists were trying to say something about which political stances they represent on immigration were the truly "American" position to take and which ones, in contrast, were a violation of the nation's core identity.

The connections between art, other imagery, and national identity have been analyzed by many scholars,[9] although sociology has generally not incorporated visual imagery into its work systematically. One notable exception was William Gamson's use of political cartoons to explore political attitudes and opinions, but he did not focus on the images themselves.[10] Howard Becker asks clearly a question that can vex sociology: "How do you use photographs and films to elaborate an argument and how do you deploy them as evidence for the argument you want to make?"[11] The methodological considerations involved in "visual sociology" focus on how and when images are convincing evidence.[12] What makes for good visual sociology—as opposed to what makes something a "good photograph" in an artistic or craft sense—is still developing. Images are evocative and multivocal, and they can communicate a great deal quite parsimoniously, but what they communicate can range widely. The messages may themselves be ambiguous, unclear, and primarily emotional. That is one of the reasons that images are so effective in political communication; they can transmit several potential meanings quite evocatively, and their emotional impact sticks with viewers.

All that said, the use of pictorial images to explore social issues, in this case immigration or American identity, is not unknown. Two examples deserve particular mention. Sociologist Leo Chavez studied the images used on magazine covers from 1965 to 1999 that dealt specifically with immigration.[13] His book is organized in part chronologically in that several chapters focus on particular time periods and show either developments in the period or how the cover images were responding to particular events (such as California's 1994 Proposition 187). Other chapters explore the varied images that are used recurringly, some of them consistently enough to be labeled "icons." This results in what Chavez calls a "discourse on immigration and the nation." In these images, not surprisingly, the Statue of Liberty makes many appearances; interestingly, Uncle Sam makes very few.

A more ambitious effort in scope is historian David Hackett Fischer's "visual history of America's founding ideas," focused on the concepts of liberty and freedom.[14] It is organized chronologically and makes use of all types of images, from photographs to posters, magazine covers, public monuments, and fine art. Given the focus on liberty, the statue makes many appearances, only some of them about immigration. Uncle Sam is a consistent feature as well, but generally not about immigration.

The cartoons presented here illustrate the immigration debate and go beyond that to make implicit comments about the nature of American society. They use two well-known icons, Uncle Sam and the Statue of Liberty, as stand-ins for what are presented to be the core values or character of the nation. In each of the cartoons, either Lady Liberty or Uncle Sam is presented in some "distress"—that is, not in complete control of the situation, or actually chagrined, or in a situation where their treatment is being presented as somehow "un-American." The inference is that the harm being done to the icon in the cartoon is a harm being done to the nation and, further, that it is a harm to some fundamental, essentially valued, property of the nation.

In this way, the images are a civil religious discourse. There is something jarring about the presentation of either figure in a way that is transgressive. This can be seen regularly in political cartoons using these two national icons. For example, an image of Uncle Sam that appeared in a cartoon protesting the first Gulf War in the early 1990s showed him mainlining an injection into his forearm like a heroin addict—with a gasoline hose as a needle. Or a recent issue of the German magazine *Der Spiegel* showed President Donald Trump with a huge bloody knife and holding the severed head of the Statue of Liberty, while other recent cartoons show President Trump grabbing Lady Liberty in a form of sexual assault that became notorious during the 2016 presidential campaign when tapes from an interview with the TV program *Access Hollywood* revealed Trump bragging about sexually grabbing women without their consent. While few would make a claim of "blasphemy" about these images, what they say about the country and the events in question is troubling; the images themselves are deeply uncomfortable. How Uncle Sam and the Statue of Liberty are portrayed are clear messages about how we as a nation are or should be. Presentations of such well-known images of the nation are deliberate (if in varying degrees of self-consciousness) attempts to say something about contemporary politics in a way that speaks to our core values and the essence of U.S. national identity. They are recognizable and resonant images and work as representations because they are so deeply embedded in our vocabulary of collective self-understanding.

Images of American National Identity

Short genealogies of the two icons of American national identity will help establish the semiotic shorthand that has developed around each of these representations of the nation. These images/icons by their very nature reduce our collective history and identity into a coherent "oneness"—a unified "personality" that Mary Douglas called a "condensation symbol."[15] They condense a history, and a potential variety of meanings and ideas, into a "whole." Their very being as single embodied figures gives a oneness to the nation and reduces its internal diversity, variation, and differences. Thus, the very use of either Uncle Sam or the Statue of Liberty "produces" a unity of national existence—in much the way one of the defining characteristics of civil religion is its function of providing national unity.[16]

Uncle Sam, United and Resolute

Uncle Sam first arose in association with the military and war efforts in the early national period in the nineteenth century (there is a common story that Samuel Wilson of Troy, New York, supplied food to the army in the War of 1812 and is often credited with being the Sam referred to; there are also reasons to doubt that specific connection). He arose alongside, and finally supplanted, another personification of the United States, Brother Jonathon. Brother Jonathan began as an image associated with Puritans in England in the seventeenth century and became connected to New England and its Yankee residents by the mid-to-late eighteenth century (including during the American War of Independence). Brother Jonathan was portrayed with a stovepipe hat and striped trousers (as was Uncle Sam later) and by the nineteenth century was associated enough with the United States so that British soldiers during the Napoleonic era referred to American troops as "Jonathans."[17]

Uncle Sam became increasingly widespread after 1865 and finally emerged in 1916 in the form with which we are so familiar (by artist James Montgomery Flagg, who used his own face in the World War I recruitment poster), indelibly associated with military (and other) recruitment efforts. During the first half of the nineteenth century, both Brother Jonathan and Uncle Sam were in use, but there is evidence they had different meanings. Winifred Morgan finds that Brother Jonathan was often thought of as a representation of the nation itself, while Uncle Sam represented the national government and its power (perhaps given its various connections to the military).[18] Interestingly, there is evidence that in the Know Nothing nativist movement in the 1850s there was an internal division between the "Jonathans" and the "Sams"; the latter were seen as more radical in their approach to politics and immigration and thus more anti-immigrant.[19] After the Civil War, Brother Jonathan began to recede in media and popular consciousness, finally wholly supplanted by Uncle Sam.

During war efforts, and generally with regard to military matters, the nation is often depicted as unified, coherent, and determined, with an aura of shared sacrifice and purpose. In these cases, Uncle Sam often has an almost belligerent resolve, and over time one can see depictions of him become increasingly muscular and less lanky (Sam also became significantly taller than Brother Jonathan was usually portrayed). Of course, no symbol or icon is univocal; numerous uses and interpretations are possible. But it is precisely the dominant use of the image that provides the interpretive frame and communicative power for those using it in other situations and for other meanings. The dominant reading of a symbol sets the terms for readings that are against the grain. Uncle Sam's history and common representation as militant, muscular, determined, and in control make it all the more eye-catching when he is presented in distress. The important point is that the America represented by Uncle Sam imagery is unified and (usually resolute). He is a representation of the nation as a whole, the United States as a nation in the sociological sense of a country where the inhabitants are marked by their "peoplehood"; there is the sense that Americans are a single people, a coherent collective. In this regard, Uncle Sam regularly is portrayed in contradistinction to people from other nations—often themselves represented as single images (for example, England's John Bull or the Russian bear) or others portrayed as a group or type of person (such as, for example, immigrants).

The Statue of Liberty—Home to All

The Statue of Liberty embodies a different, but also a deep, theme within American collective identity and national mythology (in the anthropological sense). That *mythos* is about America as a "nation of immigrants," a "land of opportunity" in which people—who are often the underprivileged or the persecuted—from other nations can find liberty and a new life. The Statue of Liberty thus often signals an American nation connected to the world but different from other nations, an America having ties to elsewhere but also embodying a new world marked by diversity. Specifically, the reference conjures those who have traveled from all over to form a new life, as well as a new nation.

The first significant point in the statue's symbolism is its placement. The statue was a gift from France for the U.S. centennial (1876) and was placed in New York Harbor in 1886. By that time, New York was fifty years into being the United States' largest city and busiest shipping port—making it the principal connection to the Eastern Hemisphere. Note that the statue was not placed outside Washington, D.C., Philadelphia, or Boston—all cities that in other periods, or for other reasons, could have been seen as *the* American city. Significantly, next to the Statue of Liberty is Ellis Island, from 1892 to 1954 a place for processing new immigrants to this country and which opened just six years after Liberty was erected. Of course, immigrants entered the country through many other cities and processing centers—notably Angel Island in San Francisco Bay—but the combination of Ellis Island and the statue made New York Harbor the most symbolically rich representation of that part of American history. Images of boats full of new immigrants passing under the raised arm of the Statue of Liberty and disembarking on Ellis Island are so common they are often represented as *the* story of immigration to the United States. The statue was placed symbolically at what became America's "front door" to the world, or at least to Europe.

A second way in which the Statue of Liberty has become connected to America's immigrant history is through the sonnet "The New Colossus" by poet Emma Lazarus, which is on a plaque on the base of the statue, added in 1893. The poem has several notable features. It was written specifically for the statue as part of a contest to celebrate and support fundraising to erect the statue. It specifically mentions welcoming newcomers who are disadvantaged but hopeful in life—the "tired," "poor," and "huddled masses yearning to breathe free." And the sonnet distinctly distances this statue and the United States' "golden door" from the old world and its conceptions of nationhood. From the sonnet's opening line ("Not like the brazen giant of Greek fame [the Colossus of Rhodes], / With conquering limbs astride . . ."), through the line describing the statue/nation as being the "Mother of Exiles," to the exclamation to "Keep, ancient lands, your storied pomp!" the sonnet separates the United States and its new world from the old. The nation is new, welcoming, and a place for common people and those without a national home. One implication is that European notions of nationhood—often connected to blood and land—are less relevant to the United States, as everyone has come from elsewhere to begin anew.

Thus, deep in this national icon and the story the image constructs is a narrative of freedom, opportunity, new beginnings, and a welcome to immigrants. An important implication of this argument, and deeply connected to the icon of Lady Liberty herself, is that of individual liberty, representing a land where people are free to make choices and even to become new persons.

The statue was not initially meant to have particular significance as a welcome to immigrants or to identify the United States as a nation of immigrants. Historically in French art, Liberty has often been depicted as a female figure, as in Delacroix's famous 1830 painting *Liberty Leading the People*, portraying France's 1830 revolution. Similarly, the French Republic is often represented as Marianne. The United States has also been represented somewhat similarly as a woman, in the form of Columbia (who also appears in a flowing robe/tunic, often with one arm held in the air, holding a torch). In each of these cases, the female figure represents liberty from tyranny, in a classical liberal sense. Indeed, little commented upon are the broken chains that lay by Lady Liberty's feet—an allusion to the recent end to slavery in the United States. As noted, the statue itself was a centennial present from France, representing the two nations' shared histories of republican revolutions in the name of a universal, rights-based, "Enlightenment-influenced" liberty.

Thus, a claim sometimes made by contemporary anti-immigration activists that the Statue of Liberty was not *originally* intended to celebrate immigration is technically correct. However, the connections between the Statue of Liberty, American national identity, and immigration developed within the first decade of the statue's existence in the United States and have been consistently employed ever since. The late 1880s marked a reacceleration of immigration to the United States, as new populations of Eastern and Southern Europeans came here to work in the expanding factories of the industrializing North and Upper Midwest. Indeed, the hegemony of Lady Liberty and Ellis Island as symbols of immigration is such that many Americans have never heard of Angel Island, a major intake center for Asian immigrants in San Francisco Bay.

The overarching point about the representations of Uncle Sam and the Statue of Liberty is that uses of the two images—and thus in many ways the images themselves—reveal two stories about American society and its national identity, particularly as that identity is relevant to issues of diversity, inclusion, and pluralism. And they are two different ways of representing when or how the nation is in danger, is acting honorably, or is acting in ways that require reform. They represent competing cultural myths of our national identity and form differing "visions of the good society."[20]

Immigration Discourse in the Current Issue Culture

Debate over immigration is not new in American politics, but neither is it always a hot political issue. Public political concerns about immigration emerge when (1) there are economic pressures or national security "events"; (2) there are highly visible immigrant "others" around whom suspicions of threat can be raised; and (3) a political group or groups are in a position to benefit from making immigration an issue. It is worth noting that the terrain upon which the issue is debated changes with the times. In certain historical periods immigrants' religious differences have been emphasized, and at other periods the racial composition of immigrants and the supposed qualities and characteristics of cultural groups have been center stage.[21]

The concerns with immigration since the mid-1990s have circled around four basic themes: (1) security, terrorism, and control of borders; (2) economic effects of immigrants, particularly on "American" workers; (3) environmental effects of increased population growth in the United States; and (4) cultural integration and diversity. More recently there has been a fifth concern, (5) an influx of new voters who will be disproportionately Democrats.[22] There are ways in which these themes are intertwined, although some of them have rather distinct constituencies (e.g., those concerned with environmental impact rarely make claims about national security or terrorism). And many scholars find underlying themes of ethnonationalism and racism in all these claims. But whatever the specific content of positions on immigration policies or whether the concern is about particular groups of immigrants, the focus here is on how any rationale is *undergirded by an implicit message about American national identity and our cultural stories about what makes America a good and moral society*. Discussions of immigration—whether calls to restrict newcomers or defenses of immigrant rights and contributions to the body politic—are informed by a moral vision of what constitutes the "good society" and how the United States should embody that ideal. Thus, there are both moral and collective identity arguments that accompany the specific political positions on immigrants and immigration. When people debate who should be able to immigrate to the United States, they are making statements about whom Americans are as a people—and that has obvious racial, ethnic, cultural, and religious dimensions. But beyond that identification, when people debate the effects of immigration or whether it is basically a good or bad thing (distinct from whom the immigrants are), they are tapping into deep streams of American political culture that offer moral visions of what kind of nation we are and what type of society we should be.

Images and Themes from 2005–6

As noted above, in early 2006 immigration became a high-profile political issue following the House's attempt to make being in this country without legal documentation a felony (it was not then and is not now) and, moreover, to punish criminally anyone in this country who might help undocumented immigrants. Those proposed bills, and the ensuing marches and political debate, have been the source of scholarly study.[23] Further, this appears in retrospect to have been a real jump in making immigration the hot-button issue that it is now, particularly the concern with undocumented immigrants and "illegal" immigration.[24] The themes illustrated here continue to be vibrant and visible.

Using the Statue of Liberty

Using the Statue of Liberty in political cartoons during the controversy about the Sensenbrenner Bill portrays aspects of the bill as an ironic and unfortunate break with national history and a violation of core American principles of openness and diversity.

Thus the image and cartoons reference a national mythology about being a "new nation" of welcome and opportunity. In three of the four cartoons discussed here, the words of Emma Lazarus's poem are juxtaposed with symbols of, or reference to, crime and law enforcement—but law enforcement as potentially oppressive and unfair, not as a system protecting all equally. In Figure 7.1, cartoonist Ben Sargent mocks the Sensenbrenner Bill with a sarcastic rendering of a police officer bringing Lady Liberty into the station, presumably as an arrested criminal. The arresting officer reads the poem's last verse, not knowing its origins, and clearly thinks it both strange and unlawful. The sergeant responds by accusing the figure of the statue of conspiring with felons (the word given added emphasis) for trying to live up to the words written on the plaque—or even just holding such ideals as important. Notably, Liberty's torch, the "golden lamp" that has been a beacon to peoples of the world, has been extinguished and smokes in her hands. Those supporting the criminalization of immigrants are actually punishing the nation, the cartoon implies, and do so out of an ignorance of the nation's identity and with a suspicion of others.

Tony Auth's cartoon in the *Philadelphia Inquirer* from March 28, 2006 (not reprinted here), associates the move to criminalize immigration with an allusion to prison walls. The cartoon depicts a concrete / cinder block wall, with strands and rings of barbed wire along the top. On the wall is a

Figure 7.1. Ben Sargent, *Austin American-Statesman*, March 28, 2006. Reprinted with permission.

sign that reads, "Give me your tired, your poor. . . ." The welcoming phrase from Lazarus's poem is not identified directly but is instantly recognizable and forms an abrupt contrast with the forbidding wall—marking the wall and its attitude as not in keeping with American principles. Auth does not put the phrase in quotation marks, potentially indicating that it is less a quotation than it is an established principle of American life that needs no adjudication or specific reference. The figure of the Statue of Liberty itself is not needed to identify that national story with this contemporary situation. An interesting question, given the brick-and-barbed-wire barrier, is whether these tired and poor are being kept in as with a prison or kept out as with a border wall. That both could be true makes the image particularly effective. The prescience for how central a physical border wall has become in the imagery associated with immigration politics since 2016 and the extent to which the Immigration and Customs Enforcement (ICE) agency's detention camps under the Trump administration kept undocumented migrants in barbed-wire camps is a bit eerie.

Figure 7.2. Mike Luckovich, *Atlanta Journal-Constitution*, May 15, 2006. Reprinted with permission.

Other examples are equally telling. On May 15, 2006, just two weeks after the massive May Day immigration rights marches, Mike Luckovich published a cartoon in the *Atlanta Journal-Constitution*. Its imagery is simple and even explained by one of the characters in the cartoon. The statue lies on her side, right on the U.S.-Mexican border, instantly being transformed from a symbol of welcome to a physical barrier to travel. On the clearly labeled Mexican side of the statue, one sombrero-clad person says to another, "They turned her on her side and made her a fence." While drawn in 2006, the cartoon also foreshadows the idea of building a wall on the southern U.S. border. The people meant to be kept out in this cartoon are directly identified as Mexicans (unlike the general allusion to immigrants in the preceding examples).

This is notable, as ostensibly the debate over the House bill was not specifically about Mexican immigrants or the border with Mexico; certainly they were not singled out in the bill itself. And yet, much of the political debate at this time was about "illegal" immigrants, and for better or worse the issue of undocumented immigration has been particularly focused on Mexico.²⁵ Also, one particularly salient point of controversy regarding the pro-immigration marches in both March and May 2006 was the number of Mexican flags being carried by marchers. Conservative critics of the protests made many objections to Mexican flags at the March demonstrations, and some questioned the extent to which the marchers actually thought of themselves as "Americans" and hence whether they should be in this country. It was salient enough that many of the organizers of the May march made a point of emphasizing that people should bring U.S. flags (which were many and highly visible in the May events).

A final example of cartoons using the Statue of Liberty comes from July 12, 2006, as the controversy over immigration moved into high gear. Mike Keefe of the *Denver Post* comments on the state of Colorado's laws, passed in the late spring / early summer of 2006, that regulated public benefits for undocumented immigrants and required business employers to obtain proof of legal status of all their employees. Keefe uses the Statue of Liberty as a compassionate national image and makes allusion to Lazarus's words as if they are a presumed motto or principle of the United States. The statue's tablet has JULY IV MDCCLXXVI replaced with "Colorado claims toughest immigration laws," while Lady Liberty herself amends Lazarus's words by saying, "Speaking for 49 out of 50

Figure 7.3. Mike Keefe, *Denver Post*, July 12, 2006. Reprinted with permission.

states, give me your tired, your poor...." Colorado's claim, rather than being applauded in this image, seems instead to exempt the state from its belonging to the America that is represented by the statue and the poem. As with the other cartoons, Liberty is used to represent what is honorable and good about the United States; political actions that undermine her message are thus betrayals of that very identity.

Portraying Uncle Sam

Not all the editorial cartoons about immigration during the 2006 period that used Lady Liberty endorsed the idea that restricting or criminalizing immigration was necessarily a bad idea. The statue, in these representations, represents a nation that is overwhelmed and distressed by the recent conditions of immigration (Leo Chavez's work shows examples of this motif).[26] But a very common motif, when the United States is being portrayed as struggling to deal with immigrants and levels of immigration, is for the nation to be embodied by Uncle Sam—and that representation of the collective is then shown as being under duress.

As noted above, economic issues are a key rationale for many who think levels of immigration have gotten out of control. Whether the idea is that low-wage immigrant labor "steals jobs" from or "drives down wages" of native-born citizens or alternatively that immigrants "cost taxpayers' money for services" and thus are a public burden, economic themes are common. Several of the 2006 cartoons call attention to economic issues and immigration, but they do so with Uncle Sam, not the Statue of Liberty.

In Nick Anderson's April 2, 2006, cartoon for the *Houston Chronicle*, Uncle Sam stands astride an opening in a border—a border again signified by the fence that many now think should separate the United States from Mexico, and again a fence topped with barbed wire. Uncle Sam clearly announces that there is no welcome here; he towers above the fence and holds a "keep out" sign. Here is the image of a unitary, determined nation defending its turf. It is not clear why there is an opening in the fence, but Uncle Sam is firmly in its path. But a different message comes simultaneously from the figure marked "employers" who stands under Uncle Sam's legs, explicitly seeking workers, presumably immigrant labor. The impression is that Uncle Sam is being undermined by

Figure 7.4. Nick Anderson, *Houston Chronicle*, April 2, 2006. Reprinted with permission.

the business executive who stands in the opening formed by his legs, welcoming low-paid immigrants, despite official policy. Or is Uncle Sam perhaps not attuned to the reality of the American economy and its needs for labor? Is the critique here aimed at business or at Uncle Sam's lack of recognition of reality, or perhaps both? It is interesting that the employer figure strikes the identical pose as Uncle Sam, including the positioning of his legs. And his pants ride up in parallel with Uncle Sam's, including revealing his socks under similarly drawn shoes. Is Anderson drawing the two figures this way just for artistic design and coherence, or is this a comment about how business is undermining the "keep out" message but actually is very much like Uncle Sam—meaning perhaps that the "keep out" sign is a symbolic sham? In any case, it is not immigrants themselves who are at issue in this cartoon but rather what this reveals as a problem with immigration—that is, immigration issues are undermining the very unity and solidarity represented by Uncle Sam imagery.

Figure 7.5. Tony Auth, *Philadelphia Inquirer*, May 1, 2006. Reprinted with permission.

Tony Auth's May 1, 2006, cartoon—the day of the "strike" by immigrants—shows another take on the economics issues connected with immigration and does so with a confused and bumbling Uncle Sam at the border. He stands looking over a fence that obviously would not keep anyone out and is trying to speak some of Emma Lazarus's words in halting Spanish ("denme los fatigados, los pobres . . . por favor"). Here Uncle Sam shows unfamiliarity with Mexico, and perhaps immigration, but recognizes the extent to which the United States is dependent upon immigrant labor and is trying to be welcoming. However, a Mexican immigrant (marked with a sombrero-style hat) is already in the United States and is behind Uncle Sam, who seems unaware. Further, the immigrant is on a labor strike (as on May 1), with the sign written in Spanish. This furthers the sense that Uncle Sam does not have control over the situation and that his outreach to potential immigrants is failing—perhaps his willingness to welcome the stranger is being taken advantage of, or perhaps the immigrant himself is ungrateful for the opportunity he has and doesn't want to work hard. Interestingly, Uncle Sam here is clean-shaven, shorter, and more portly—more like Brother Jonathan was in the 1830s and 1840s. This is not the towering, if disconnected and unaware, figure of Nick Anderson's cartoon (Figure 7.4), but unimposing as well as ineffective. It increases the image of Uncle Sam being feeble—his feeble Spanish behind a feeble fence. He is not an imposing figure that would scare off any foreign enemies.

In a cartoon from April 27, 2006, just two days after some major pro-immigration marches, conservative cartoonist Glenn McCoy uses Uncle Sam to show a different problem with immigration (cartoon not reprinted here). In this depiction, Uncle Sam is in a school room teaching a class, labeled on the blackboard as "Assimilation 101." The room looks more like an elementary school classroom than a college classroom, with a pencil sharpener and a small American flag on the wall. The students, clearly from Mexico (one has a Mexican flag on the back of his shirt with the words, "Mexico—love it and leave it"), mangle the words to the national anthem by singing "José, can you see," substituting a common Spanish name for the anthem's opening words. Sam sits behind the teacher's desk with his head in his hand in the proverbial pose of the frustrated school teacher, and his thought bubble says, "I give up." It is interesting that Sam is teaching a class—trying to be helpful to immigrants rather than just forbidding. But this attempt to help appears fruitless. The class itself is one on assimilation—teaching immigrants how they should adapt to American life and culture, but it is "101," the most elementary, introductory-level course. And the use of specifically Mexican immigrants to illustrate the problem with Sam's approach is striking, the clear implication being that these students either cannot or will not assimilate. The image also subtly calls to mind the concerns many have that undocumented immigrants place burdens on school systems and that school systems are themselves failing the nation, especially in terms of integrating different groups within society. That Mexican immigrants are unwilling or unable to learn English and assimilate is a manifestly clear message and connects with the political activism in recent years that has called for English to be made the U.S. national language.

A final example is a June 17, 2006, cartoon by Olle Johansson (not reprinted here). It offers another view of Uncle Sam on the southern border (alluded to by saguaro cacti on the landscape). Again, the immigrant is represented as Mexican, with a sombrero and a large black mustache, and he dashes across a nonvisible border—a completely ineffectual boundary. As with the Anderson cartoon above (Figure 7.4),

Uncle Sam stands at the border and holds a sign with a forbidding command, in this case "stop" in bold black and red. And yet, again as in Figure 7.4, the immigrant runs through Uncle Sam's legs, heightening the sense of Sam being humiliated and shamed. Uncle Sam is not as directly distressed or befuddled as in some portrayals, in part because we see only the lower half of his body, again alluding to him as very tall. But that height is apparently a liability in understanding what is going on, literally, on the ground. He is clearly not in control of the border and is undermined as people go through his legs. Our society—our unified peoplehood—is under threat.

As noted above, Uncle Sam has no specific historical connection to the nation's immigrant story. Nonetheless, there are many nineteenth- and early twentieth-century cartoons that show him as threatened by or as a formidable barrier to unsavory examples of immigrants. He often guards the border, or stands on a coast by an ocean. On occasion, Uncle Sam is also portrayed as welcoming, a figure who would protect the vulnerable including those seeking to come to the country. Uncle Sam's origins in war mobilization make him a symbol of unity, militance, and tough-minded resolve toward the outside world. How easily the threat of immigration is shown as coming from the southern border and Mexico in these cartoons is notable, as is the consistent representation of Mexicans as small compared to Uncle Sam. Significantly, while the Mexicans may consistently be smaller than Uncle Sam, they are often fast and devious.

The American Good Society

As a result of a highly moralized political culture, American national identity is intimately tied to notions of the country as a "good society." The United States does not have a truly secular political language (e.g., secularist Marxian political language never generated widespread support in the United States). Arguably, it is the basic moral and ontological categories of Protestantism that still shape American public discourse and collective life. Even when American political discourse is not explicitly religious, it is deeply moralized, and for many Americans there seems to be little difference in that distinction.

Thus, not only does American political discourse contain visions of a general public good, or an idealized good society, as an assumption for politics and policy, these visions are connected to national identity. It may well be true that the United States is not alone in envisioning itself as a moral nation or articulating its national narrative in civil religious terms. But that does not negate the power of that notion in American politics and culture, nor is that a claim that all visions of the good society are similar, across societies.

The United States' particular history as a nation of peoples whose descendants left other homelands has made immigration integrally entwined with national identity. Almost all participants in the immigration debate would agree that national identity is a particular type of "accomplishment" for Americans and one that is in need of periodic reaccomplishment. For many Americans, in many periods of history, national identity has not *necessarily* been rooted in blood, race, or land—as is the case for so many societies that view themselves as "God's peoples." It is true that there are racialized versions of American identity that have left out people of color; those ideas can be countered by the argument that "anyone" can potentially become American. True, this idea often comes with assimilationist assumptions. But while not downplaying the central features of racism and racial exclusion in the United States, there have been historical periods when many American publics would reject the idea that national identity is something ascribed, inherited, and immutable.

American identity is often articulated both by everyday citizens and by scholars, as a matter of principles, ideas, or "American values." But the interpretation of those principles and values proceeds from, and often leads to, different notions of the good society, with different legitimating myths that make the nation exceptional. Is America a covenanted "people," connected by a culture, who must protect its own from the rest of a potentially dangerous world? Or is it a nation that is open, ever changing, and dynamic precisely *because* it has never limited itself to one people? Is it a place of "progress," where the individual dynamism that accompanies diversity produces a collective good? Are Americans' connections to other societies and cultures a matter of *heritage* that everyone must cast off (to some extent) for this nation to exist, or are those connections a matter of *identity*, in which many individual people and groups form a nation out of their vibrant interactions and fluidity?

Conceptions of the good society and national identity are the foundational building blocks of the immigration debate, just as they are foundational for other issues. "Who are we?," these conceptualizations ask, and "what kind of society do we want to have?" The answers to these questions can be civil religious in orientation, as they connect the nation's history and destiny to the transcendent. The questions, and their answers, often shape what Americans think is the appropriate stance toward worldly action. The answers get told in national stories that legitimate the nation as distinct, even special. They can legitimate the existing social order, or they can challenge the nation to become better than it is. They are the American civil religion in practice.

NOTES

1 One can see this argument, both explicitly and implicitly, in much recent research. See, for example, Carol M. Swain, ed., *Debating Immigration* (New York: Cambridge University Press, 2007); Daniel J. Tichenor, *Dividing Lines: The Politics of Immigration Control in America* (Princeton, NJ: Princeton University Press, 2002); Aristide R. Zolberg, *A Nation by Design: Immigration Policy in the Fashioning of America* (New York: Russell Sage Foundation, 2006); Peter Schrag, *Not Fit for Our Society: Immigration and Nativism in America* (Berkeley: University of California Press, 2010); David M. Reimers, *Unwelcome Strangers: American Identity and the Turn Against Immigration* (New York: Columbia University Press, 1998).

2 Robert N. Bellah, "Civil Religion in America," *Daedalus* 96 (1967): 1–21.

3 Will Herberg, *Protestant-Catholic-Jew: An Essay in the Sociology of Religion* (Garden City, NJ: Anchor Books, 1955).

4 Rhys H. Williams, "Immigration and National Identity in Obama's America: The Expansion of 'Culture Wars' Politics," *Canadian Review of American Studies* 42, no. 3 (2012): 322–46.

5 N. J. Demerath III and Rhys H. Williams, "Civil Religion in an Uncivil Society," *Annals of the American Academy of Political and Social Sciences* 480 (July 1985): 154–66.

6 Phillip E. Hammond, "Constitutional Faith, Legitimating Myth, Civil Religion," *Law & Social Inquiry* 14, no. 2 (1989): 377–91.

7 Robin Dale Jacobson, *The New Nativism: Proposition 187 and the Debate over Immigration* (Minneapolis: University of Minnesota Press, 2008). See also Lina Newton, *Illegal, Alien or Immigrant: The Politics of Immigration Reform* (New York: New York University Press, 2008).

8   Rhys H. Williams and Timothy J. Kubal, "Movement Frames and the Cultural Environment: Resonance, Failure, and the Boundaries of the Legitimate," *Research in Social Movements, Conflict, and Change* 21 (1999): 225–48.
9   Alison D. Howard and Donna R. Hoffman, "A Picture Is Worth a Thousand Words: Building American National Identity through Art," *Perspectives on Political Science* 42 (2013): 142–51.
10 William A. Gamson, *Talking Politics* (New York: Cambridge University Press, 1992).
11 Howard Becker, "Afterword: Photography as Evidence, Photographs as Exposition," in *Picturing the Social Landscape: Visual Methods and the Sociological Imagination*, ed. Caroline Knowles and Paul Sweetman (London: Routledge, 2004), 193–98, 196.
12 John R. Hall, Blake Stimson, and Lisa Tamiris Becker, eds., *Visual Worlds* (London: Routledge, 2005), 2. See also Becker, "Afterword"; Douglas Harper, *Visual Sociology* (New York: Routledge, 2012); Roman R. Williams, ed., *Seeing Religion: Toward a Visual Sociology of Religion* (New York: Routledge, 2015).
13 Leo R. Chavez, *Covering Immigration: Popular Images and the Politics of the Nation* (Berkeley: University of California Press, 2001).
14 David Hackett Fischer, *Liberty and Freedom: A Visual History of America's Founding Ideas* (New York: Oxford University Press, 2005).
15 Mary Douglas, *Natural Symbols* (London: Barrie & Rockliff, 1970).
16 Rhys H. Williams and Todd Nicholas Fuist, "Civil Religion in a Neoliberal Age," *Sociology Compass* 8, no. 7 (2014): 929–38.
17 Kenneth Hopper and William Hopper, *The Puritan Gift: Triumph, Collapse and Revival of an American Dream* (New York: I. B. Tauris, 2007), 63.
18 Winifred Morgan, *An American Icon: Brother Jonathan and American Identity* (Newark: University of Delaware Press, 1988), 81.
19 John P. Senning, W. W. Danenhower, Henry S. Jennings, and Buckner S. Morris, "The Know-Nothing Movement in Illinois 1854–1856: Read before the Illinois State Historical Society, Springfield, Illinois May 18, 1912," *Journal of the Illinois State Historical Society* 7, no. 1 (April 1914): 7–33.
20 Rhys H. Williams, "Visions of the Good Society and the Religious Roots of American Political Culture," *Sociology of Religion* 60, no. 1 (1999): 1–34.
21 Rhys H. Williams, "Religion and Immigration Post-1965: Race, Culture Wars, and National Identity," in *The Wiley-Blackwell Companion to Religion & Politics in the U.S.*, ed. Barbara A. McGraw (Malden, MA: Wiley-Blackwell, 2016), 278–90.
22 Janet Armitage, "The Immigration Reform Movement in the Contemporary United States: The Organization of a Movement" (PhD diss., Department of Sociology, Southern Illinois University, Carbondale, 2002). See also Swain, *Debating Immigration*; Rhys H. Williams and James C. Park, "'Some May Call It Racism, We Call It Stopping Immigration': Race in Immigration Reform Discourse" (paper, Eastern Sociological Society, Boston, 2006); Williams, "Immigration and National

Identity"; Ediberto Roman, *Those Damned Immigrants: America's Hysteria over Undocumented Immigration* (New York: New York University Press, 2013).

23 Stephen P. Davis, Juan R. Martinez, and R. Stephen Warner, "The Role of the Catholic Church in the Chicago Immigrant Mobilization," in *¡Marcha! Latino Chicago and the Immigrant Rights Movement*, ed. Amalia Pallares and Nilda Flores-González (Urbana: University of Illinois Press, 2010), 79–96; Otto Santa Ana and Sandra L. Treviño, "A May to Remember: Adversarial Images of Immigrants in U.S. Newspapers during the 2006 Policy Debate," *Du Bois Review* 4, no. 1 (2007): 1–26.

24 Williams, "Immigration and National Identity."

25 Evidence of this can be seen in public opinion polling. See Jeffery M. Timberlake and Rhys H. Williams, "Stereotypes of Immigrants from Four Global Regions," *Social Science Quarterly* 93, no. 4 (2012): 867–90.

26 Chavez, *Covering Immigration*.

8

George Washington, Miguel Hidalgo, and Transnational Civil Religion at the U.S.-Mexico Border

ELAINE A. PEÑA

George Washington and Miguel Hidalgo Must Embrace

Around ten o'clock the evening of Friday, February 19, 2010, a firefight between Los Zetas, one of northern Mexico's most powerful drug cartels, and Mexican law enforcement officers broke out underneath the Juárez-Lincoln International Bridge at the port of Laredo (Laredo, TX, USA and Nuevo Laredo, Tamaulipas, Mexico).[1] Soon after the news broke, a team of federal, municipal, and civil society actors from both sides of the border gathered in a secure location in Laredo to evaluate the situation. Although they were accustomed to meeting on a monthly basis as part of post-9/11 border security protocol, the gathering that evening was different. The 112th annual George Washington's Birthday Celebration—a century-spanning, cross-border tradition featuring an international parade, a carnival, a jalapeño eating contest, a Princess Pocahontas pageant, a Society of Martha Washington pageant, and a Noche Mexicana gala sponsored by the League of United Latin American Citizens (LULAC)—was in full swing. That very evening, Martha debutantes wearing jewel-encrusted colonial dresses were curtsying for a packed house of families and friends less than a couple of miles from the bridge. Moreover, hundreds of people had already set up camp just down the street from the international bridge to secure a good seat for the parade the next morning.

Those gathered at the emergency meeting had to map out how to proceed, and, most pressingly, to decide if the International Bridge Ceremony should go on as planned at seven o'clock the next morning. Staged between the United States and Mexico in the middle of the Juárez-Lincoln International Bridge, the ritual currently features the participation of child ambassadors, high-profile appointed and elected officials, law enforcement officers, clergy from both sides of the border, as well as two men portraying George Washington and Miguel Hidalgo, the men often called the "father of the nation" for the United States and Mexico, respectively (see Figure 8.1). Could international bridge and ritual stakeholders representing Laredo and Nuevo Laredo guarantee the safety of bridge ceremony participants? Should the ceremony's official torchbearers—the two *abrazo* ("embrace" in Spanish) children representing the United States dressed in early American colonial garb (imagine George and Martha Washington in miniature) and the two abrazo children representing Mexico outfitted in a charro suit and a china poblana dress—participate in the ritual, much less lead their delegations? Authorities finally concluded around four o'clock that morning that the ceremony could and should go on as scheduled.[2] Securing the border was the group's primary objective. But proceeding with the ceremony was also an opportunity to communicate to drug cartel actors that the proximity and future threat of violence was not going to "muscle us off of our own bridge,"[3] and, by extension, not going to force the suspension of the International Bridge Ceremony—a prominent feature of regional historical memory and recurring evidence of that port of entry's shared history of cooperation during times of crisis.[4]

This chapter uses the place and pace of that decision to think about the resiliency and adaptability of civil religious expression in a border environment.[5] It draws on cross-border ethnographic and archival research to show how Laredoans (residents of Laredo) and *neolaredenses* (residents of Nuevo Laredo) repurpose civil religious discourses to negotiate the real and perceived threat of violence—to "express something that *could not* [or perhaps *should not* for fear of retribution] be placed into words."[6] While acutely aware of the specific challenges posed by an international border environment (e.g., multiple jurisdictions, different languages, different cultural referents and national heroes and heroines), this study rallies scholars to press forward with an analytic model that keeps materiality (e.g., border infrastructure) and ephemerality (e.g., ritual) in productive tension with one another.[7] Informed by regional approaches to the study of borders that challenge methodological nationalism and "nation as container" thinking, this chapter reckons with civil religion's implicit reliance on cultural oneness and demonstrates

CIVIL RELIGION AT THE U.S.-MEXICO BORDER | 165

Figure 8.1. Miguel Hidalgo and George Washington walking toward the International Bridge Ceremony, Juárez-Lincoln International Bridge, 2013. Photo credit: E. A. Peña.

how transnationally produced expressions of civil religion can exceed categorical thinking about the nation-state.[8] One of the key takeaways from this chapter is the idea that paying attention to the comanagement of civil religious narratives and symbols in an international setting not only problematizes American and civil religion's geographic aversion to border spaces but also opens up the concept's transnational potential. Moreover, studying border-based articulations of civil religion (American and otherwise), particularly when those performances are carried out under duress, can productively expand how we think about the concept's relationship to crisis.

First Things First: Why Commemorate Washington's Birthday at the U.S.-Mexico Border?

Initially organized by members of the Improved Order of Red Men (IORM) Yaqui Tribe 59—a brotherhood that claims the Sons of Liberty

Figure 8.2. IORM members and municipal officials play up Native America at the border, Washington's Birthday Celebration International Parade, 1934. Image courtesy of the Washington's Birthday Celebration Association.

as ideological antecedents—the first George Washington's Birthday Celebration at the port of Laredo in 1898 featured a reenactment of the Boston Tea Party, an international parade, a meeting on the international bridge, and a fireworks display featuring Washington's likeness adorned with a halo. Fraternity members chose versatile expressive strategies and "extratextual registers" to remind spectators that the soil underneath their feet was no longer solely Mexican.[9] They used their elite status as Laredo's mayor, sheriff, and district attorney to publicly invoke their belief in Washington as a national hero and as the only white man to gain access to the "Indian Heaven."[10] Their staging choices, particularly Washington's apotheosis at the close of the inaugural celebration, evoked American civil religion's most generative symbols and narratives.[11]

Although the celebration is no longer organized by IORM Yaqui Tribe 59 members, border actors at the port of Laredo still use expressions of civil religion to commemorate Washington's birthday. As noted in the opening vignette, Laredoans and neolaredenses continue to "play Indian," stage eighteenth-century tableaux vivants, and meet in the middle of the international bridge.[12] The content of the celebration, including how and where border actors choose to articulate their respective patriotic claims, have changed over time (e.g., the celebration still closes with a spectacular fireworks display but no longer features Washington's likeness). Organizers' careful selection of participants year to year is a form of "symbolic stock-taking."[13] The young woman chosen to portray Princess Pocahontas each year, for example, does not participate in the bridge ceremony. Like each of the one hundred eleven Indian Princesses chosen before her, however, she does receive the key to the city of Laredo from the mayor during the grand parade (see Figure 8.2). The sustained and rhythmic emplacement of civil religious discourse on the bridge and on the streets of Laredo and Nuevo Laredo during the festivities is dynamic and complex. But tracing change "by slow unconscious accretion," however unquantifiable, is worth considering.[14]

Groups of border elites linked by property and intermarriage continue to maintain majority control over the celebration's "organizational vehicles."[15] Like their IORM predecessors and the protagonists of other studies of the structure of social life in America, they select history carefully. Members of the Washington's Birthday Celebration Association (WBCA), the International Good Neighbor Council (IGNC–Laredo), and the Consejo Internacional de Buena Vecindad (CIBV–Nuevo Laredo) oversee the International Bridge Ceremony. They follow strict protocol throughout the process. Choosing the abrazo children each year, for example, is highly regulated; the WBCA maintains a contract with IGNC and CIBV members to ensure the quality of the selection. All three organizations follow international diplomatic guidelines set out in a protocol book published by a Texas state senator (now in its third edition) to stage the bridge ceremony as well as the abrazo children's official announcement and presentation events. Abrazo parents have leeway when designing their children's costumes, but they must not take too many liberties (e.g., the Virgin of Guadalupe is an appropriate symbol, Frida Kahlo's likeness is not) (see Figure 8.3). As Haberski reminds us, "Civil religion is manufactured by the same people who wish to use it as a means to evaluate themselves. That arrangement is fraught with peril because civil religion is not a set of laws but a collection of myths."[16]

Figure 8.3. Mexican abrazo children, Nuevo Laredo, Washington's Birthday Celebration, International Bridge Ceremony, 2014. Photo credit: E. A. Peña.

International and Comparative Approaches to the Study of Civil Religion

During prolonged periods of violence, the WBCA, IGNC, and CIBV members have scaled back on face-to-face visits and sponsoring events in Nuevo Laredo proper. Even then, members of those organizations continued to cross the border and work closely with federal and municipal authorities to ensure that security concerns would not compromise the festivities. In the port of Laredo's case, the impact of drug cartel violence is magnified by its geographic position at the northern end of the Pan-American Highway (Mexican Federal Highway 85) and U.S. Interstate 35—a NAFTA superhighway. Located at one of the hemisphere's busiest inland ports, Laredo and Nuevo Laredo are ground zero for an ever-changing roster of actors and business interests. The Sinaloa Cartel's shifting of its drug trafficking operations to the Texas-Tamaulipas border in 2003 presented the biggest challenge. The move initiated a bloody power grab among competing cartels (e.g., Tijuana, Juárez, Sinaloa-Sonora, and the Gulf Cartel) vying for direct access to distribution routes.[17] Street warfare in Nuevo Laredo among cartel members and Mexican federal, state, and municipal law enforcement officers struggling to maintain rule of law on the pavement (and within their own organizations) ensued. Port of Laredo residents as well as refugees and economic migrants making their way from the interior of Mexico and Central America to the United States have had to cope with acts of violence and trauma—beheadings, mass shootings, kidnappings, disappearances, and extortions—and the everyday fear of living in or in close proximity to a war zone.[18] Considering the day-to-day impact of drug cartel violence on that border environment along with its impact during extraordinary occasions such as on the eve of the International Bridge Ceremony necessarily stretches civil religion's relationship with crisis. Paying attention to moments of crisis that traverse international boundary lines shows that civil religion need not be linked to millennial fears or a loss of confidence in the state.[19]

Those lines of inquiry do not inform early thinking about comparative and international approaches to the study of civil religion. In *Varieties of Civil Religion*, for example, Bellah and Hammond were searching for distinction without depth. They relied on binary opposites to explain the differences between American civil religion and civil religion in Japan and other countries. Bellah was quick to point out that American civil religion is not better. Japan's version is traditional and hierarchical while America's is modern and egalitarian.[20] In the case of Mexico, Hammond explained the impossibility of Mexican civil religion based on the Mexican Republic's absolute and conflictual separation between church (Catholic) and state. Moreover, the modes of transmission used to communicate Mexican civil religion like public education and the courts not only make apolitical claims but also lack the "transcendental language" that civil religion needs to be successful.[21] In short, Mexico does not have "institutionalized religious liberty."[22]

The International Bridge Ceremony presents us with a distinct interpretation of Mexican civil religion. Hammond's analysis of the separation of church and state and Mexico not only lacks nuance (and a discussion of property) but also fails to address intranational differences. At the port of Laredo, and other border-crossing zones, civil religion manifests itself differently. Take, for example, the symmetrical choreography and use of civil religious symbols during the International Bridge Ceremony. Miguel Hidalgo's presence on the bridge fulfills several cultural and national expectations. Hidalgo, like Washington, is often identified as a "[Pan] American Saint."[23] As Victor Turner rightly suggests, Hidalgo's contribution to Mexican history cannot be enumerated: "The conceit that led [Hidalgo] to rejoice in the title and uniform of 'Captain-General of America' is forgiven, and his final public repentance for having allowed so much slaughter is forgotten. The symbol has swallowed up the man, and it is a symbol of *communitas*, of Mexico regarded in the mode of fellowship rather than structure."[24] Like Washington, his life has been mythologized to meet nationalism's expectations. It could be argued that Miguel Hidalgo, as George Washington's counterpart at the International Bridge Ceremony, represents a coequal interpretation of American civil religion from a Mexican perspective. Washington's and Hidalgo's places in North American history and post–World War II interpretations of binational collaboration are examples of "extreme historical revisionism."[25] Yet their roles in the International Bridge Ceremony and their roles in allowing border residents to "consciously and purposefully re-enact the past" serve a greater purpose.[26]

It is not arbitrary that George Washington and Miguel Hidalgo appear to meet at the exact midpoint of the international bridge. The Mexican federal agency Secretaria de Comunicaciones y Transportes and the City of Laredo International Bridge department have managed their respective ends of the bridge since the privately owned Laredo Bridge Company was dissolved in 1946.[27] The ritual is meticulously choreographed to reflect and respect that ownership. Indeed, every inch is accounted for; flags are placed and displayed to mark American and Mexican spaces. The Mexican and American military bands—which play each other's national anthems—must be equally enthusiastic. Neither country should be upstaged. The rank of the Mexican official, for example, must match the rank of the U.S. official. If the governor of Texas decides not to attend the event, as Rick Perry did during his tenure, then governors of Tamaulipas, Coahuila, and Nuevo León cannot be present. Those "mirror-imaging" techniques create the semblance of a one-to-one correlation. In the moment of the ceremony, the United States and Mexico are on an even playing field.

Politicians, diplomats, and business elites may imbue the International Bridge Ceremony with political capital, but the abrazo children are the protagonists. Although practiced in some form since 1898, the International Bridge Ceremony recovered prominence when it began to feature the children in 1969.[28] Well groomed and well prepared, the abrazo children make highly effective cultural ambassadors. Bellah's initial thinking about civil religion pinpointed key moments in American history (e.g., the American Revolution, the Civil War, the Vietnam War) and traced, for example, how themes of death, sacrifice, and rebirth were "written into the civil religion" with the life and death of Lincoln.[29] A sense of rebirth is enfleshed into the civil religion of the border with the participation of children. Front and center, the children's perceived innocence and earnestness lend an air of irreproachability to the ritual. Their involvement mitigates the moment when Mexican bridge ceremony participants and media personnel who do not have dual citizenship or possess a Border Crossing Card are discouraged (physically blocked) from walking north, onward to the United States, after the ceremony (see Figure 8.4).[30] The children may not provide bridge spectators with a moment of rebirth, as Bellah would have it, but the exchange is generative. Made possible by the expectation of meeting in the middle every year to commemorate Washington's birthday—as mandated by a "ritual calendar"—the children's embrace is a reoccurring moment when spectators, on the Mexican and American ends of the bridge, can contemplate moving forward with a renewed sense of possibility.[31]

Lloyd Warner's scholarship is also instructive here. His analysis of mid-twentieth-century parades in New England suggests that "the condensation of collective experience expressed in the forty-two tableaux [in Yankeetown] was much greater than the condensation of an individual's dream ... the images of this procession dealt with a span of time which covers the total meaning of the lives of tens of thousands of individuals who had lived, died, and passed on their collective and individual significance to those now living."[32] Atop the Juárez-Lincoln International Bridge, delegations from both sides of the border are not reflecting the value of one human lifetime or one span of time. Including nationally and internationally renowned luminaries like Hidalgo and Washington signals that the ritual is more than local. Presenting four children dressed in patriotic garb signals collective cleansing and tran-

Figure 8.4. Law enforcement officers blocking northbound traffic after the ceremony. Washington's Birthday Celebration, International Bridge Ceremony, 2014. Photo credit: E. A. Peña.

shistorical renewal. Having the children meet face to face in the middle of the international bridge demonstrates their willingness to play together; in that moment, their innocence is more powerful than difference, crisis, or the sins of the past.

Calibrating Transnational Civil Religion

For Bellah, envisioning transnational civil society requires the creation of "a genuine transnational sovereignty."[33] He proposes that American civil religion's transnational potential "would necessitate the incorporation of vital international symbolism into our civil religion. . . . Fortunately, since the American civil religion is not the worship of the American nation but an understanding of the American experience in the light of ultimate and universal reality, the reorganization entailed by such a new situation need not disrupt the American civil religion's continuity."³⁴ This reading of transnational civil religion differs from Bellah's vision in significant ways. At the port of Laredo, the processes through which the International Bridge Ceremony is produced and maintained are transnational, but the ritual itself is not. Throughout the year, and especially in the months leading up to the celebration, WBCA, IGNC, and CIBV associates crisscross the international boundary line to plan, fundraise, and promote the event. Those actors operate transnationally. Their efforts, not the product, are transnational. They do not traverse the international boundary line during the ritual. Indeed, one of the most important aspects of the rite is to designate a meeting place to differentiate Mexican space and American space. The two nations do not fuse to create "transnational sovereignty." They do not share national symbols; they exchange them.

The transnational potential of the International Bridge Ceremony, however, is actualized year-round because preparation draws on cross-border lines of communication and well-rehearsed collaboration scenarios. And, as described above, transnational cooperation can take center stage during the festivities proper. In denying a transnational criminal organization like the Zetas an opportunity to "muscle us off of our own bridge," border actors stood by civil religious symbols and discourse to generate a united front. The idea that civil religion's transnational potential is firmly attached to border infrastructure—a point of view that differs from scholarship that frames transnational civil religion as a diasporic project—is also key here.³⁵ The variance is based on the international bridge not only as the site of action but also as infrastructure that is internationally co-owned. Because the bridge is managed jointly by the Mexican federal government and the City of Laredo, both entities have equal authority and share a vested interest in protecting their property.³⁶ Taking place between two nations, the International Bridge Ceremony encourages us to see the importance of infrastructure (the bridge) and to identify the underlying dynamics of socioeconomic partnerships at the port of Laredo. The content of the ritual itself may overemphasize separate national identities, but the ritual's reliance on binational participation and cross-border cooperation, particularly during times when crisis is shared across international boundary lines, invites further reflection on the concept's transnational promise.

Conclusion

This analysis has shown how civil religious symbols—heroes, icons, and capstone events—can be shared, resignified, and exchanged across national boundary lines in ways that do not, at first glance, necessarily undermine or detract from ideas of "oneness" that condition significations of American civil religion. The participation of bridge ceremony actors, whether George Washington in adult size or in miniature, for example, or the iconic portrayal of Miguel Hidalgo carrying a banner with the Virgin of Guadalupe's image, is carefully choreographed to communicate a one-to-one exchange—an act of embodied reciprocity, not borrowing—played out, literally and precisely, between nations and among carefully selected participants. This analysis has demonstrated how the ritual can unequivocally reinforce national boundaries and distinguish national identities, but it has also illuminated how the production process is anything but insular.

On a broader level, this chapter has also tested American religion and civil religion's confidence in proper geography. While idiosyncratic, the International Bridge Ceremony links the port of Laredo to places across the "American landscape" where invoking historical narratives, luminaries, and symbols renews localized ties to the nation.[37] At the U.S.-Mexico border, as in storied places like Yankeetown, national holidays (e.g., Memorial Day, Presidents' Day) invite residents to festively engage the past to create their present.[38] To be clear, it is not that civil religious discourse mitigates binational tensions or counteracts long-standing citizenship and class-based hierarchies. Border enactments can convey the semblance of national unity, international balance, and/or border control, even when the power to organize those rituals lies primarily in the hands of actors based on one side of the border.[39] Border rituals, inflected with civil religious symbols or not, can also reinforce differences based on language (e.g., Spanish or English), history (e.g., Miguel Hidalgo or George Washington), and patriotic customs (e.g., Zogist salute or palm over heart), even when the relevance of those distinctions varies on a day-to-day basis. Similarly, civil religion's underlying logic, as developed by Bellah and other Durkheimian sociologists, is problematic even if that cohort of thinkers emphasized cohesion to protect societal ties buoyed by pluralism.[40] Moving forward, it will be difficult for us to untether ourselves entirely from that legacy and even more so if we avoid tackling two fundamental problems. The proposal here is twofold: continue to expand the contours of American religion with research that challenges implicit notions of proper geography and continue to challenge American civil religion's reliance on "oneness," "self-containment," and center/periphery logic with increased attention toward the ways in which civil religious expression can be indebted to cross-border and transnational practices.

NOTES

1 U.S. embassy cable 10NUEVOLAREDO44, Gun Battle between Mexican Army and Zetas at International Bridge (February 22, 2010); Interview, State Department Official, Washington, D.C., August 2014; Interview, Nuevo Laredo Municipal Official, October 2013; Interview, Former CBP Agent, December 2015; Interview, WBCA Member, March 2014.
2 Law enforcement had swept the scene and had arranged for additional on-site security measures (e.g., additional snipers and plain-clothes personnel). Attendees had also checked in with their informants on the ground to acquire a fuller picture of the threat. According to a *Laredo Morning Times* article published on February 20, 2010, a spokesperson for the Laredo Police Department later related that "talk of a curfew or bridge closures were mentioned [but ultimately deemed] premature."
3 Interview, Laredo Municipal Official, March 2014; Participant observation, City of Laredo/WBCA Security Meeting, City Public Works Building, January 8, 2014.
4 In addition to drug cartel violence, border residents have used the International Bridge Ceremony to work through a wide range of crises, including recovering from natural disasters and protecting the port of entry's economic security. E. A. Peña, ¡*Viva George! Celebrating Washington's Birthday at the US-Mexico Border* (Austin: University of Texas Press, 2020).
5 Robert N. Bellah, "Civil Religion in America," *Daedalus* 96, no. 1 (1967): 1–21; Robert N. Bellah and Phillip E. Hammond, *Varieties of Civil Religion* (San Francisco: Harper & Row, 1980). See also Roger Stump, "Toward a Geography of American Civil Religion," *Journal of Cultural Geography* 5, no. 2 (March 1985): 87–95; Arthur E. Farnsley II, N. J. Demerath III, Etan Diamond, Mary L. Mapes, and Elfriede Wedam, *Sacred Circles, Public Squares: The Multicentering of American Religion* (Bloomington: Indiana University Press, 2005); Mark Silk, "Defining Religious Pluralism in America: A Regional Analysis," *Annals of American Academy of Political and Social Sciences* 612 (July 2007): 64–81; Arthur Remillard, *Southern Civil Religions: Imagining the Good Society in the Post-Reconstruction Era* (Athens: University of Georgia Press, 2011); Thomas A. Tweed, *"America's Church": The National Shrine and Catholic Presence in the Nation's Capital* (New York: Oxford University Press,

2011); and Rhys H. Williams, "Civil Religion and the Cultural Politics of National Identity in Obama's America," *Journal for the Scientific Study of Religion* 52 (June 2013): 239–57. See also Wilbur Zelinsky, "Nationalism in the American Place-Name Cover," *Names: A Journal of Onomastics* 31 (1983): 1–28, and Tamar Frankiel, "Ritual Sites in the Narrative of American Religion," in *Retelling U.S. Religious History*, ed. Thomas A. Tweed (Berkeley: University of California Press, 1997), 57–86.

6 P. C. Johnson, "Savage Civil Religion," *Numen* 52, no. 3 (2005): 289–324.

7 Staying on or as close to border infrastructure as possible, it highlights the materiality of the international bridge (see D. Newman, "The Lines That Continue to Separate Us: Borders in a 'Borderless' World," *Progress in Human Geography* 30, no. 2 [2006]: 144) and the ritual's reliance on "mirror-imaging" techniques (Daphne Berdahl, *Where the World Ended: Re-unification and Identity in the German Borderland* [Berkeley: University of California Press, 1999], 150). "Mirror-imaging" acts (e.g., inauguration ceremonies, flag-folding rituals) feature symmetrical choreography that communicates participants' respective ties to nation. This approach differs from those of "borderlands" scholars who often emphasize the far-reaching effects of international boundary lines to trouble the "precise correspondence between nation, state, and territory" (Thomas M. Wilson and Hastings Donnan, eds., *A Companion to Border Studies* [Oxford: Blackwell, 2012], 10). From thinking through "poetic" formulations that characterize religious production in the borderlands (L. D. León, "Metaphor and Place: The U.S.-Mexico Border as Center and Periphery in the Interpretation of Religion," *Journal of the American Academy of Religion* 67, no. 3 [1999]: 543) to examining institutions that strategically envision borderlands as a common geographic space (A. M. Martínez, *Catholic Borderlands: Mapping Catholicism onto American Empire, 1905–1935* [Lincoln: University of Nebraska Press, 2014]) and focusing on the creative repurposing of landscape, symbol, and ritual beyond the boundary line proper (L. M. Sarat, *Fire in the Canyon: Religion, Migration, and the Mexican Dream* [New York: New York University Press, 2013]; see also Pierrette Hondagneu-Sotelo, Genelle Gaudinez, Hector Lara, and Billie C. Ortiz, "'There's a Spirit That Transcends the Border': Faith, Ritual, and Postnational Protest at the U.S.-Mexico Border," *Sociological Perspectives* 47 [June 2004]: 133–59), borderlands-oriented studies illuminate the vastly creative ways religion envisions its relationship to territory.

8 E. A. Peña, "The U.S.-Mexico Transborder Region: Cultural Dynamics and Historical Interactions. Carlos G. Vélez-Ibáñez and Josiah Heyman, Eds. Tucson: University of Arizona Press, 2017. 408 Pp: Book Reviews," *American Ethnologist* 45, no. 3 (2018): 426–27.

9 J. L. Modern, "Commentary: How to Read Literature, Win Friends, Influence People, and Write about American Religion," *American Literary History* 26, no. 1 (2014): 192–93.

10 E. A. Peña, "More Than a Dead American Hero: Washington, the Improved Order of Red Men, and the Limits of Civil Religion," *American Literary History* 26, no. 1 (2014): 61–82.

11 Bellah, "Civil Religion in America," 11; see also David Morgan and Sally M. Promey, *The Visual Culture of American Religions* (Berkeley: University of California Press, 2001); and Peter Gardella, *American Civil Religion: What Americans Hold Sacred* (New York: Oxford University Press, 2014).
12 P. Deloria, *Playing Indian* (New Haven, CT: Yale University Press, 1998). Washington's Birthday Celebration currently boasts thirty activities over a four-week period and counts on sixteen affiliate organizations. Highlights include the Society of Martha Washington presentation and ball, a Princess Pocahontas pageant, a Mr. South Texas award (a former recipient includes George W. Bush), a Noche Mexicana gala, a Jalapeño Festival, and an International Bridge Ceremony. To give a sense of the spectacle, bejeweled colonial gowns and Indian costumes may cost anywhere between five thousand and fifty thousand dollars. To learn more about the festivities, see E. Young, "Red Men, Princess Pocahontas, and George Washington: Harmonizing Race Relations in Laredo at the Turn of the Century," *Western Historical Quarterly* 29, no. 1 (1998): 48–85; S. Green, *A Celebration of Heritage* (Laredo, TX: Border Studies, 1999); E. A. Peña, "Depoliticizing Border Space," *e-misferica* 3, no. 2 (2006); N. Cantú, "Dos Mundos: Two Celebrations in Laredo, Texas—Los Matachines de la Santa Cruz and the Washington's Birthday," in *Global Mexican Cultural Productions*, ed. Rosana Blanco-Cano and Rita Urquijo-Ruiz (New York: Palgrave Macmillan, 2011); E. A. Peña, "Reveling in Patriotism: Celebrating America on the US-Mexico Border during the Mexican Revolution," in *Open Borders to a Revolution: Culture, Politics and Migration*, ed. Jaime Marroquin, Adela Pineda, and Magdalena Mieri (Washington, DC: Smithsonian Institution, 2013); and E. A. Peña, "More Than a Dean American Hero: Washington, the Improved Order of Red Men, and the Limits of Civil Religion," *American Literary History* 26, no. 1 (2014): 61–82.
13 W. Lloyd Warner, *The Family of God: A Symbolic Study of Christian Life in America* (New Haven, CT: Yale University Press, 1961), 96–97.
14 Bellah and Hammond, *Varieties of Civil Religion*, 30, 32.
15 Bellah and Hammond, *Varieties of Civil Religion*, 44.
16 Raymond J. Haberski Jr., *God and War: American Civil Religion since 1945* (New Brunswick, NJ: Rutgers University Press, 2012), 6.
17 Tony Payan, "The Drug War and the U.S.-Mexico Border: The State of Affairs," *South Atlantic Quarterly* 105, no. 4 (2006): 863–80; Freddy Mariñez Navarro and Leonardo Vivas, "Violence, Governance, and Economic Development at the U.S.-Mexico Border: The Case of Nuevo Laredo and Its Lessons," *Mexican Studies / Estudios Mexicanos* 28, no. 2 (2012): 377–416; Guadalupe Correa-Cabrera, "Security, Migration, and the Economy in the Texas–Tamaulipas Border Region: The 'Real' Effects of Mexico's Drug War," *Politics & Policy* 41, no. 1 (2013): 65–82; see also Cory Molzahn, Viridiana Ríos, and David A. Shirk, "Drug Violence in Mexico: Data Analysis through 2011" (San Diego: Trans-Border Institute, University of California San Diego, 2012); and G. Hernández y Hernández, "Análisis de la política de seguridad en México 2006–2012," *Política y Cultura* 44 (2015): 159–87.

18 Stephanie Brophy, "Mexico: Cartels, Corruption and Cocaine: A Profile of the Gulf Cartel," *Global Crime* 9, no. 3 (2008): 248–61; Adam Isacson and Maureen Meyer, "Beyond the Border Buildup: Security and Migrants Along the U.S.-Mexico Border" (Washington Office on Latin America, April 12, 2012).
19 Robert N. Bellah, "Religion and Legitimation in the American Republic," *Transaction* 15 (1978): 16–23.
20 Bellah and Hammond, *Varieties of Civil Religion*, 28–30; see also Jane Naomi Iwamura, "Japanese Americans and the Birth of a New Civil Religion," *American Quarterly* 59, no. 3 (2007): 937–68.
21 Bellah and Hammond, *Varieties of Civil Religion*, 53–54.
22 Bellah and Hammond, *Varieties of Civil Religion*, 66.
23 Bellah and Hammond, *Varieties of Civil Religion*, 47.
24 Victor Turner, *Dramas, Fields, and Metaphors: Symbolic Action in Human Society* (Ithaca, NY: Cornell University Press, 1974), 100.
25 Geraldo Cadava, *Standing on Common Ground: The Making of a Sunbelt Borderland* (Cambridge, MA: Harvard University Press, 2013), 53–54.
26 Paul Nugent, "Cyclical History in the Gambia/Casamance Borderlands: Refuge Settlement and Islam from c. 1880 to the Present," *Journal of African History* 48 (2007): 221–43.
27 Minutes of the First Meeting of the Board of Trustees of Laredo Bridge System, February 18, 1946, Laredo Public Library, box 144.
28 The *abrazo* children were not incorporated into the International Bridge Ceremony program until 1969. City staff members of the Laredo Health Department in conversation with members of the International Good Neighbor Council (IGNC) and its sister organization in Mexico—the Consejo Internacional de Buena Vecindad (CIBV)—initiated the change. Those organizations are the outgrowth of the Texas Good Neighbor Commission (TGNC), established by Texas governor Coke R. Stevenson in 1943. Unlike the Monroe Doctrine (1823) or Roosevelt's Good Neighbor Policy (1933), the TGNC was a regional initiative that was targeted toward assuaging tense race relations and advocated for the fair treatment of Mexicans and other Latin Americans. In 1954, the IGNC/CIBV was created to assess relations between Texas and Mexican border states—Tamaulipas, Nuevo Leon, Coahuila, and Chihuahua. The TGNC was terminated in 1991, but IGNC and CIBV are still active in the United States and Mexico. Records, Texas Good Neighbor Commission, Archives and Information Services Division, Texas State Library and Archives Commission.
29 Bellah, "Civil Religion in America," 9–10; see also Haberski, *God and War*.
30 This was not always the case. Until 1976, all bridge ceremony participants and border residents at large were allowed to cross into the United States without restriction for one day during George Washington's Birthday Celebration, a practice known as *paso libre* (free passage). Thousands of Mexican citizens crossed into the United States without having to show documentation. It was understood that those Mexican citizens would return to Mexico after they had watched the parade,

made purchases, eaten at local restaurants, and perhaps visited with family members for the day. Although there was no way to ensure that they would not stay in the United States permanently, *paso libre* was an integral and celebrated component of Washington's Birthday Celebration since 1957. The *paso libre* phenomenon exemplifies the celebration's power to both facilitate and temper cross-border movement. See E. A. Peña, "Paso Libre (Open Border): Border Enactment, Infrastructure, and Crisis Resolution at the Port of Laredo (1954–1957)," *Drama Review* 61, no. 2 (2017): 11–31.

31 Catherine L. Albanese, "Dominant and Public Center: Reflections on the 'One' Religion of the United States," *American Journal of Theology and Philosophy* 4, no. 3 (1983): 83–96, 91.
32 Warner, *Family of God*, 94.
33 Bellah, "Civil Religion in America."
34 Bellah, "Civil Religion in America."
35 Tricia R. Hepner, "Religion, Nationalism, and Transnational Civil Society in the Eritrean Diaspora," *Identities* 10 (2003): 269–23.
36 The port of Laredo moves close to $500 billion in import/export trade annually. See Texas Department of Transportation, "2012 International Trade Corridor Plan" (December 1, 2012), http://ftp.dot.state.tx.us and Laredo Development Foundation, "Laredo Monthly Economic Indicators 2002–2013" (September 11, 2013), www.ldfonline.org.
37 Michael Pasquier, "Religion and the American Landscape," *Religion Compass* 7, no. 4 (2013): 137–48.
38 W. Lloyd Warner, *American Life: Dream and Reality* (Chicago: University of Chicago Press, 1953); Warner, *The Family of God: A Symbolic Study of Christian Life in America* (New Haven, CT: Yale University Press, 1961).
39 Jisha Menon, *The Performance of Nationalism: India, Pakistan, and the Memory of Partition* (Cambridge: Cambridge University Press, 2013), 47–49; see also Eve Darian-Smith, *Bridging Divides: The Channel Tunnel and English Legal Identity in the New Europe* (Berkeley: University of California Press, 1999); and Suk-Young Kim, *DMZ Crossing: Performing Emotional Citizenship along the Korean Border* (New York: Columbia University Press, 2014).
40 Rhys H. Williams, "Civil Religion and the Cultural Politics of National Identity in Obama's America," *Journal for the Scientific Study of Religion* 52, no. 2 (2013): 242.

9

Civil Religion in Indianapolis

ARTHUR E. FARNSLEY II

From its founding in the early nineteenth century until at least the middle of the twentieth, Indianapolis had a white Protestant establishment that constituted the core of the city's civic life. During that first century, these white Protestants and their churches provided the dominant public culture that shaped the city's morals, laws, and social life.

The city was platted by Alexander Ralston, an associate of Pierre L'Enfant, the architect who designed Washington, D.C. Ralston shared L'Enfant's basic pattern with a circular street at the center, surrounded by an expanding grid of streets running due north-south and east-west and four spokes running out at forty-five-degree angles. Because Indianapolis was a planned city from the outset, it was easy to imagine and maintain a fixed, symmetrical design.

Protestant churches were the most prominent buildings surrounding the Circle, with as many as five church buildings there in the nineteenth century. Some planners even dreamed the governor's mansion could be built in the center of the Circle to symbolize the way religion surrounded and supported civic order. However, when the governor's wife said she did not want her washing to be visible to everyone from every side, that dream was never realized.

In the early twenty-first century it is sometimes difficult to imagine the degree to which these white Protestants saw their establishment as the true American way of life or to envision the ease with which their leaders made public pronouncements about what was decent and proper. They saw their own values as normative. Sermons by prominent pastors were printed in the newspaper. Easter sunrise services led by Protestant ministers were held on the Circle. For civic leaders in Indiana, there was no line separating white Protestant values from national, patriotic ones:

together these symbolized what it was to be a true American living in an all-American city.

Such terms were not meant as platitudes. Many Americans were deeply concerned about an influx of immigrants and about what they perceived as lawlessness and disorder in America's growing cities. Beginning in the 1880s, large numbers of Eastern European Jews and Catholics from across Europe migrated to the United States and settled in cities. Not long after the turn of the century, Jews and Catholics constituted a numerical majority in cities like Chicago and Detroit. This rapid rise in nonnative population coincided with a host of urban problems that scandalized the Protestant establishment, with many Protestants wondering aloud whether Jews or Catholics could ever be true Americans.

In the early twentieth century immigrants made up only 10 percent of Indianapolis, a place with an "almost total absence of the foreign floating element."[1] And the Protestant establishment went to great lengths to define the boundaries of citizenship and proper civic, moral order. In 1915, the Indianapolis Church Federation published an open letter in which they described the city as "wide open" where "the saloons are veritable death traps to scores of young boys and girls" but still can "continue their business unmolested." Prostitution was also identified as a pressing social problem.[2]

In 1905, local clergy advocated ever more strongly for Sunday closing laws, challenging the new entertainments that were cropping up such as vaudeville, theater, and baseball. In 1916 the superintendent of the Methodists in Indianapolis said, "The opportunity is at hand to grip this city religiously as it has never been gripped before."[3] But in truth, many of the clergy must have realized their grip was already slipping. Soon after Sunday baseball was outlawed as part of a moral crusade that included Prohibition, the legislature passed the Brolley Bill to quickly reinstate it.[4]

In the early twentieth century, many Protestants were skeptical about assimilation by Catholics or Jews; they questioned whether these faiths were compatible with American ideals of liberty and freedom. Said a 1908 editorial in the *Indianapolis News*, "The growth of new religious sects in Indianapolis has been so rapid that the adherents of straight and old-fashioned creeds wonder what will come next." During World War I, concerns about how to best Americanize immigrants provided the larger context within which notions of American identity and patriotic concern were articulated. But the post–World War II era represented a sea change in this thinking because discussions about religion and citizenship came under the umbrella of a much wider context, dominated more by fears of communists without rather than immigrants within.

Post–World War II Indianapolis was also forced to confront racial segregation and prejudice. Like much of the urban Midwest, the city saw a rapid influx of African Americans from the Upland South in the early twentieth century. Also like the rest of the country, by the mid-twentieth century Hoosiers had to acknowledge problems of residential separation and significant inequality of opportunity in income, education, and other social goods. Urban poverty was an undeniable problem, and the development of the Interstate Highway System served both to build artificial walls through existing urban neighborhoods and to allow whites to flee downtown on a thoroughfare to suburban living.

The 1950s were a time of enormous social change in Indianapolis, as elsewhere. Church attendance reached historic highs, but it was already becoming clear that the white, Protestant, establishment churches could not play the culturally central role they had played in the late nineteenth and early twentieth centuries. Catholics were here to stay. Black churches were asserting their social and political influence as the civil rights movement gained momentum. Jews, though small in number, were gaining social and economic influence too. As middle-class white people left the downtown for, literally, greener pastures in the suburbs, they entered new political jurisdictions with separate administrative structures, including schools.

Patriotism and Sports as the City's Social Glue

The story of American metropolitan areas becoming physically larger and administratively diffuse throughout the twentieth century, with middle-class whites removing themselves to new jurisdictions, is an oft-told one.[5] All cities are conglomerations of overlapping commercial and social interests playing out on multiple levels: individual, family, neighborhood, region, and metropolis. Some of these interests are centripetal, pushing people together in the center, but others are centrifugal, driving them toward the periphery.

As white citizens moved toward the suburbs in the middle of the twentieth century, the city made conscious efforts to create a central urban core capable of holding the spreading metropolis together. In 1944, George Kuhn, chairman of the Mayor's Committee on Post-War Planning, spoke to a group of three hundred fifty business leaders at Block's Department Store, urging them to respond to decentralization. He recommended expanding roads and highways, creating more parking spaces, undertaking smoke abatement to improve air quality, redeveloping slums, beautifying streams and rivers, and constructing a large public auditorium.[6]

Indianapolis's civic leadership worked hard to maintain a commercial core, but they also sought to build an urban identity and create a sense of shared citizenship by appealing to values that were not purely commercial. In the 1920s Indianapolis deliberately emphasized the sacrifice of military veterans to build a sense of common enterprise in a city that was still very white and highly nativist. By the 1950s, the city began to redefine these same memorials to highlight a sense of common citizenship, in opposition to fascism and communism, even as the downtown became significantly more diverse and as Protestant whites, especially, moved outward. It later used sports to create a shared identity and to build shared interests and values across racial, socioeconomic, and ethnic lines. The link between the two—patriotism and sport—proved to be a key feature of the city's social integration, a central feature of the city's identity. Whether this rises to the level of civil religion is a theoretical question best approached by telling the story.

Promoting Patriotism as Civil Religion

In 1902, the Soldiers and Sailors Monument was dedicated in the center of the Circle, which was thereafter known as Monument Circle. In 1919, Indianapolis pressed hard to host the national headquarters of the American Legion, an organization chartered by Congress that same year to serve World War I veterans. The Legion was temporarily headquartered in New York City, but Washington, D.C., hoped to become the permanent host. At the national meeting of the Legion in Minneapolis in November 1919, D.C. got the most votes, but not a clear majority, on the first ballot. Indianapolis lobbied hard and won outright on the second ballot.

As part of its commitment to house the Legion headquarters, Indianapolis agreed not only to build an enormous World War I monument patterned on the Mausoleum at Halicarnassus but in fact to build an entire War Memorial Plaza with a cenotaph, fountain, and obelisk in addition to the War Memorial, the American Legion headquarters, and two outbuildings. This plaza was not constructed on some abandoned property near the edge of town but along Meridian Street, the city's busiest thoroughfare bisecting Monument Circle from north to south. The U.S. federal building sat just to the south of the plaza, also along Meridian. The Scottish Rite Cathedral was built across Meridian to the west. All of the buildings were constructed in a grand neoclassical style using Indiana limestone, the same stone used to build the Pentagon and the Empire State Building.

While these buildings were doubtless meant to create a sense of public purpose and common citizenship, the proximity of the Scottish Rite Cathedral, a Masonic organization, reminded everyone that citizenship was still normatively white and Protestant, just like Freemasonry.

There is no evidence that city planners consciously intended the war memorials as a way to manage diversity. For one thing, the War Memorial Plaza plan came about when Indianapolis was still heavily nativist and fully racially segregated. In fact, the 1920s were the heyday for Ku Klux Klan activity in Indiana,[7] so the plaza was built at a time of overt resistance to pluralism. But in the mid 1940s, as World War II came to a close, Indianapolis made a clear, measured change from being a city with a dominant white Protestant core—clearly visible in the churches, Masonic buildings, and public ceremonies—to being a city whose downtown emphasized the shared values of commerce and citizenship as patriotism. The city embraced a specifically American version of civil religion in an attempt to create a common sense of purpose by leveraging existing patriotic symbols. As Jan Shipps said in her essay "Religion" in the *Encyclopedia of Indianapolis*, "These are a critical feature of this city's civic spirit, part of its vitality and essence."[8]

As other chapters in this volume make clear, civil religion need not mean only patriotism, nationalism, flag waving, and an emotional appeal to military sacrifice, and it assuredly does not *require* linkage to whiteness or Protestantism. It is clear Bellah did not mean to promote this vision of a common good, and for the rest of his life he resisted this interpretation of his work.

But civil religion *can* refer to this Fourth of July version of America, and in the case of Indianapolis, it did mean this. Many have criticized this patriotic vision of civil religion as uncritical and unhelpful, a way to protect dominant groups at the expense of subordinate ones. While this criticism contains undeniable truth, it is also true that in Indianapolis this same vision broke down some kinds of barriers and united citizens by emphasizing common enemies: Nazism and godless communism. The city did this by honoring a type of community service and sacrifice that was in principle available to all Americans through the military.

The War Memorials

Most communities have war memorials. The dedication of the Soldiers and Sailors Monument in 1902 marked the beginning of Indianapolis's attempt to define its all-American status with monuments. The Soldiers and Sailors Monument was built to honor Indiana's role in the Civil War.

Figure 9.1. Soldiers and Sailors Monument. Photo credit: Nathaniel Wynne.

Figure 9.2. Indiana War Memorial. Photo credit: Nathaniel Wynne.

But this monument at the exact center of the city was a harbinger of much bigger things to come.

Construction of the War Memorial Plaza, including the headquarters of the American Legion, set this vision very literally in Indiana stone. The words engraved into the external walls of the Indiana War Memorial after World War I leave no doubt. Above the doors to the north and the south it reads, "To vindicate the principles of peace and justice in the world." And the main inscription says, "To commemorate the valor and sacrifice of the land, sea and air forces of the United States and all who rendered faithful and loyal service at home and overseas in the World War; to inculcate a true understanding and appreciation of the privileges of American citizenship; to inspire patriotism and respect for the laws to the end that peace may prevail, justice be administered, public order maintained and liberty perpetuated."

The memorial's Shrine Room on the second floor is its true centerpiece. A symbolic bronze casket sits below an enormous American flag, with pale blue lighting offering the effect of stained glass. The atmosphere could not reasonably be termed anything less than "worshipful." Everyone is called to reflect on the military sacrifice and the shared values for which it is offered.

The Soldiers and Sailors Monument, the American Legion, and the War Memorial Plaza all reinforce the civil religion of American patriotism, but the city did not stop there. After World War II, the city and state moved to incorporate the veterans of that war into the World War Memorial. But the city also moved to create a new memorial to the men who in 1945 lost their lives on the cruiser U.S.S. *Indianapolis*, the same ship immortalized in the below-deck conversation in the movie *Jaws*. It took fifty years, but in 1995 the national monument to the *Indianapolis*

Figure 9.3. Indiana War Memorial Shrine Room. Photo credit: Nathaniel Wynne.

was built downtown along the canal. In 2007, an *Indianapolis* museum opened in the War Memorial. In 1999, Indianapolis dedicated the Medal of Honor Memorial with the names of each Medal of Honor recipient—3,436 at the time—etched into it. This was also built along the canal directly across from the Indiana State Museum, adjacent to Indiana Military Park. Indianapolis is second only to Washington, D.C., in the number of war monuments built in the twentieth century. As one local architect said when the Medal of Honor Memorial was unveiled, "For the sake of downtown real estate development, let us hope there are no more world wars."

Promoting Sports as Civil Religion

The second half of the twentieth century saw a different kind of downtown development also aimed at bringing different kinds of people together, but with an eye toward the city's national profile. The war memorials helped to create a shared identity for residents, but they were never going to promote the city's core identity to the rest of the nation because most cities and states consider themselves patriotic and all-American. To build a reputation as a national city and to stimulate downtown business development, civic leaders made a conscious choice to become the Amateur Sports Capital of America. In 1969, the Amateur Athletic Union relocated to the city. By 1990, the governing bodies of eight Olympic sports had located to the city with funding assistance from the Lilly Endowment, the city's most powerful foundation.[9]

The centerpiece of this plan was building venues to host the Pan Am Games in 1987. The city and state governments, local businesses, and the Lilly Endowment all made various large investments toward this end. Some of the biggest investment was in infrastructure to be located at Indiana University–Purdue University Indianapolis (IUPUI), on downtown's western edge, most notably a track for athletic events, a natatorium for world championship swimming events, and upgrades for the former Doubletree Hotel on campus, which became a conference center with a museum dedicated to art about sports. Other new infrastructure was built downtown, including an ice rink in Pan Am Plaza, another entire city block set aside for the Pan Am Games.

These structures changed the city's national profile to some degree, though the long-term effects of those changes varied by sport and by venue. No national events are now held at the running track, which has relatively limited seating. The track was later named for Michael Carroll, the Lilly Endowment official most responsible for bringing the Pan Am Games to Indianapolis, who died in a tragic midair collision on September 11, 1992. The ice rink at Pan Am Plaza closed permanently in 2014. The natatorium, however, went on to host many U.S. swimming and diving national trials and is, at this writing, being fully renovated. The direct, lasting effects of these venues has been mixed.

But they foretold a changing attitude toward downtown development and fit hand in glove with other sports-related changes going on in the city. In the early 1980s, Indianapolis businesses, foundations, and the city government also made an investment of roughly eighty million dollars in a downtown stadium large enough to host an NFL football team, even though the city had no team to host. Half of this money was raised in public debt, half in private financing. But once the Hoosier Dome (RCA Dome) was in place, the city wasted no time convincing Robert Irsay to relocate his Baltimore Colts to town in 1984, a move that still stings Baltimoreans. Although the city already had an NBA team, one of only four teams to move from the start-up ABA to the NBA when the younger league dissolved, the arrival of an NFL team marked this relatively small city as "big league."

Indianapolis did not stop there. In 1997, Indianapolis outbid Kansas City for the NCAA headquarters that had been located in Kansas City since 1955. New buildings were constructed along the downtown canals and the White River near the State Museum, Military Park, the zoo, and the space that would later be the Medal of Honor Memorial. During its more than twenty years in Indianapolis, the NCAA has expanded its reach, built new buildings, and consolidated its influence in the city. Indianapolis cemented its major city status by hosting Super Bowl XLVI in 2012. It became one of the smallest cities to host this gigantic event, and the Colts' home field, Lucas Oil Stadium, became the second smallest host stadium. Fifty thousand Indianapolis residents served as volunteers over the two weeks leading up to the Super Bowl.

Indianapolis is a city of 950,000 in a nine-county metro area of about 1.9 million (thirty-third among U.S. metropolitan statistical areas). Civic leadership saw sports as a way to build local community spirit and to create a sense of the city's national importance despite it being only midsized among the country's big metropolitan areas. These developments were intentional and carefully planned. Taxpayers within local and state governments, along with foundations and businesses, paid a high price to shape the impressions of residents and visitors alike. It is important to remember that Indianapolis *bid* for the American Legion and NCAA headquarters. The city built a huge football stadium with the intention of securing a team. City leaders committed significant resources to house national sports offices in hopes of reinforcing the city's internal identity and promoting a particular external identity to those who lived elsewhere.

The commitment to sports as a commercial enterprise and tool for urban development fit with other plans to make downtown a place where suburbanites not only would want to come but, for many activities, would be forced to come. Midwestern cities like Cleveland (Richfield Coliseum) and Detroit (Palace of Auburn Hills) built some sports stadiums away from their downtowns, a pattern repeated recently when the Atlanta Braves moved from downtown Atlanta to Cobb County in the northern suburbs. Civic leaders in Indianapolis ensured this would not happen. Nearly every major public development in Indianapolis was kept directly downtown, including every sports stadium. Beyond this, plans were constantly made and remade to create more downtown retail and parking. Large, newly built sports stadiums made Indianapolis a more attractive venue for conferences and tourism, so the convention center was expanded. Hotels, restaurants, and downtown shopping would support, and be supported by, the sporting businesses.

The first large-scale attempt at a downtown shopping mall was the renovation of the old railroad depot, Union Station, whose redevelopment ran side by side with the development of Pan Am Plaza and the building of the Hoosier Dome. The Colts arrived in 1984, Union Station opened as a restaurant and shopping venue in 1986, and the Pan Am Games were held in 1987.

Union Station faltered. The opening of a new shopping center, Circle Centre Mall, in 1995 signaled the end of shopping at Union Station. Circle Centre was developed by Simon Properties. Not only were the Simon brothers, Herb and Mel, Indianapolis residents, they had the deep pockets of national real estate developers. They were also the owners of the NBA's Indiana Pacers.

During this period downtown also boasted a renovated symphony theater on Monument Circle and a new repertory theater just off the Circle. The Lilly Endowment provided funds for the glass-enclosed Artsgarden above the busy intersection of Washington and Illinois streets.

The economic development of downtown Indianapolis is not so different from similar developments elsewhere, but the revitalization efforts that surrounded it were unusually tightly—intentionally tightly— focused on sports and surrounded by the monuments to patriotism. The development of IUPUI as the state's urban campus, founded in 1969 next door to existing medical, nursing, and dental schools, ran directly parallel to these other efforts at economic development. Slowly and deliberately, Indianapolis created a public identity for itself as an urban center, gradually shedding the moniker "India-no-place."

In *Sacred Circles, Public Squares*, my co-authors and I made the argument that the city's growth and economic development could be understood as a tension between two countervailing social forces: public efforts by elites to strengthen the city's core and private, personal movement toward the city's periphery.[10] Put another way, it was clear this city, like most others, was becoming a "place of places," but there was an especially strong effort in Indianapolis to make certain the city had a center capable of exerting a strong gravitational pull.[11]

Sports were critical to creating such a center. Today, Indianapolis has a highly concentrated set of downtown entertainment and arts venues and hotels. When Indianapolis hosted Super Bowl XLVI, it was only the fourth cold-weather city ever to host and surely the only one in recent memory where visitors could walk from the football stadium to the basketball stadium to the AAA baseball stadium to the NCAA headquarters and to nearly every hotel and restaurant. They could also walk to the Indiana State Museum, Eiteljorg Museum of Western and Indian Art, the Repertory Theater, and the symphony. When Dallas or New York City hosts the Super Bowl, the stadiums are not even in those cities. In Indianapolis, everything listed here is within, or adjacent to, one downtown square mile that also includes the state capitol building and its offices. Only two public institutions of consequence are not within walking distance of the Circle—the Indianapolis Museum of Art, built on the grounds of an old Lilly family mansion, and the Children's Museum, built three miles north of downtown in hopes of revitalizing a deteriorating urban neighborhood (and, perhaps coincidentally, across the street from the Lilly Endowment).

In an era of residential diffusion and the development of many regional centers around edge cities, Indianapolis fought to maintain a post–World War II downtown as the core for which everything else is periphery. Only the wealthiest edge city, the northern suburb of Carmel, makes significant efforts toward distinguishing itself as a "center" in its own right, most recently by making a very large investment in a performing arts complex. But it is extraordinarily unlikely Carmel could ever host the city's sports teams, much less the patriotic monuments and war memorials.

Traditional Religion Moves Outward

Imagine a European visitor to Indianapolis being shown the city via hot air balloon. What structures might she pick as the cathedral, the center? The largest, most prominent structures are the state capitol building, the government buildings that surround it, Lucas Oil Stadium (second home to the NFL's Colts after the Hoosier Dome), and the War Memorial Plaza flanked by the Scottish Rite Cathedral. The monuments and rituals of both patriotism and sports are easily identifiable as very traditional American forms of civil religion. The values embodied in these could, in principle if not always in practice, be shared across racial, ethnic, and socioeconomic lines, which suited them well as the symbols of unity during the changes of the second half of the twentieth century.

Indianapolis's public presentation of these shared values corresponded to a change in the public role for traditional religious congregations, especially churches. Some churches were literally closed and moved to make room for the War Memorial Plaza. For others, the economic pressure to sell out to other interests around the Circle was just too strong. Traditional religion did not disappear by any means, but it certainly relocated. By the mid-twentieth century there was only one church left on Monument Circle: Christ Church Cathedral, the Episcopal congregation that was home to the city's most prominent and wealthy citizens, the Lilly family.

The case of Second Presbyterian Church makes the point very nicely. The church was founded in 1823 as First Presbyterian Church, but by 1838 broke into Old School and New School factions. The New School faction created Second Presbyterian, located on the northwest quadrant of the Circle (not yet Monument Circle). Henry Ward Beecher, brother of Harriet Beecher Stowe, was the pastor of this important congregation. In 1870 the church moved to the "suburbs," as their website describes it, all the way to the corner of Pennsylvania and Vermont streets, roughly half a mile north.

As War Memorial Plaza was developed, Second Presbyterian was clearly in the way. Other downtown churches moved farther north along with their white, upper-middle-class parishioners, but Second Presbyterian insisted it had a ministry to the whole city, including the downtown, and refused to go.

The matter was settled in true Indianapolis fashion: In 1959, Lilly corporate vice president and Second Presbyterian elder Charles Lynn offered the church twenty acres at 7700 North Meridian, highly valuable real estate in a city where the wealthy were moving northward. If twenty acres were not enough, he also offered them one million dollars toward construction of the new building. This offer proved irresistible, and Second Presbyterian cleared off the developing War Memorial Plaza in 1959 when their new building was completed. The downtown building was razed in 1960. Second Presbyterian continued to play a leading role in the city, home church to residents such as Peyton Manning and the locale for the historic funeral service of Ryan White, an Indiana teenager who died in 1990 of AIDS-related complications and became a symbol for public education and nondiscrimination regarding HIV/AIDS.

In the end, Second Presbyterian went where many of the central downtown white churches went—northward with their better-off, mostly white constituents. As the population dispersed into specific neighborhoods, suburbs, and edge cities, congregations relocated to those areas or, more often, new congregations emerged while the older ones nearer the city center closed their doors or changed hands. Just as neighborhoods developed specific characteristics tied to specific demographics, congregations came to reflect their immediate neighbors.

Congregations have always reflected a high degree of racial, ethnic, and socioeconomic homogeneity. The movement of churches away from the downtown core did not in any way cause this phenomenon. But that movement did signal a change nonetheless: Some churches, especially the biggest white Protestant churches—had imagined themselves to speak for the public at large, to represent a shared religious vision for the common, public good. By the mid-twentieth century it was clear they did not—they represented the particular values and choices of the people who attended them. The city needed different kinds of shared values located in different, more potentially inclusive institutional settings.

Some churches continued to occupy high-profile public roles, as is true in any city. Some large mainline Protestant churches still wielded considerable political and social sway, not least because of their influential members. Similarly, certain Black churches became public voices during the civil rights movement. But it was clear these churches spoke for specific social groups with particular interests. Moreover, Catholic churches, synagogues, and eventually white evangelical churches developed voices of their own.

Some have argued that religion became highly privatized and individualized over the course of the twentieth century. Perhaps, but it is not necessary to make such a strong individualistic argument to claim that churches became more localized and particularized over that period. Sometimes they coalesced around geographic proximity; other times they coalesced around specific ideas or attitudes (the rise of Open and Affirming churches regarding LGBTQ issues represents the latter trend). Traditional religion became *particularized*, and other types of more generalizable values grounded in other institutions replaced their role as symbols of the city's shared values.

The National Context for Patriotism and Sports in Indianapolis

> I think it should be clear from the text that I conceive of the central tradition of the American civil religion not as a form of national self-worship but as the subordination of the nation to ethical principles that transcend it in terms of which it should be judged. I am convinced that every nation and every people come to some form or religious self-understanding whether the critics like it or not. Rather than simply denounce what seems in any case inevitable, it seems more responsible to seek within the

civil religious tradition for those critical principles which undercut the ever present danger of national self-idolization.
—Bellah on his 1967 *Daedalus* article in *Beyond Belief* (1991)

Bellah clearly wanted to distinguish his view of civil religion from "a form of national self-worship." He argued that every nation does in fact have a self-understanding that is religious in the Durkheimian sense and further that it was worthwhile to consider which rituals, texts, practices, values, and beliefs made up the American version of this self-understanding. Debate about what *should* be included was inevitable. Bellah himself hoped that America was built on a shared sense of community responsibility capable of offsetting what he saw as excesses of liberal individualism. He offered his clearest vision of the problems of individualism in *Habits of the Heart* and clarified his prescriptions in *The Good Society*.[12]

Some critics of Bellah's work have argued that, in the end, no realistic definition of *actual* American civil religion can be separated from conservative, nationalistic visions of individual choice, free enterprise, and especially nationalist commitment to America as an imperial, militaristic power. The best definition of American civil religion, according to these critics, is in fact the one Bellah hoped to counter. The very concept has been thoroughly colonized by nationalist conceptions of patriotism.

There have also been many attempts to show how contemporary sports serve the totemic, community-building religious function Durkheim described in his *Elementary Forms*. The basic outline of this argument is easy to see: Contemporary individuals lack the organic, ascribed sense of belonging (Tönnies's *gemeinschaft*) common in earlier social situations.[13] Some of them are drawn toward a new kind of belonging with others who share their affinity with sports teams. This affinity often crosscuts other elective relationships such as citizenship in a city, state, or region or perhaps a shared membership in a high school or college community. The sports teams are the elite warriors of the shared community; the mascots are the totems. The more crosscutting the shared identities are—place, ethnicity, social class, political membership, personal membership—the stronger the bonds shaped around sports can be. But in the end, participation is voluntary and, as befits such an individualistic society, the costs of entering or leaving the community are relatively low.

This idea has been developed and elaborated many times in the literature.[14] While it is undeniably true that many organizations—professional sports corporations, universities, and others—have commercialized these ties as part of a broader American culture of consumerism, this does not make the sense of belonging any less real. Saying that sports are big business and that their ultimate aim is to make money does not mean the fans are not really fans with deep personal commitments. Economic exchange is an integral part of community building in any society; it does not invalidate other kinds of social bonds.

These most obvious ways of thinking about civil religion—what Bellah called "national self-worship" in the form of patriotism and a consumer-oriented vision of sports—are in fact the channels through which Indianapolis elites attempted to create the city's core civic identity over the course of the twentieth century. In the early twenty-first, it is worth considering how these changes played out. Such a discussion requires some analysis of Bellah's *ethical principles* and the ways they are challenged or reinforced by these attempts to hold the community together. In the end, there is no Archimedean point from which to judge: we can only ask what the community intended to do, what actually happened, whether intended or not, and what consequences followed. Whether the sum of these efforts constitutes civil religion is a subjective claim, something we know when we see, as Justice Potter Stewart famously said of pornography.

Patriotism

Washington, D.C., has the most war memorials and monuments of any city in America. Its architecture and statues promote a sense of gravity and humility that is clearly meant to be sacred in the broadest meaning of the term—"Our lives, our fortunes, and our sacred honor." Indianapolis drew on that reserve of shared responsibility when it built its War Memorial Plaza, meant to evoke the same spirit in the citizens of Indiana generally and Indianapolis specifically. World War I created a new public awareness of America's leadership role in the world, and the War Memorial Plaza emblazoned that awareness in engraved letters.

War memorials undoubtedly enshrine exclusivity and violence, but it matters whether citizens perceive them as emblems of patriotism or nationalism. The distinction between these terms is not always recognizable in normal conversation, but the difference is significant. At one level, war memorials glorify patriotism, a celebration of a country's values and the level of commitment its members have to those values. In principle, patriotism is about *citizenship* and *can* include every citizen based on political membership rather than race, ethnicity, or culture. It is creedal. Indeed, one of the country's citizenship values can be pluralism. But at another level the memorials glorify nationalism, a celebration of a country's identity and culture that usually reflects the mores and traditions of the dominant group, in this case white Protestant Christians.

The War Memorial Plaza, built in the 1920s, is an interesting case. It was built at the height of Ku Klux Klan activity in central Indiana, activity that was at least as much about nativism as about racial purity. So while the War Memorial Plaza is not overtly racist or Protestant, there is no evidence that it was meant to build inclusivity across ethnic or racial lines. However, the plaza and the ideals it embodied were available, post–World War II, as the city gradually emphasized a citizenship-based patriotism over culture-bound nationalism as a way to build unity in an expanding, diversifying metropolis. Over the course of the twentieth century the downtown core evolved from a center of churches, mostly white and Protestant, to a center of patriotism where the "others" were Nazis and communists. While this shift may not have been framed as an outreach program to Catholics, Jews, Blacks, and other immigrants, it can be seen to have had that effect. Everyone could in principle sacrifice on behalf of America because of their shared membership—their citizenship. Their citizenship was, at some ideal level, grounded in the belief that each individual's life and liberty was essential to the whole. Everyone was included, at least ideally, in the new synthesis, just as they were increasingly included in the military itself.

This is not to imply the city's racial, ethnic, religious, and socioeconomic divisions were miraculously healed. This argument does not require such rosy optimism. Patriotism provided a frame of reference by tying the values of sacrifice and freedom to other values such as pluralism and equality of opportunity, however imperfectly, as ways of imagining the shared interests of citizens.

This is also not to imply that the violence inherent in prejudice or discrimination disappeared but to show how publicly sanctioned violence was transferred toward different public goals with various perceived enemies. Even blood sacrifice was for shared ideals, not for "blood and soil." Although terms like "people," "shared ideals," "patriotism," and "nationalism" are often interchanged in imprecise usage, the difference between nationalism and patriotism used here is clear: Indianapolis tried to create greater social *inclusion* for its citizens by shifting the excluded group to enemies of a project that was ultimately political rather than cultural, racial, or ethnic. It emphasized patriotism over nationalism as a way to think about citizenship and membership.

Did this synthesis work, even judged by its own standards of greater inclusion and equality of opportunity? Indianapolis is undeniably less segregated by race or religion than it was in the early twentieth century, but it is also still very segregated by race and even more by socioeconomic status. There is no need to overstate the results to claim that after World War II Indianapolis began the long, slow process of confronting religious, racial, and cultural pluralism, and patriotism played a role in the process. Indianapolis had the patriotic infrastructure in place for that task and gradually shifted from nativism toward anticommunism.

It is unclear how this attempt to create a new synthesis based on political values and institutions will work in the twenty-first century. America is experiencing a new wave of nativism, though the starting point is now necessarily less white and European simply because of demographic changes. There is a significant nationalist movement, aligned with a fringe white supremacist movement, still arguing for "blood and soil," but we do not know yet just how many Americans have at least some sympathy for this vision of America or how strongly the liberal tradition will resist it. Muslims, especially, are finding it difficult to claim membership as citizens because their allegiances and motives are treated with the same suspicion Catholics and Jews received a century earlier. Latinx citizens are often swept up in debates about the limits of legal immigration and the definition of citizenship. And the Black Lives Matter movement reminds us just how frequently racial inequality and injustice determine social outcomes.

A liberal optimist can hope the process of inclusion is a virtuous cycle and the arc of justice bends toward inclusion, toward universal values embodied in the principle of citizenship, in the very long run. But a pessimist—or is that a realist?—might argue that liberal appeals to common citizenship are ultimately a pragmatic fiction used repeatedly in the struggle to negotiate political coalitions by blurring some boundaries while bringing others into sharper relief. From World War II to the Cold War, Nazis then communists became the high-definition "other" against which a practical, liberal coalition could be built. Today, we continuously redefine us and them in the interest of building politically effective coalitions and momentary political attention shifts to whomever makes up the "swing" constituency at the time, paying special attention to that constituency's perceptions of the other.

Sports

Much has been said about the ways sports teams and their mascots serve as solidarity-building totems and provide a sense of community identity because sports provide the occasion for individuals to participate in something greater than themselves. Fans dress in uniforms, chant in unison, and lose themselves in the act of cheering for shared goals (pun intended). It all seems classically Durkheimian, a functional way to think of religion, or at least something religion-like, that includes collective effervescence.[15]

Sports also provide a model of and for other American values such as competition, leadership, and teamwork. Sports are a morality play where the victor deserves the spoils through hard work, careful planning, and superior execution. In short, sports ritualize many of the same cultural forces at work in both the free market and military campaigns. Sports are highly meritocratic and are, like the military, much more racially integrated than most American institutions—though ownership of sports teams is much less integrated than participation is.

But building a city's sporting reputation involves more than a hyperactive sense of team spirit. Professional sports leagues are tightly controlled monopolies with the highest imaginable barriers to entry. The big leagues each have around thirty teams. Cities that host these teams mark themselves as national, or at least regional, centers that are attractive to businesses and convention planners. (The Indianapolis metropolitan area is ranked thirty-third by population and so is very near the lower boundary among likely cities for sports franchises, especially since some very large cities have more than one.) Almost all cities with large sports venues also have large convention centers—the Indianapolis Convention Center is currently seventeenth in terms of available square footage. These cities tend to have airports serving international destinations and serve as hubs for business and social endeavors far beyond sports. There are a few exceptions—Green Bay, Wisconsin, has an NFL team for particular historical reasons—but the presence of professional sports teams generally validates a big-city reputation and is part of a city's marketability.

National headquarters do the same. When Indianapolis political and business leaders committed money, both public and private, to win the rights to host the American Legion and the NCAA headquarters, they made a statement about the city's public goals. Public investments in sporting venues like Lucas Oil Stadium (Colts) and Bankers Life Fieldhouse (Pacers) are similar. Analysts disagree about the direct knock-on economic effects of sports teams on their host cities, wondering how much additional money fans really spend on hotels, restaurants, and other tourism. But this analysis often misses the larger point. Indianapolis was a city known primarily for its five-hundred-mile auto race, an event held once a year in a venue far from downtown at a facility owned by a privately held family corporation. While the city still proudly trumpets the Indianapolis 500, in the second half of the twentieth century it invested very large sums to make sure its eggs were not all in one basket. Building an NFL stadium in a city with no football team is very literally a leap of faith in the civic power of sport. This was not about direct, dollar-for-dollar return on investment but about creating a sense of local prominence and a local people's sense of themselves, which civic leaders hoped would pay dividends far beyond the teams' direct economic impact. Yes, the owners of the Colts and the Pacers make money as the values of their franchises increase, even if they lose money on particular seasons, but that private gain is not the goal of the public investment. The public goal is to create a larger sense of identity, and significance, for a place. The owners benefit from the monopoly of their leagues, but the city cannot change that; it can only compete on the playing field it has.

The "religious" function served by sports in Indianapolis goes beyond the fact that Colts fans all dress in blue, share emotion-laden hopes, and participate in widely shared rituals. Sports, like patriotism, help define the way Indianapolis residents think of themselves and their lives together. This self-definition does not carry the weight of race, ethnicity, or traditional religion, but the professional teams create a sense that Indianapolis is a player on a national stage, a worthy capital whose residents are citizens of such an enterprise. The teams' presence cuts against perceptions of the city as parochial or provincial.

In 2017, the National Endowment for the Humanities supported a seventeen-month seminar to help community college instructors use religion, and specifically Indianapolis religion, more effectively in their classrooms. In a conversation between these instructors and three Russian Jewish immigrants, the discussion stopped cold when the oldest of the immigrants referred to Indianapolis as "parochial." The instructors, all city residents, clearly thought of their city as a capital and an urban hub; they were surprised to hear an immigrant who had lived there for forty years dismiss it as relatively unimportant.

Does this sense of the city as a national metropolis, a Super Bowl city, matter to its residents or to local culture? The city's self-designated monikers tell the story: the Railroad City (Indianapolis had the nation's first Union Station, where tracks of different gauges met); Crossroads of America (Indianapolis has always sought connections because it is geographically isolated); 100% American City (in the 1920s Indianapolis claimed the highest native-born population; the rise of the Ku Klux Klan in Indiana is closely related); Toolmaker to the Nation (the city became the supply hub for the automotive industry, among other things); Circle City (a reference to the circle in Ralston's design and a recurring theme in city life); and finally Amateur Sports Capital of the World. City elites very intentionally meant their investments to symbolize the city on the national landscape. They proudly proclaimed Indianapolis the Silver Buckle on the Rust Belt.

It is impossible to prove these slogans and the ideas behind them affect residents' sense of themselves, but there are reasons to believe people in Indianapolis imagine their city to be important, plural, and diverse, especially in relation to the rest of Indiana. In a state with seven Republican congressional representatives and only two Democrats, Indianapolis (Seventh District) has one of the Democrats. And he is Black, and Muslim. Roughly 30 percent of the citizens in the Seventh District are Black, so race cannot be the only deciding factor, though obviously that matters a great deal. Likewise, when the state of Indiana attempted to allow citizens to refuse to participate in gay marriages based on religious conviction in one of the nation's many state-level Religious Freedom Restoration Acts, Indianapolis balked, strongly emphasizing the degree to which all are welcome because, among other reasons, this was good for business. In this case, Indianapolis's interests, backed by the state's globally oriented corporations such as Lilly and Cummins, won against the more conservative, traditional interests of much of the rest of the state, and the law was reworded to ban discrimination.

In no way does Indianapolis's *relative* liberalism and inclusivity prove that sports helped create the city's sense of itself as a diverse metropolis. Indianapolis has clear historical reasons for being more diverse and clear commercial interests for being more welcoming and less "traditional" than the rest of the state. And in this, it is not much different from cities across Middle America. But it is very clear that the city's elite meant to create a metropolitan identity and that the sports teams were part of that effort. The teams, along with the NCAA headquarters, were an intentional investment by private businesses, foundations, and government.

Emotional attachment to a city's sports teams and the sense of place it creates hardly rise to the level of patriotism as a kind of emotional attachment—who would be willing to die for the Colts?—so it is reasonable to wonder whether even a functional definition of religion applies here as readily as it does to patriotism. But the two overlap. Patriotism infuses sports, especially professional sports, and that relationship has been crisply clarified in the past few years. Long ago, professional sporting events commenced with a small color guard carrying a normal-sized American flag onto the field, after which fans sang, or listened to, the national anthem. Today at NFL games, a field-sized flag is held by veterans or current military members, and almost all performances of the national anthem involve a salute to veterans. Larger events, including the Indianapolis 500, often have military flyovers where fighter jets put an exclamation point on the end of the national anthem, just in case anyone missed the connection between the military, patriotism, and the highly competitive event about to take place.

We know now that the U.S. military has been funding the NFL's tributes to troops and the field-sized flags drawn out before games, and the military has always underwritten the flyovers, so some of this linkage is intentional and blatantly tactical.[16] Patriotism and sports are used to create a sense of common citizenship as well as to build support for military veterans.

But during the 2016 NFL season, the limits of this shared mythology became obvious when Colin Kaepernick took a knee during the playing of the national anthem before a football game. Other players followed suit. Together, these players turned this most symbolic linkage of sports, patriotism, and militarism on its head, using their high visibility to raise questions about the treatment of Black people by police and the ongoing problems of racism in America more generally. They amplified many of the concerns of the Black Lives Matter movement, which arose as a response to police brutality against African Americans. In so doing, they shined a bright light on the complexity of shared values and thus exposed the limits of patriotism or sports in uniting Americans.

Without once questioning the importance of citizenship or the attendant values of sacrifice, freedom, equality of opportunity, or even military service, the players drew attention to the fact that these values and their benefits were not uniformly or universally distributed. They raised questions about implicit bias, white privilege, and systemic racism. Just as the civil rights movement had done decades earlier, they criticized the synthesis of patriotism and sports not by challenging the legitimacy of the underlying values or even the ideal of universality in those values but by pointing out that practice looks very different from theory or creed.

Conservative politicians criticized the protestors for being antipatriotic and therefore antimilitary or antiveteran. This animosity demonstrates just how closely tied military service is to patriotism and citizenship because the protestors themselves never mentioned veterans and their other remarks contained nothing about the military. But for many, any criticism during a flag ceremony, no matter the target, equates to criticism of the military, and such criticism is presumed to be inherently un-American. Vice President Mike Pence, a former Indiana congressional representative and governor, made an elaborate show of attending the beginning of a Colts game so he could leave in protest of the protests.[17]

Others heralded the free speech of the players and praised them for using their public platform to draw attention to unequal treatment. The protests did not create a new boundary in political dialogue, but they exposed an existing boundary that was slightly less obvious than some others because of Americans' shared commitments to patriotism and sport. But the fact that this venue became central, that the mix of patriotism and sports made it precisely the place where Black people could most publicly raise questions about common citizenship, points out just how deeply this relationship between sports and patriotism runs.

Patriotism, Sports, and American Ideals in an All-American City

John F. Kennedy's Inaugural Address of January 20, 1961, serves as an example and a clue with which to introduce this complex subject. That address began,

> We observe today not a victory of party but a celebration of freedom—symbolizing an end as well as a beginning—signifying renewal as well as change. For I have sworn before you and Almighty God the same solemn oath our forebears prescribed nearly a century and three-quarters ago.
>
> The world is very different now. For man holds in his mortal hands the power to abolish all forms of human poverty and to abolish all forms of human life. And yet the same revolutionary beliefs for which our forebears fought are still at issue around the globe—the belief that the rights of man come not from the generosity of the state but from the hand of God.

And it concluded,

> Finally, whether you are citizens of America or of the world, ask of us the same high standards of strength and sacrifice that we shall ask of you. With a good conscience our only sure reward, with history the final judge of our deeds, let us go forth to lead the land we love, asking His blessing and His help, but knowing that here on earth God's work must truly be our own.

Bellah began his 1967 essay with these quotes. He saw in these three uses of "God" a way to think about America's own civil religion: freedom, forebears, solemn oath, strength, and sacrifice. As Kennedy said, "Here on earth God's work must truly be our own."

Bellah was well aware that critics, especially from the left, would say that American civil religion ultimately boiled down to military imperialism and capitalism. At the very least, America's shared identity emphasized a kind of faith in individual choices now often called neoliberalism. But Bellah never stopped believing that America harbored other, community-oriented values that shone through in some forms of traditional religion and in some forms of political discourse and engagement. These are the principles he hoped America would use to judge itself.

American values encompass both sides of a spectrum, with liberty on one side and equality on the other. America embodies an ongoing tension between the good of the individual and the good of community. These need not be mutually exclusive, but surely we now know that they are not fully coextensive. Sometimes something has to give. No one understood this better than Bellah, who spent his life preaching the value of communitarianism and emphasizing instances where societies, from Japan to America, promoted the common good over individual goods.

The question of whether patriotism and sports constitute a civil religion in Indianapolis must be set in this context. It is easy enough to argue that patriotism, at least, was meant to emphasize the common good over individual goods. But even here there is a caveat: the common goods of nationalism and imperialism are not the ones Bellah had in mind. The war memorials emphasize citizenship as self-sacrifice. The sacrifice was necessary to keep evil at bay, to differentiate between us— even if "us" could be conceived more broadly—and them. Even if the original meaning was particular to the city's mostly white citizens, the underlying theme is universal. The casket in the Shrine Room reads, "The True Patriot Best Supports His Government by Creating Friendliness through Kindness and Generosity Wherever Fate May Carry Him."

The emphasis on veterans had a similar universalizing effect. If anything is truly a sacred cow in America, it is respect for veterans. Even if national policy about veterans' health care or the quality of veterans' institutions is uneven, Americans are prone to say that they honor and respect veterans' contributions. This emotional connection, this appeal to shared sacrifice, might be more widely embraced than any other shared value.

The city also appealed to sports as a way to build a shared public identity and to create an urban core capable of linking disparate parts of an expanding city. To be sure, professional sports are commercial enterprises, monopolies, that enrich owners through public subsidy. But they are never only this. Professional sports are a model of ideal enterprise American society wishes to sanction; they promote the capitalist values of individual achievement and success through managed cooperation, in addition to being successful business ventures themselves. They are racially integrated at a level far beyond most other public ventures. They also include, or are co-opted by, the kind of patriotism that involves high respect for the military and equates citizenship and patriotism with martial strength. This is especially true in the NFL, where it is difficult to tell where patriotism stops and sporting events begin.

The city's business and philanthropic elite placed their bets, often with public funding, that having an NFL team and a sixty-eight-thousand-seat stadium would boost Indianapolis into a higher tier as a convention city, a place of national consequence. This had the extended effect of building a shared public identity not based on race, ethnicity, or socio-economic status. It is impossible to document how precisely this shared identity was intended as a secondary effect; it is always hard to quantify the ways in which culture is created. But it is important to remember that civil religion works much the same: shared ideals and practices can be nudged and nurtured, but they develop as they will. Elites play an outsized role, and other members of society accept the dominant ideas to differing degrees.

The point is not that sports are democratizing in every sense. Many Indianapolis residents cannot afford to attend Colts games. And public funding is certainly being used to fuel private gain. Still, sports create a common interest, something that people from all backgrounds and walks of life can discuss. Professional sports bring people in the city together in a way the arts, movies, and even television do not. When the Colts finally made it to the Super Bowl in February 2007, the city experienced a moment of common identity. It experienced another in 2012 when those fifty thousand Indianapolis residents served as volunteers for the Super Bowl, doing everything from acting as downtown docents to knitting Colts-colored scarves for the other volunteers who worked out in the cold.

Critics convinced that American civil religion will always boil down to elevation of either the individual and capitalism, on the one hand, or militarism and imperialism, on the other, could easily use the case of

Indianapolis to make their point. All the ingredients are present. Moreover, in a state that is 85 percent white,[18] the white privilege implicit in picturing America in certain ways has received relatively little critical attention in most public conversations within Indiana, though there is reason to believe the most recent Black Lives Matter protests are creating some change. The values of national pride linked to individualism, capitalism, and even militarism are considered traditional and normative; any challenges—even questions about the application of the values rather than the values themselves—are repudiated as criticism of essential American ideals.

The important question is not whether Indianapolis can be used to make the point that American civil religion is about such values—it can—but whether the city's mixture of sports and patriotism could meaningfully be called civil religion in any other way. Is there any sense in which the city's focus on patriotism and sports can be understood as representing "the subordination of the nation to ethical principles that transcend it in terms of which it should be judged"?

An affirmative answer, admittedly optimistic, should not be dismissed out of hand. The builders of the war memorials meant to enshrine principles such as liberty, peace, prosperity, and public order in a city that was, at the time, remarkably homogeneous. One might argue that values like those inherently benefit those who are already privileged, leaving less room for those whose historical conditions provide less advantageous starting places. Equality is not glorified to the same extent, but if the war memorials are understood as representing the essence of the liberal tradition, then a certain amount of equality of opportunity comes with the package.

In the middle of the twentieth century, the turn to citizenship as the standard for inclusion benefitted non-European Americans. Participation in the armed forces reinforced that shared citizenship. It is not necessary to be Pollyanna; residential segregation post–World War II and white flight to the suburbs were significant factors in maintaining economic inequality. Still, many of the gaps between Americans of European descent and others narrowed over the decades following the war for a multitude of reasons.

In a society as diverse as the United States, liberalism will always emphasize citizenship, in the sense of membership in the body politic, over other kinds of social identities associated with race, ethnicity, or even social class. People are entitled to vote and to receive society's benefits—education, health care, public protection—because they are citizens, full-fledged members. One can argue that the second half of the twentieth century saw a turn toward political citizenship represented by patriotism and national service that bent national discourse away from the earlier emphasis on race or religion as the normative markers of Americanness, at least for many people.

Obviously, any observed change must be measured over time and carefully qualified. However, change can be real even if it is slow and even if multiple counterexamples can be presented. Greater emphasis on patriotism and sports did not complete a shift toward a more egalitarian notion of membership in the city, but there are good reasons to believe they helped to begin that shift.

The twentieth century also saw a rise in public benefits guaranteed by the state and federal governments: Medicare and Social Security led the way in building security for retirees, but other programs such as Medicaid and AFDC also arose to mitigate poverty among younger generations. As these benefits of citizenship got broader and more expensive, debates about the requirements for claiming citizenship shifted their focus to benefit entitlement. People of non-European origin could, in principle, become U.S. citizens, but not without a host of regulations that changed according to economic and political conditions.

Not surprisingly, then, national debates about membership, citizenship, and nationalism shifted their focus once again toward immigration and its limits. In the twenty-first century, membership in America comes with many more social guarantees funded by taxes. Immigration is now discussed in terms of its cost in public programs in addition to the same concerns about possible changes to the culture that have been repeated for generations as succeeding waves of immigrants negotiated their social position.

Although white Christian nationalism still carries considerable weight,[19] there can be little doubt that a liberal view of citizenship as membership, in principle available across racial, ethnic, or religious lines, is a powerful counterweight. The liberal, pluralistic view of citizenship was bolstered by military service, especially in World War II, but later in Korea, Vietnam, and the Middle East. Indianapolis embraced this vision of citizenship by emphasizing patriotism as sacrifice, creating a civil religious identity that went beyond older ideas that white, Christian, Protestant values were necessarily normative.

Conclusion

When Bellah said "I conceive of the central tradition of the American civil religion not as a form of national self-worship but as the subordination of the nation to ethical principles that transcend it in terms of which it should be judged," he did not immediately follow by specifying which principles those were. Reasonable people could disagree, and the principles surely vary from society to society and from time to time even within societies. So we must ask, what American principles "undercut the ever present danger of national self-idolization" over the course of the twentieth century?

Bellah had certain communitarian notions, such as mutual care, in mind, but it seems clear that values such as freedom, individualism, membership as citizenship, and sacrifice for the greater good are also core American principles. Each of these can be co-opted to fund an ethnocentric worldview that privileges particular races and religions, but each can also be used to sustain a liberal worldview that is in principle more open to all. A community full of citizen-members, each paying proportionate costs and reaping proportionate benefit, is a legitimate way to envision a liberal version of the American dream.

Seen in that light, the growth of Indianapolis's war memorials and a disproportionately large emphasis on sports relative to the size of the population helped hold an expanding city together as a community even as whites moved outward to the suburbs and racial and religious particularism threatened to keep the city separated. The development of a community bound by shared symbols, rooted in national values that transcend particular differences, is not the only way to interpret developments within Indianapolis over the course of the twentieth century, but such an interpretation fits the available facts.

Belaboring the power of these values to transcend difference or emphasizing unity in the face of very real segregation and difference paints an unbalanced portrait of Indianapolis in the twenty-first century. However, emphasizing only difference, separation, and chaos does the same. Certain forces—economic, political, cultural, and racial—acted centrifugally, pushing the city away from any meaningful center or core. But other forces acted centripetally, creating a real geographic core and a sustaining civic identity. Shared national values such as liberty, sacrifice, duty, citizenship, and patriotism are key components of that ideology. Their careful use helped the city transition from a white, Protestant, Christian core to a more pluralistic one, even as residency and political borders expanded.

NOTES

1 David Bodenhamer and Robert Barrows, *Encyclopedia of Indianapolis* (Bloomington: Indiana University Press, 1994), 55.
2 *Indianapolis News*, June 12, 1915.
3 *Indianapolis News*, January 4, 1916.
4 *New York Times*, February 25, 1909.
5 Jan Shipps calls the city's shared celebrations "cultural glue" in her essay in Bodenhamer and Barrows, *Encyclopedia of Indianapolis*, 170ff.
6 Post-War Planning Committee, *The Post War Plan for Indianapolis* (Indianapolis: Post-War Planning Committee, 1944), 12.
7 Bodenhamer and Barrows, *Encyclopedia of Indianapolis*, 879.
8 See Jan Shipps's essay "Religion" in Bodenhamer and Barrows, *Encyclopedia of Indianapolis*, 181.
9 Bodenhamer and Barrows, *Encyclopedia of Indianapolis*, 252.
10 Arthur E. Farnsley II, N. J. Demarath III, Etan Diamond, Mary L. Mapes, and Elfriede Wedam, *Sacred Circles, Public Squares: The Multicentering of American Religion* (Bloomington: Indiana University Press, 2004).
11 I use "place of places" advisedly. In *Sacred Circles, Public Squares*, we used the term "multicentering," but the term itself received considerable thoughtful criticism.
12 Robert N. Bellah, Richard Madsen, William M. Sullivan, Ann Swidler, and Steven M. Tipton, *Habits of the Heart: Individualism and Commitment in American Life* (Berkeley: University of California Press, 1985); Robert N. Bellah, Richard Madsen, William M. Sullivan, Ann Swidler, and Steven M. Tipton, *The Good Society* (New York: Knopf, 1991).
13 Ferdinand Tönnies, *Community & Society* (Gemeinschaft Und Gesellschaft) (East Lansing: Michigan State University Press, 1957).
14 Joseph Price, *Rounding the Bases: Baseball and Religion in America* (Macon, GA: Mercer University Press, 2006); Michael Novak, *Joy of Sports, Revised: Endzones, Bases, Baskets, Balls, and the Consecration of the American Spirit* (New York: Madison Book, 1993); Berkley Center for Religion, Peace & World Affairs, "National Anthem Protests and American Sports as Civil Religion" (September 11, 2018), https://berkleycenter.georgetown.edu.

15 Émile Durkheim, *The Elementary Forms of the Religious Life: A Study in Religious Sociology* (London: G. Allen & Unwin, 1915).
16 Andrew Mach, "Report: Defense Dept. Paid NFL Millions of Taxpayer Dollars to Salute Troops," *PBS NewsHour*, May 10, 2015, www.pbs.org.
17 Jim Ayello and Emma Kate Fittes, "Vice President Mike Pence Leaves Colts Game after 49ers Players Kneel during Anthem," *Indianapolis Star*, October 8, 2017, www.indystar.com.
18 U.S. Census 2017 estimate.
19 Samuel Perry and Andrew Whitehead, *Taking Back America for God: Christian Nationalism in the United States* (Oxford: Oxford University Press, 2020); Sarah Posner, *Unholy: Why White Evangelicals Worship at the Altar of Donald Trump* (New York: Random House, 2020).

ACKNOWLEDGMENTS

This volume emerged from a conference held at the Center for the Study of Religion and American Culture (RAAC) in Indianapolis in November 2016. That seemed like a portentous time to review and discuss the fifty years since the publication of Robert Bellah's first essay on civil religion and the decades of scholarship that were unleashed. That things have been more tumultuous over the past several years than we could have predicted then is a bit of an understatement.

Nonetheless, our contributors rose to the challenge, producing chapters that examine the birth and development of thinking about American civil religion, while also speaking to issues relevant to the idea in our current national situation. We haven't, collectively, given up on the concept, but we recognize and explore some of the very real challenges to it.

As editors, we are deeply appreciative to the volume's contributors for their willingness to engage these ideas and revise their chapters (often twice or more). It has been a fulfilling experience for us in that way. We are especially grateful to Lauren Schmidt, Programs and Operations Manager of the RAAC, for her work on the conference, and to Nate Wynne, Program Coordinator at RAAC, for shepherding the manuscript through its various electronic phases.

As always, Jennifer Hammer of New York University Press has been a pleasure to work with, simultaneously enthusiastic about ideas and exacting in her expectations for quality scholarship. Further, she engaged two enormously helpful (anonymous) reviewers to read and comment on the manuscript. Our thanks go to them.

And, of course, we thank those who are not directly connected to this particular scholarly effort but make our living worthwhile: Rhys thanks Kelly Moore. Ray thanks Shenan Kroupa. Philip thanks Kate McGinn.

ABOUT THE CONTRIBUTORS

ROSEMARY R. CORBETT is a Faculty Fellow with the Bard Prison Initiative.

KORIE LITTLE EDWARDS is Associate Professor of Sociology at the Ohio State University.

ARTHUR E. FARNSLEY II is Senior Research Fellow in the Center for the Study of Religion and American Culture at Indiana University–Purdue University Indianapolis.

PHILIP GOFF is Director of the Center for the Study of Religion and American Culture and Chancellor's Professor of American Studies and Religious Studies at Indiana University–Purdue University Indianapolis.

PHILIP GORSKI is Professor of Sociology at Yale University.

RAYMOND HABERSKI JR. is Professor of History and American Studies at Indiana University–Purdue University Indianapolis.

ELAINE A. PEÑA is Associate Professor of American Studies at the George Washington University.

ARTHUR REMILLARD is Professor of Religious Studies and Director of the Wolf-Kuhn Ethics Institute at Saint Francis University.

MARK SILK is Professor of Religion in Public Life at Trinity College.

WENDY L. WALL is Associate Professor of History at Binghamton University, State University of New York.

RHYS H. WILLIAMS is Professor and Chair of the Department of Sociology at Loyola University Chicago.

INDEX

ACR. *See* American civil religion
Adams, James Truslow, 132, 136n40
Adams, Jasper, 43–44
Adams, John, 40, 46n19; on general Principles, 43, 47n34; on Numa, 37–38
affirmative action legislation, 66
African Americans, 14; Black Lives Matter, 98, 111–12, 203, 207; Du Bois as, 25, 99, 106, 116n29; Jim Crow and, 87, 103, 129. *See also* King, Martin Luther, Jr.; Obama, Barack Hussein
Albanese, Catherine, 39–40
Aldrich, Winthrop, 119, 127
Allen, Danielle, 132–33
alt-right, 30
Amateur Athletic Union, 188
Amateur Sports Capital of America, 188
Amateur Sports Capital of the World, 201
American Academy of Arts and Sciences, 1
American Academy of Religion, 72n44
The American Adam (Lewis), 136n37
American civil religion (ACR), 3, 5–6, 14, 20–21, 28. *See also specific topics*
American Covenant (Gorski), 22
American exceptionalism, 15, 33
American flag, 186, *187,* 202–3
American Indians, 95–96; assimilation and integration of, 99; inferiority of, 102; IORM as, 165–67, *166;* oppression of, 100; Pocahontas as, 167
American Legion, 183–84, 186, 190, 200
Americanness, 52, 64, 142, 208
American presidents, 7, 11, 28, 97, 138–39. *See also specific presidents*

American principles, 109
American values, 210
"America's Civil Religion" (Herberg), 135n19
Anabaptists, 80
Anderson, Nick, 154–55, *155,* 157–58
Angel Island (San Francisco Bay), 146, 148
anti-Catholicism, 123–24
anticommunism, 198
"Apostle of Liberty," 83
Appelbaum, Yoni, 78
Arlington National Cemetery, 53
art, 142. *See also* Statue of Liberty; Uncle Sam
Asad, Talal, 72n45
assimilation and pluralism theory, 99
atheism, 90
Augustine (saint), 25
Auth, Tony: Statue of Liberty by, 150–51; Uncle Sam by, *156,* 156–57

Balaban, Barney, 127
Bayle, Pierre, 35
Becker, Howard, 142
Beecher, Henry Ward, 193
Bellah, Robert, 2, 72n44, 73n48, 169; "Civil War and Civil Religion" by, 54; *Daedalus* by, 1, 96–99, 125, 194–95; "Flaws in the Protestant Code" by, 52, 60; *Habits of the Heart* by, 59, 96, 195; "The Kingdom of God in America" by, 57, 71n18; "Religion and the Legitimation of the American Republic" by, 56–57. *See also specific topics*

217

Berger, Peter L., 135n28
Black Americans. *See* African Americans
Black feminist perspective: of academy, 96, 109; American presidents in, 97; assimilation and pluralism theory in, 99; blindness in, 101; on civil religion term use, 114–15; on covenant theology, 95–96, 98–101, 112; CRT in, 106–7; Cruse and, 99–100; CWT in, 104–10; *Daedalus* related to, 96–99; on diversity, 110–12; Du Bois and, 99, 116n29; elite White men in, 105–6; eugenics and, 102–3; on exclusion and oppression, 99–101; God in, 97; hope in, 96, 98, 109, 111; on hyper-racial segregation, 112; on ideological foundations, 112–13; on immigration, 103; of intellectuals, 106; of Jim Crow, 103; on legitimacy, 113; limitations in, 104; of manifest destiny, 101–2; mass incarceration in, 104; objectification in, 100–101; of people of color, 95–96, 99–104; on philosophy, 113; on religion term use, 113–14, 115; revolutionary world in, 98; of RLDP, 111–12; on sacred, 114; on socialization, 115; standpoint of, 104–5, 115; structures in, 95; tests in, 97–98; on truth, 114; of underbelly, 101–4; unfortunate exceptions in, 100; whiteness in, 95, 107–8; on whiteness theoretical perspective, 95; of women, 100–101
Black Lives Matter, 98, 111–12, 203, 207
Blankenship, Anne, 89–90
blood, 30–31
blood religion, 26
Border Crossing Card, 171
borderlands, 176n7. *See also* International Bridge Ceremony
Border Protection, Anti-terrorism, and Illegal Immigration Control Act of 2005 (HR 4437). *See* Sensenbrenner Bill
border rituals. *See* International Bridge Ceremony
Bortolini, Matteo, 2–3, 5
Boston, Mass., 83
boycott/protest marches, 140–41
The Broken Covenant (Bellah). *See* covenant theology
Brophy, Thomas D'Arcy, 127
Brother Jonathan, 144–45
Buddhist monk, 52–53
Buddhists, 9
Burke, Edmund, 41
Bush, George H. W., 29; on immigration, 138–39
Bush, George W., 29, 138–39, 140
Butler, Jon, 119

Canavan, Francis, 65
Carroll, Michael, 189
Catholic Bishops, 57–58
Catholic Relief Services, 64–65
Catholics: in Indianapolis, Indiana, 181, 182; Muslim Americans compared to, 69, 70; in Protestant hegemony, 62–65; Protestants compared to, 67; self-sacrificing service related to, 57–59
Center for World Religions, 51
Chavez, Leo, 142–43, 154
Chernus, Ira, 76
Chesterton, G. K., 63
Chinese Exclusion Act of 1882, 103
Chipley, William, 85–86
Christianity: Adams, John, on, 47n34; Gordon, S. B., on, 48n40; Republicans related to, 43
Christian libertarianism, 131, 135n14
Christian nationalism, 88–89; from Trump, 12–13
Christian Right, 58; Reagan and, 29, 57
CIBV. *See* Consejo Internacional de Buena Vecindad
CIBV-Nuevo Laredo. *See* Consejo Internacional de Buena Vecindad

citizenship, 163, 205; liberalism related to, 207–9; nationalism and, 208–9. *See also* war memorials
civic republicanism, 20–21
civil religion, 82; in practice, 15; term use of, 57. *See also specific topics*
civil religion decentering: diversity in, 82; divisions in, 82–89; Marsden in, 78, 79; pacifists in, 79; philosophy on, 81; power in, 80, 82; sacrifice in, 78; Trump in, 78; understanding of, 79–80
"Civil Religion in America" (Bellah). *See specific topics*
"Civil Religion in an Uncivil Society" (Demerath, III, and Williams), 81
"Civil Religion in Theological Perspective" (Richardson), 114
civil religious corruption, 28–29
civil religious tradition and rivals, 25–28
civil rights, 53
Civil Rights Act (1964), 8
civil rights movement, 138, 203
Civil War, 22–23, 85–86, 98, *185*, 185–86
"Civil War and Civil Religion" (Bellah), 54
Clark, Tom, 127
Clinton, Bill, 29, 33n16
Clinton, Hillary, 12
Cold War, 2, 7–8, 88, 120–21
Collins, Patricia Hill, 104–5, 108
Colorado, *153*, 153–54
Columbia (fictional character), 147
common good, 131
communism, 123; Jews and, 66; nativism related to, 122, 198
community service: military/militarism compared to, 63, 70, 185; in Protestant hegemony, 63–65
Consejo Internacional de Buena Vecindad (CIBV), 167–68, 173, 178n28
Consejo Internacional de Buena Vecindad (CIBV-Nuevo Laredo), 167

consensus: language of, 130; in origins problem, 121, 122, 123–24, 131; politics of, 11, 14
conservative corporate leaders, 135n14
conservativism, 126, 128, 132, 153, 157
Considerations on the Government of Poland (Considerations) (Rousseau), 36–37, 40, 46n19
Constitution, 22–23, 46n12; invocation for, 38; separation in, 27
Contested Truths (Rodgers), 130
covenant theology, 4–6, 25, 28; African American *men* in, 106; Black feminist perspective on, 95–96, 98–101, 112; Clinton, B., and, 29; diversity in, 110–11; happiness related to, 20–21; individualism and, 57; prescription in, 55–56; Revolutionary generation and, 22–23; values and, 159
critical race theory (CRT), 106–7
critical whiteness theory (CWT), 104, 108; epistemology in, 105–6, 109; Obama and, 109–10
CRT. *See* critical race theory
Cruse, Harold, 99–100
cultural conversation, 131, 136n37
cultural glue, 210n5
cultural identity, 136n37
culture wars: contention of, 139; immigration related to, 139; political gridlock from, 19; politics of partisanship in, 131
CWT. *See* critical whiteness theory

Daedalus (Bellah), 1, 125, 194–95; Black feminist perspective related to, 96–99
Declaration of Independence, 27, 39, 118; Allen on, 132–33; separate and equal in, 37
Demerath, N. J., III, 81
Democratic Party, 28
Democrats, 28, 128, 138; immigration related to, 149
diplomatic history, 126–27, 135n26

diversity, 89–91; Black feminist perspective on, 110–12; in civil religion decentering, 82; in covenant theology, 110–11; in origins problem, 123; questions related to, 77, 92n5
Douglas, Mary, 144
Douglass, Frederick, 22
drug trafficking, 168–69
Du Bois, W. E. B., 25, 99, 106, 116n29
Durkheim, Émile, 10, 126, 195, 199
Durkheimian theory, 59

education, religious identity related to, 9–10
Edwards, Korie L., 111
Eisenhower, Dwight, 44
elites, 19, 76, 107–8
elite White men, 105–6
Ellis Island, 146–47
Ellsworth, Oliver, 42
emotionalism, 142
employers, for immigrants, 154–55, 155
epistemology, 105–6, 109
equality, liberality and, 205
ethnonationalism, 33, 149
eugenics, 102–3
evangelicals, 3, 31, 32; Israel and, 74n72; Protestant, 8, 9, 12, 61, 74n72; white, 30, 194

Farnsley, Arthur E., II, 191, 210n11
fascism, 131–32
Fellowship of Reconciliation (FOR), 130
Fiorenza, Francis Schüssler, 73n53
First Amendment, 42, 61, 73n48
Fischer, David Hackett, 143
Flagg, James Montgomery, 145
"Flaws in the Protestant Code" (Bellah), 52, 60
flaws of the religious right, 73n53
FOR. *See* Fellowship of Reconciliation
Foucault, Michel, 80

founding fathers, 13–14, 20–21, 27; God of, 97; Jefferson as, 128; Serra as, 89; Washington as, 83
founding myth, 22–23, 25
France, 38–39, 42; French Revolution, 41, 47n26; Statue of Liberty from, 147–48
Franklin, Benjamin, 46n12, 54, 59
Freedom Train, 118–20; FOR and, 130; Jim Crow and, 129
free passage (*paso libre*), 178n30
French Revolution, 41, 47n26
Freneau, Philip, 40, 47n23

Gamson, William, 142
gay marriages, 202
gender, 32
gender theory, 108
generalized Christianity: Adams, Jasper, on, 43–44; Eisenhower on, 44; *Ruggles* case in, 42–43, 48n39; Rush on, 42–43; universal transcendent religious reality in, 45
general Principles, 43, 47n34
Gingrich, Newt, 66–67
God, 57, 71n18, 121, 131; in Black feminist perspective, 97; Kennedy on, 204
God and War (Haberski), 126
Good Citizen, 118–19
good society, 149; national identity in, 159–60
Gordon, Milton, 99
Gordon, Sarah Barringer, 43, 48n40
Gorski, Philip, 22
Grady, Henry, 86
Gray, Francis, 83
Gulf War, 143

Haberski, Ray, 126, 167
Habits of the Heart (Bellah), 59, 96, 195
Hamilton, Alexander, 38, 40, 43, 47n27
Hammond, Phillip, 57, 169, 170
Handy, Robert, 6
Haney-Lopez, Ian, 107

Hart-Celler Act. *See* Immigration and Nationality Act of 1965
Hauerwas, Stanley, 7
Hebraic and Christian archetypes, 132
Hebrew Scriptures, 20, 21, 22; prophets of, 26
Hegy, Pierre, 5
Herberg, Will, 120, 124–26, 130–31, 135n19; *Protestant-Catholic-Jew* by, 124–25, 138
heritage, 159–60
Herzog, Jonathan P., 121, 134n13
Hidalgo y Costilla, Jose Miguel, 83–84, 163–64, 165, *165*, 170, 174
Hindus, 9
history: diplomatic, 126–27, 135n26; self-sacrificing service in, 51–52
HIV/AIDS, 193
Holand, Hjalmar, 87–88
Hollinger, David, 136n40
hope, 32; in Black feminist perspective, 96, 98, 109, 111; liberal optimists and, 198–99
Hughes, Langston, 129
human equality, 24
Hutchinson, Anne, 88–89

ICE. *See* Immigration and Customs Enforcement
idealism and materialism tension, 73n56
identity, 77; of culture, 136n37; religious, 9–10; sports related to, 195–96, 206. *See also* national identity
IGNC. *See* International Good Neighbor Council
IGNC-Laredo. *See* International Good Neighbor Council
"I Have a Dream" speech (King, Jr.), 131
illegal immigration, 140, 150, 152–53
images and themes from 2005-2006, 149–50
immigration, 8–9; Black feminist perspective on, 103; cross-cutting cleavages on, 138; culture war related to, 139; current issues in, 148–49; Democrats related to, 149; Ellis Island related to, 146–47; employers for, 154–55, *155*; Hart-Celler Act on, 138; illegal, 140, 150, 152–53; legitimating myths related to, 139; national identity related to, 137, 149, 159; nationalism and, 208; National Origins Act and, 137–38; polarization on, 138; Republicans and, 138–40; strike by, 156, *156*. *See also* Statue of Liberty; Uncle Sam
Immigration and Customs Enforcement (ICE), 151
Immigration and Nationality Act of 1965 (Immigration Act of 1965) (Hart-Celler Act), 8, 132, 136n40, 138
Improved Order of Red Men (IORM), 165–66, *166*
Indiana Military Park, 188
Indianapolis, Indiana, 15, 209–10, 210n5; Amateur Sports Capital of the World, 201; American Legion in, 183–84, 186, 190, 200; Catholics and Jews in, 181, 182; immigrants in, 181–82; Ku Klux Klan in, 184, 197, 201; Monument Circle of, 180, 183–84; names of, 201; parochialism of, 201; planning of, 180; privatized religion and, 194; race in, 201–2; Scottish Rite Cathedral in, 184, 192; Second Presbyterian Church in, 193; segregation in, 198; suburbia in, 182–83; for Sunday closing laws in, 181; symbolism of, 201; urban development in, 190–94; War Memorial Plaza in, 186–88, 192–93, 197; war memorials in, 183–88, *185*, *186*, *187*, 197, 207; white Protestants in, 180–81, 184, 194. *See also* patriotism
Indianapolis, U.S.S., 187–88
Indianapolis Church Federation, 181

222 | INDEX

Indianapolis sports, 199; Amateur Athletic Union in, 188; community spirit from, 189–90; emotional attachment to, 202; IUPUI in, 188, 191; monopoly in, 200; national self-worship and, 194–95; NBA in, 189, 190–91; NCAA in, 189–90, 200; NFL in, 206; Pan Am Games in, 188–89; Super Bowl XLVI, 189, 191, 206
Indiana Republicans, 201
Indiana's whiteness, 207
Indiana University-Purdue University Indianapolis (IUPUI), 188–90
Indiana War Memorial, *186*, 186–87
individualism: covenant theology and, 57; liberal, 195; Protestant hegemony and, 60, 61; self-sacrificing service or, 55–56
International Bridge Ceremony, 15, 175n4, 176n7; drug cartels and, 163, 164, 168–69, 173; George Washington actors at, 163–64, *165*, 170, 174; IORM at, 165–67, *166*; LULAC and, 163; Mexican *abrazo* children in, 164, 167, *168*, 171–72, 178n28; Miguel Hidalgo actors at, 164, *165*, 170, 174; origins of, 165–66; *paso libre* in, 178n30; preparation for, 173
International Good Neighbor Council (IGNC), 167–68, 173, 178n28
International Good Neighbor Council (IGNC-Laredo), 167
IORM. *See* Improved Order of Red Men
Ireland, John, 88
Islamic Relief USA, 70
Islamic Society of North America (ISNA), 67–70
Israel, 20, 22, 74n72
"Is There a Common American Culture?" (Bellah), 72n44
IUPUI. *See* Indiana University-Purdue University Indianapolis

Jacobins, 46n14
Jakobsen, Janet, 72n45

Japan, 53, 169
Japanese Americans, 89–90
Jefferson, Thomas, 39, 43
Jeremiah (prophet), 20, 55, 62
Jews, 9, 94n45, 103, 127, 201; communism and, 66; in Indianapolis, Indiana, 181, 182; Protestants and, 74n72
Jim Crow, 87, 103, 129
Johansson, Olle, 157–58
John Paul II (pope), 58–59, 62
Johnson, Lyndon B., 66, 126
Jones, Donald, 2–3
Juárez-Lincoln International Bridge, 163–64. *See also* International Bridge Ceremony
Judeo-Christian, 64, 94n45, 124–25

Kaepernick, Colin, 203
Keefe, Mike, *153*, 153–54
Kelly, Megyn, 31
Kennedy, John F., 7, 28, 63; election of, 64, 65; on God, 204; Inaugural Address of, 204; self-sacrificing service and, 53–55
Kensington Runestone, 87–88
King, Martin Luther, Jr., 23, 71n18, 79, 131
"The Kingdom of God in America" (Bellah), 57, 71n18
Know Nothing nativist movement, 145
Kruse, Kevin M., 121, 135n14
Kuhn, George, 183
Ku Klux Klan, 184, 197, 201

Lady Liberty. *See* Statue of Liberty
language, 174; of consensus, 130; sacred vocabulary, 133; Spanish, *156*, 156–57; symbols as, 141
Lanthenas, François, 38–39, 46n14
Laredo, Texas, 163–67, 174, 175n2. *See also* International Bridge Ceremony
Lawler, Margretta, 129
Lazarus, Emma, 150–51, *151*, *153*, 153–54; strike and, 156, *156*

League of United Latin American Citizens (LULAC), 163
legitimating myths, 139
L'Enfant, Pierre, 180
Lewis, R. W. B., 136n37
LGBTQ, 194, 202
liberal individualism, 195
liberalism: citizenship related to, 207–9; nationalism and, 26; neoliberalism, 58–59, 65, 67, 205; of Reagan, 28–29; secular, 28
liberal optimists, 198–99
liberal secularism, 13
libertarianism, 19
libertine liberalism, 26
Liberty, 147–48. *See also* Statue of Liberty
Lincoln, Abraham, 4, 54, 118, 126; death of, 171; on slavery, 98; on Union, 22–23
Lincoln, Bruce, 92n5
Lippy, Charles, 42
Long, Charles, 76–77
Luckovich, Mike, 152, *152*
LULAC. *See* League of United Latin American Citizens
lynching, 87
Lynn, Charles, 193

Machiavelli, 35–36, 45n1
Madison, James, 27
mainline Protestantism, 2, 8, 64, 194
Malcolm X, 99, 106
manifest destiny, 101–2
Manufacturing Religion (McCutcheon), 72n45
marginalization, 87–91
Marianne (fictional character), 147–48
Marsden, George, 78, 79
Martin, Luther, 38
Martinez, Antonio Jose, 84
Mathews, Donald, 87
Mathisen, James, 6
McCarthy, Joseph, 50–51

McCoy, Glenn, 157
McCutcheon, Russell, 72n45, 77
Medal of Honor Memorial, 188
megachurches, 8
memorials. *See* war memorials
Mennonites, 79
Mexican *abrazo* children, 164, 167, *168*, 171–72, 178n28
Mexico, 152–53, 157–58. *See also* International Bridge Ceremony
military/militarism, 52; community service compared to, 63, 70, 185; diplomatic historians on, 126–27; ethics and, 56; nationalism and, 195; patriotism as, 208–9; sacrifice of, 53, 54–55, 183; sports related to, 202–3, 206. *See also* Uncle Sam; war memorials; *specific wars*
military veterans, 129, 183, 187, 202, 205
Mirror-imaging acts, 176n7
Moore, Charles Chilton, 90
moral debts, 19–20
morals, 28, 47n27
Morgan, Winifred, 145
Morrison, Norman, 53
multicentering, 210n11
Mumford, Lewis, 131–32
Muslim Americans, 198; Catholics compared to, 69, 70; Community Service Program of, 67–69; loyalty of, 68–69; murder of, 69; 9/11 and, 68; Obama and, 68; Peace Corps related to, 69–70; threats against, 70
Muslims, 9, 30
MuslimServe Call to Action 2010, 69
myths, 25, 87–89, 139, 159; nationalism and, 170

national community service, 52
National Endowment for the Humanities, 201

national identity: art related to, 142–44; in good society, 158–60; *heritage* and, 159–60; historical development for, 13; immigration related to, 137, 149, 159; legitimating myths related to, 139; myths and, 159; race and, 159. *See also* Statue of Liberty; Uncle Sam

nationalism: Christian, 88–89; citizenship and, 208–9; collective self-worship as, 27; cultural conversation and, 131, 136n37; ethnonationalism, 33, 149; immigration and, 208; liberalism and, 26; military/militarism and, 195; myth and, 170; patriotism as, 187–88, 192, 195, 197–98, 203–4; political theology of, 25; secularism and, 13; war memorials as, 197, 205

National Origins Act of 1924, 137–38

national quota system, 138

national self-worship, 194–95, 196, 209

Native Americans. *See* American Indians

nativism: anti-Catholicism as, 123–24; anti-communism from, 198; communism related to, 122, 198; decline of, 138; Ku Klux Klan from, 197; Protestant, 59, 64, 65

Nazism, 103, 185, 199

neoliberalism, 58–59, 65, 67, 205

"The New Colossus" (Lazarus), 147, 150–51, *151*, *153*, 153–54; in Spanish, 156, *156*

New South, 85–86

Niebuhr, Reinhold, 73n56

9/11, 29, 68, 163

Nixon, Richard, 4, 53

nones (religious), 9–10

nonviolence, 71n18

Norwegians, 87–88

Novak, Michael, 66–67

Numa Pompilius, 36–38, 80–81

Obama, Barack Hussein, 97; CWT and, 109–10; on national community service, 52, 68; reconciliation of, 23; Wright and, 110

One Nation, Divisible (Silk and Walsh), 84

one nation divided: Kensington Runestone in, 87–88; New South in, 85–86; origin myths in, 87–89; Reconstruction in, 86–87; Santa Fe in, 83–84

"one nation under God," 131

One Nation Under God (Kruse), 121

origins problem: African Americans in, 129; American Way in, 120, 123; analysis of, 121–22; applications in, 120–21; conscientious objectors and, 128–29; consensus in, 121, 122, 123–24, 131; definitional fuzziness in, 121; diplomatic historians in, 126–27; diversity in, 123; fascism and communism in, 122–23; Freedom Train in, 118–20, 127–30; institutionalization in, 119–20; Judeo-Christian in, 124–25; nativism in, 122, 123–24; New Deal in, 122; pilgrimage in, 119; prescription for, 121–22, 130–31; religious right in, 125

Orsi, Robert, 80

Our Declaration (Allen), 132–33

pacifists, 79

Paine, Thomas, 41

palladium, 39, 46n16

Pallas Athena, 46n16

Parsons, Talcott, 50

paso libre (free passage), 178n30

past and future: elites in, 19; moral debts and, 19–20; Trump in, 19; truths about, 19–20

patriotism, 207; as military/militarism, 208–9; as nationalism, 187–88, 192, 195, 197–98, 203–4; secularism and, 19; in Washington, D.C., 196

Peace Corps, 54, 64–65; Muslim Americans related to, 69–70

Pellegrini, Anne, 72n45

Pence, Mike, 203

People v. Ruggles (1811), 43–44, 48n39

Pershing, John, 30
Pew Research Center poll, 69
place of places, 210n11
Plato, 85
Pledge of Allegiance, 2
Plutarch, 48n35, 48n40
Pocahontas, Princess, 167
Poland, 36–37, 45n8
political cartoons: civil religious discourse in, 143–44; harm in, 143; visual sociology in, 142–43. *See also* Statue of Liberty; Uncle Sam
politics of consensus, 11, 14
power, 108; in civil religion decentering, 80, 82
Preston, Andrew, 126–27
Progressive Movement, 24–25
Proposition 187, 140
Protestant-Catholic-Jew (Herberg), 124–25, 138
Protestant evangelicals, 8, 12, 61, 74n72
Protestant hegemony: affirmative action legislation in, 66; American Enterprise Institute in, 65–66; bias in, 60; Catholics in, 62–65; community service in, 63–65; cultural codes related to, 61; First Amendment related to, 61; homogeneity as, 60; individualism and, 60, 61; Judeo-Christian and, 64; Muslim Americans and, 67–70; national cultures and, 60; Novak in, 66–67; pluralism as, 60, 63; religious dissent and, 60; "strong society, weak state" in, 67
Protestantism: good society and, 158; mainline, 2, 8, 64, 194
Protestant nativism, 59, 64, 65
Protestants, 8; Catholics compared to, 67; Jews and, 74n72; Republicans as, 9; secularism and, 64–65; self-sacrificing service and, 59–60
protest marches, 140–41
Prothero, Stephen, 91

public opinion polling, 162n25
public theology, 50
Puritans, 21, 125; Brother Jonathan related to, 144–45

race: CRT, 106–7; in Indianapolis, Indiana, 201–2; national identity and, 159
racial and ethnic exclusion and oppression, 99–101
racial integration, 112; in sports, 199
racism, 32–33
radical secularism, 26–28
Ralston, Alexander, 180
Reagan, Ronald, 66; absolution from, 28, 33n15; Christian Right and, 29, 57; on immigration, 138–39; liberalism of, 28–29
Reflections on the Revolution in France (Burke), 41
regions: communities and, 76–77; elites and, 76; political identities and, 77; Puritans related to, 77; traditions and, 76; 'we' related to, 76–77
"Religion" (Shipps), 184
Religion and Human Evolution (Smith), 50
"Religion and the Legitimation of the American Republic" (Bellah), 56–57
"Religion by Region" (Silk and Walsh), 84
Religious Freedom Restoration Acts, 202
religious identity: American politics related to, 9–10; education related to, 9–10; nones, 9–10
Religious Leadership and Diversity Project (RLDP), 111–12
religious nationalism, 25–27
religious nationalism secularization, 30–32
religious right, 19, 29, 33, 57, 58; alt-, 30; in problem of origins, 125; Protestants as, 66; young evangelicals as, 32
Remillard, Arthur, 125
The Republic (Plato), 85
Republican presidents, 138–39

Republicans, 19; Christianity related to, 43; civic, 20–21; immigration and, 138–40; in Indiana, 201; morals of, 28, 47n27; Protestants as, 9; Reagan as, 28; tradition and, 36, 40. *See also* Trump, Donald

The Restructuring of American Religion (Wuthnow), 125

Revolutionary War, 21–22, 98, 144–45

Richardson, Herbert, 114

Richey, Russell, 2–3

rituals, 7, 54–55, 63, 70, 101, 121; of sports, 199, 200–201; Washington's birthday celebration as, 83, 167, 177n12, 178n30. *See also* International Bridge Ceremony

RLDP. *See* Religious Leadership and Diversity Project

Robertson, Pat, 29

Rodgers, Daniel T., 130

Romulus (king), 81

Roosevelt, Franklin Delano, 66

Rousseau, Jean-Jacques, 2, 4, 20, 81; bizarre hybrid of, 45n5; Christianity and, 40, 47n23; civil religion from, 10, 119–20; *Considerations* by, 36–37, 40, 46n19; on Russia and Poland, 45n8; on utilitarian context, 35–37

Rush, Benjamin, 42–43

Russia, 36, 45n8

sacrament of communion, 62–63

sacred canopy, 135n28

Sacred Circles, Public Squares (Farnsley), 191, 210n11

sacred vocabulary, 133

sacrifice. *See* self-sacrificing service

Samuel (prophet), 22

Santa Fe, New Mexico, 83–84

Sargent, Ben, 150, *151*

Schlafly, Phyllis, 32

Scottish Rite Cathedral, 184, 192

secular form of religious nationalism, 30

secularism/secularity/secularization: of ACR, 20; humanists and, 29; nationalism and, 13; of national shrines, 53; patriotism and, 19; Protestants and, 64–65; radicalism related to, 25–28; of religious nationalism, 30–32; scripture related to, 23; values of, 38–39

secular liberalism, 28

Sehat, David, 7

self-sacrificing service: Catholics related to, 57–59; civil rights and, 53; Franklin on, 54; at Harvard, 50–51; in history, 51–52; individualism or, 55–56; John Paul II on, 58–59; Kennedy and, 53–55; Peace Corps as, 54; Protestants and, 58–59; self-interest or, 52–59; Tocqueville and, 56–57; Vietnam War related to, 52–53; war in, 52–53, 55

Sensenbrenner, James, 140

Sensenbrenner Bill: boycott/protest marches against, 140–41; immigration quote reform in, 8; passage of, 138, 141; Statue of Liberty related to, 141–42, 150–54, *151*, *152*, *153*; Uncle Sam related to, 141–42, 154–58, *155*, *156*

Serra, Junípero, 89

Shipps, Jan, 184, 210n5

Shrine Room, 186–87, *187*, 205

Silk, Mark, 82; on Numa Pompilius, 80–81; *One Nation, Divisible* by, 84

slavery, 3–4, 22–23, 24; Statue of Liberty and, 147–48

Smith, Wilfred Cantwell, 50–51, 62

The Social Contract (Rousseau), 10, 35, 81

Social Texts (Jakobsen and Pellegrini), 72n45

sociologists, 2–3, 5, 11, 20

Soldiers and Sailors Monument, 183–85, *185*, *186*, *187*

Spirit of 1776. *See* Freedom Train

The Spiritual-Industrial Complex (Herzog), 121

sports: community identity from, 199, 206; identities related to, 195–96, 206; military related to, 202–3, 206; racial integration in, 199, 206; rituals of, 199, 200–201. *See also* Indianapolis sports
state actors, 127, 135n26
Statue of Liberty, 15, 139; by Auth, 150–51; choice of, 141–42; freedom related to, 147; by Keefe, 153, 153–54; Lazarus on, 150–51, 151, 153, 153–54; location of, 146–47; by Luckovich, 152, 152; national identity and, 148; poem on, 147; by Sargent, 150, 150; slavery and, 147–48; symbolism of, 146–48; Trump with, 143
Stewart, Potter, 196
Stewart, W. G., 87
symbols, 144, 170, 201; as language, 141. *See also* International Bridge Ceremony; Statue of Liberty; Uncle Sam

terrorism, 29, 30, 31, 68, 140; immigration and, 149
Texas Good Neighbor Commission (TGNC), 178n28
Thich Quang Duc, 52–53
Tillich, Paul, 50, 62
Tocqueville, Alexis de, 56–57
traditionalists, 23–25
transnational civil religion. *See* International Bridge Ceremony
Trinity United Church of Christ, 110
Trump, Donald: on *Access Hollywood*, 143–44; anti-Islamic campaign of, 69; Christianism of, 31; Christian nationalism from, 12–13; in civil religion decentering, 78; doubts of, 19; geopolitics of, 30–31; interpretations about, 30; Pershing and, 30; preparation for, 29; secular form of religious nationalism of, 30–31; Statue of Liberty with, 143; white evangelicals for, 30, 31
Trumpism, 30, 31–32
Turner, Victor, 170

Uncivil Religion, 58
Uncle Sam, 15; by Anderson, 154–55, 155, 157–58; by Auth, 156, 156–57; choice of, 141–42; in first Gulf War, 143; by Johansson, 157–58; by McCoy, 157; origins of, 144–45, 158; Sensenbrenner Bill related to, 141–42, 154–58, 155, 156; symbolism of, 145–46, 158; Wilson, S., as, 144–45
Updegraph v. Commonwealth (1824), 43, 48n35
U.S.-Mexican border, 152–53, 157–58. *See also* International Bridge Ceremony
utilitarian context: Albanese on, 39–40; civil theology in, 36; Ellsworth on, 42; Lanthenas on, 38–39, 46n14; Machiavelli in, 35–36; Rousseau on, 35–37; Warren on, 41–42; Washington on, 41
utilitarian ideology, 94n45

Varieties of Civil Religion (Bellah and Hammond), 57, 169
veterans, military, 129, 183, 187, 202, 205. *See also* war memorials
Vietnam War, 3, 4, 7, 51; to self-sacrificing service related, 52–53
Virgil, 37
visual sociology: Chavez in, 142–43; emotionalism of, 142; Fischer in, 143
voting rights bill, 126

Walker, Randi Jones, 84
Wallace, George, 79
Walsh, Andrew, 84
Warburton, William, 35
War Memorial Plaza, 186–88, 192–93, 197
war memorials, 183–85, 185, 186, 207; Medal of Honor Memorial, 188; as nationalism, 197, 205; Shrine Room of, 186–87, 187, 205
Warner, Lloyd, 171
War of Independence (Revolutionary War), 98, 144–45

Warren, Mercy, 39, 41–42
Washington, D.C. patriotism, 196
Washington, George: as "Apostle of Liberty," 83; birthday celebration of, 83, 167, 177n12, 178n30; "Farewell Address" of, 39, 40, 41, 46n15, 47n27; as founding father, 83; Hidalgo and, 163–64, 165, *165*, 170; International Bridge Ceremony and, 163–64, *165*, 170, 174; on utilitarian context, 41
Washington's Birthday Celebration Association (WBCA), 167–68, 173
Weber, Max, 11
Weems, Mason Locke (Parson), 41
Weller, Dylan, 7
West Florida, 85–86
Whillock, Rita Kirk, 81–82
White, Ryan, 193
white evangelicals, 30, 31, 194
whiteness, 105–6, 207; in Black feminist perspective, 95, 107–8
whiteness theoretical perspective, 95

white people's centrality, 116n29
white Protestants, 8; in Indianapolis, Indiana, 180–81, 184, 194
white supremacist movement, 198
white transparency, 107–8
"who belongs," 137
Wilcox, Brad, 32
Williams, Rhys, 81
Wilson, Charles Reagan, 85
Wilson, James, 38
Wilson, Samuel, 144–45
Wilson, Woodrow, 103
Winthrop, John, 21
World War I, 64
World War II, 4, 53, 64, 122, 170, 184; Japanese Americans in, 89–90
Wright, Jeremiah, 23, 110
Wuthnow, Robert, 94n45; on competition, 125; conservativism of, 126; on legitimating creed, 130

young evangelicals, 32

www.ingramcontent.com/pod-product-compliance
Lightning Source LLC
Chambersburg PA
CBHW020406080526
44584CB00014B/1194